THE UNIVERSITY OF CHICAGO
STUDIES IN SOCIAL SCIENCE

Edited by
A COMMITTEE OF THE SOCIAL
SCIENCE DEPARTMENTS

NUMBER XVII

THE SOCIAL SCIENCE STUDIES are an expression of community of interests of the social sciences. The publication of these studies is one of the results of a comprehensive program of research which has been undertaken by a group or conference of departments. The formation of this conference is an outgrowth of the belief that the social sciences should engage more actively and systematically in co-operative consideration of their problems and methodology. This does not imply any diminution of interest in the development of their special fields. The Studies, therefore, are to include the results of scientific investigations usually associated with the fields of each of the participating departments. But they will also include the results of joint investigations of several or all of these departments as well as studies in related fields.

CHICAGO

AN EXPERIMENT IN SOCIAL
SCIENCE RESEARCH

THE UNIVERSITY OF CHICAGO PRESS
CHICAGO, ILLINOIS

THE BAKER & TAYLOR COMPANY
NEW YORK
THE MACMILLAN COMPANY OF CANADA, LIMITED
TORONTO
THE CAMBRIDGE UNIVERSITY PRESS
LONDON
THE MARUZEN-KABUSHIKI-KAISHA
TOKYO, OSAKA, KYOTO, FUKUOKA, SENDAI
THE COMMERCIAL PRESS, LIMITED
SHANGHAI

THE SOCIAL SCIENCE RESEARCH BUILDING

CHICAGO

AN EXPERIMENT IN SOCIAL SCIENCE RESEARCH

T. V. SMITH
LEONARD D. WHITE
Editors

THE UNIVERSITY OF CHICAGO PRESS
CHICAGO · ILLINOIS

PREFACE

At the expiration of five years of intensive study of some aspects of urban life in Chicago and its region, as well as of a few studies reaching far beyond the city and its environs, the Local Community Research Committee believed it wise and expedient to take thought of its experience and accomplishments. An experiment in co-operative research in an urban complex had been launched in 1923. What were its results? How much the wiser were the researchers? What of the city? And what of the morrow?

Long-time planning in the field of social science research in a great university is beset with difficulties, however essential to the most effective utilization of resources. Believing that the outlines of future effort might become clearer by inspection of the past, and by some broad appreciation of the ground traversed and results achieved and habits established, the Committee directed four of its members, Mr. T. V. Smith, Mr. E. W. Burgess, Mr. C. E. Merriam, and Mr. L. D. White, to proceed with this volume.

Its primary object is therefore to instruct ourselves as to our progress in the task undertaken five years ago. It may, however, have some interest to social science researchers in other institutions, and especially in those wherein research councils have been or may be established. While no member of the Local Community Research Committee would venture to assert that its organization or procedures are more than tentative, they have neverthe-

vii

less been operating for half a decade, with results set out in the following chapters.

The reader may be helped by a few words of explanation. The name, "Local Community Research Committee," was originally devised when the sole function of the group was with research within or related to the city of Chicago, broadly construed. Later the Laura Spelman Rockefeller Memorial generously supplemented its original gift to enable the conduct of research whether local or otherwise. This accounts for the somewhat anomalous case, by way of illustration, of a research assistant in the Tyrol studying the causes of war under the authority of the Local Community Research Committee.

The chapters comprising this book were written by various members of the faculty, as indicated in the Table of Contents. They were written under the pressure of a very great burden of university work, by men and women who have many responsibilities. Mr. Park wrote the first chapter on the Pacific Ocean, en route to the South Sea. Mr. Burgess completed his contribution en route to Los Angeles. If, therefore, the revision which was jointly accomplished by Mr. T. V. Smith and Mr. White leaves something to be desired as to style and content, let the facts provide what excuse may be possible.

There are a few cases in which a given research is referred to more than once. This is not an oversight but a reflection of the fact that some studies illustrate two or more points, or are of importance in two or more contexts.

The text is not intended to be exhaustive, merely illustrative. We have been able, however, to include most of the research which has been undertaken, although often giving much less space than a project deserved. In particular, there is no exhaustive report of the many developments of research technique which have been a highly valuable part of our work. The advances in methods of social science research made by Thurstone in psychometrics, by Schultz in price determination and statistical method, by Sapir in linguistics, by Gosnell in the manipulation of large numbers of voters, by Lasswell in the application of the psychiatric interview to politics, and by other members of the group in their special fields are full of interest, and may be traced in their publications.

TABLE OF CONTENTS

xi

CHAPTER I

THE CITY AS A SOCIAL LABORATORY

I. HUMAN NATURE AND THE CITY

The city has been described as the natural habitat of civilized man. It is in the city that man developed philosophy and science, and became not merely a rational but a sophisticated animal. This means, for one thing, that it is in the urban environment—in a world which man himself has made—that mankind first achieved an intellectual life and acquired those characteristics which most distinguish him from the lower animals and from primitive man. For the city and the urban environment represent man's most consistent and, on the whole, his most successful attempt to remake the world he lives in more after his heart's desire. But if the city is the world which man created, it is the world in which he is henceforth condemned to live. Thus, indirectly, and without any clear sense of the nature of his task, in making the city man has remade himself.

It is in some such sense and in some such connection as this that we may think of the city as a social laboratory.

As a matter of fact civilization and social progress have assumed in our modern cities something of the character of a controlled experiment. Progress tends to assume that character, for example, wherever fact-finding precedes legislation and reforms are conducted by experts rather than by amateurs. Social surveys and bureaus of municipal research are evidences of a form of politics that has become empirical rather than doctrinaire.

1

The social problem is fundamentally a city problem. It is the problem of achieving in the freedom of the city a social order and a social control equivalent to that which grew up naturally in the family, the clan, and the tribe.

Civilized man is, so to speak, a late arrival. Viewed in the long perspective of history the appearance of the city and of city life are recent events. Man grew up and acquired most of his native and inheritable traits in an environment in which he lived much as the lower animals live, in direct dependence upon the natural world. In the turmoil of changes which has come with the evolution of city and civil life he has not been able to adapt himself fundamentally and biologically to his new environment.

As long as man lived within the limits of the tribe, custom and tradition provided for all the ordinary exigencies of life and the authority of natural leaders was sufficient to meet the recurrent crises of a relatively stable existence. But the possibilities of human life widened with the rise of the urban community. With the new freedom and the broader division of labor, which the new social order introduced, the city became the center and the focus of social changes that have steadily grown in extent and complexity until every metropolitan city is now a local center of a world-economy, and of a civilization in which local and tribal cultures now in process of fusion will presently disappear altogether.

In a city where custom has been superseded by public opinion and positive law, man has been compelled to live by his wits rather than by his instinct or tradition. The result is the emergence of the individual man as a unit of thought and action.

The peasant who comes to the city to work and live is, to be sure, emancipated from the control of ancestral custom, but at the same time he is no longer backed by the collective wisdom of the peasant community. He is on his own. The case of the peasant is typical. Everyone is more or less on his own in a city. The consequence is that man, translated to the city, has become a problem to himself and to society in a way and to an extent that he never was before.

The older order, based as it was on custom and tradition, was absolute and sacred. It had, besides, something of the character of nature itself; it had grown up, and men took it as they found it, like the climate and the weather, as part of the natural order of things. The new social order, on the other hand, is more or less of an artificial creation, an artifact. It is neither absolute nor sacred, but pragmatic and experimental. Under the influence of a pragmatic point of view education has ceased to be a form of social ritual merely; politics has become empirical; religion is now a quest rather than a tradition, something to be sought rather than to be transmitted.

Natural science came into existence in an effort of man to obtain control over external and physical nature. Social science is now seeking, by the same methods of disinterested observation and research, to give man control over himself. As it is in the city that the political problem, that is, the problem of social control, has arisen, so it is in the city that the problem must be studied.

II. THE FIRST LOCAL STUDIES

It is the detailed and local studies of man in his habitat and under the conditions in which he actually lives, that have contributed most to give the social sciences that realistic and objective character which they have assumed in recent years.

The first of these local studies were, as might be expected, practical rather than theoretic. They were the studies of health and housing; studies of poverty and crime. They became the basis for a whole series of reforms: model tenements, playgrounds, vital statistics. They created a new and romantic interest in the slum. A new literature grew up, telling us how the other half lived, giving us at the same time a new sense of the fact that poor people and immigrants were human like ourselves.

Social settlements, established about near the close of the nineteenth century in England and America, became outposts for observation and for intimate studies of social conditions in regions of the city that up to that time had remained *terra incognita*, except for those pioneer students of urban sociology—politicians and the police. *Hull House Maps and Papers*, published by Jane Addams and her associates, in Chicago, 1895, and *The City Wilderness*, and *Americans in Process*, by Robert Woods, of the South End House, Boston, a few years later, were in the nature of an exploration and recognizance, laying the ground for the more systematic and detailed studies which followed. Notable among these were the series of inquiries into housing conditions in Chicago under the direction of Sophonisba P. Breckinridge and Edith Abbott begun in 1908 at the request of the chief sanitary inspector of Chicago and under the auspices of the department of social investigation (Russell Sage Foundation) of the Chicago School of Civics and Philanthropy. Early studies included the housing of non-family groups of men; families in furnished rooms; the Twenty-ninth Ward back of the yards; the West Side revisited; South Chicago at the gates of the steel mills; the problem of the Negro; two Italian districts; among the Slovaks in the Twentieth Ward; Lithuanians in the

Fourth Ward; Greeks and Italians in the neighborhood of Hull House.[1]

Meanwhile Charles Booth had begun, some time about 1888, his epoch-making study of life and labor in London,[2] followed in 1901 by Rountree's more minute study of poverty in New York.[3] These were case studies on a grand scale. The thing that characterized them was a determined and, as it seemed, somewhat pedantic effort to reduce the descriptive and impressionistic statements of investigators and observers to the more precise and general formulations of a statistical statement. Booth said:[4]

No one can go, as I have done, over the description of the inhabitants of street after street in this huge district (East London), taken house by house and family by family—full as it is of picturesque details noted down from the lips of the visitor to whose mind they have been recalled by the open pages of their schedules—and doubt the genuine character of the information and its truth. Of the wealth of my material I have no doubt. I am indeed embarrassed by its mass and by my resolution to make use of no fact that I cannot give a quantitative value. The materials for sensational stories lie plentifully in every book of our notes; but, even if I had the skill to use my material in this way—that gift of the imagination which is called "realistic"—I should not wish to use it here. There is struggling poverty, there is destitution, there is hunger, drunkenness, brutality and crime; no one doubts that it is so. My object has been to attempt to show the numerical relation which poverty, misery and depravity bear to regular earnings and comparative comfort, and to describe the general conditions under which each class lives.

[1] Series of articles on Chicago housing conditions in the *American Journal of Sociology*, XVI (1910–11), 145–70; 289–308; 433–68; XVII (1911–12), 1–34; 145–76; XVIII (1912–13), 241–57; 509–42; XX (1914–15), 145–69, 289–312; XXI (1915–16), 285–316.

[2] Charles Booth, *Life and Labor of the People of London* (9 vols.) (London, 1892), p. 97.

[3] B. Seebohm Rountree, *Poverty: A Study of Town Life* (London, 1901).

[4] Booth, *op. cit.*, I, 5–6.

It was not, however, Booth's statistics, but his realistic descriptions of the actual life of the occupational classes—the conditions under which they lived and labored, their passions, pastimes, domestic tragedies, and the life-philosophies with which each class met the crises peculiar to it—which made these studies a memorable and a permanent contribution to our knowledge of human nature and of society. What we have then, finally, in these volumes, is a minute and painstaking account of the phase of modern civilization at the end of the nineteenth century, as manifested in the life of the London laborer. These volumes were a sociological study; they have become a historical document.

The thing which gave the greatest impetus to local studies in the United States was the establishment of the Sage Foundation in 1906, and the publication in the period from 1909 to 1914 of the findings of the Pittsburgh Survey. Pittsburgh was chosen by Paul U. Kellogg and his collaborators for investigation because it was regarded as a particularly flagrant illustration of the working out of forces and tendencies that had their origin in the rapidly expanding industrial life of America. Pittsburgh was conspicuously and exclusively an industrial city. America was in process of industrial transformation. Pittsburgh offered itself as clinical material for a study of American civilization. It seemed possible to exhibit, in a single city, just how the industrial organization of that time affected the personal and cultural life of a people. This was the purpose for which the Survey was undertaken.

The Pittsburgh Survey was timely. It appeared at a moment when, in every part of the United States, thoughtful people were seeking light upon problems that no longer yielded to the traditional technique embodied in the forms and traditions of party politics. It was a time when reformers were seeking to keep reforms out of politics, that is, out of party politics. The Pittsburgh Survey offered a new method for political education and collective action in local affairs, a method that did not raise party issues and did not involve anything so revolutionary as a change in the control of local government.

Social surveys now came into vogue, and local studies of a sort were undertaken in every part of the country. The wide range of interests with which they thought to deal is indicated by the subject matter of some of the more important of them. *The Springfield Survey*, which undertook to cover the whole field of social politics: public health, education, social service in all its various aspects;[1] the *Survey of Criminal Justice in Cleveland*, published in 1922, and the study of race relations in Chicago after the race riot, published in the same year under the title of *The Negro in Chicago*, are examples.

These surveys have, as regional studies invariably do, the characteristics of local and contemporary history. They emphasize what is unique and individual in the situations investigated. But they are at the same time case studies. Conditions in one city are described in terms that make them comparable to conditions in other cities. They do not yield generalizations of wide or general validity, but they have furnished a body of materials that raise issues and suggest hypotheses which can eventually be investigated statistically and stated in quantitative terms.

III. THE URBAN COMMUNITY

In all, or most, of these investigations there is implicit the notion that the urban community, in its growth and

[1] *The Springfield Survey; A Study of Social Conditions in an American City.* Directed by Shelby M. Harrison. 3 vols. (New York: Russell Sage Foundation, 1918–20).

organization, represents a complex of tendencies and events that can be described conceptually, and made the object of independent study. There is implicit in all these studies the notion that the city is a thing with a characteristic organization and a typical life-history, and that individual cities are enough alike so that what one learns about one city may, within limits, be assumed to be true of others.

This notion has been the central theme of a series of special studies of the Chicago Urban Community, some of which have already been published, others of which are still in progress.[1] Among these, three, *The Hobo*, by Nels Anderson, *The Ghetto*, by Louis Wirth, and *The Gold Coast and the Slum*, by Harvey W. Zorbaugh, deal each with one of the so-called natural areas of the city. *The Hobo: A Study of the Homeless Man* is unique in so far as it investigates the casual laborer in his habitat, that is to say in the region of the city where the interests and habits of the casual laborer have been, so to speak, institutionalized. *The Ghetto*, on the other hand, is a study of the Jewish quarter, but it is at the same time the natural history of an institution of Jewish life, an institution that grew up and flourished in the Middle Ages but has persisted in some fashion down to the present day. It has persisted, however, because it performed a social function, making it possible for two unassimilated peoples to live together, participating in a single economy, but preserving, at the same time, each its own racial and cultural integrity. *The Gold Coast and the Slum*, finally, is a study of the Lower North Side, which is not so much a natural area, as a congeries of natural areas, including, as it does, "Little

---

[1] Robert E. Park, E. W. Burgess, *et al.*, *The City* (Chicago, 1925).

Sicily," "The Gold Coast," and an extensive region of rooming-houses between.[1]

A region is called "a natural area" because it comes into existence without design, and performs a function, though the function, as in the case of the slum, may be contrary to anybody's desire. It is a natural area because it has a natural history. The existence of these natural areas, each with its characteristic function, is some indication of the sort of thing the city turns out upon analysis to be—not as has been suggested earlier, an artifact merely, but in some sense, and to some degree, an organism.

The city is, in fact, a constellation of natural areas, each with its own characteristic milieu, and each performing its specific function in the urban economy as a whole. The relation of the different natural areas of the city to one another is typified in the relation of the city and its suburbs. These suburbs are, apparently, mere extensions of the urban community. Every suburb, pushing outward into the open country, tends to have a character which distinguishes it from every other. The metropolis is, it seems, a great sifting and sorting mechanism, which, in ways that are not yet wholly understood, infallibly selects out of the population as a whole the individuals best suited to live in a particular region and a particular milieu. The larger the city, the more numerous and the more completely characterized its suburbs will be. The city grows by expansion, but it gets its character by the selection and segregation of its population, so that every individual finds, eventually, either the place where he can, or the place where he must, live.[2]

[1] See pp. 126 and 133 for maps showing the local communities of Chicago.

[2] See the article by E. W. Burgess, "The Growth of the City," in R. E. Park, et al, The City, pp. 47–62.

Recent studies in Chicago have revealed to what an extraordinary extent this segregation may go. There are regions in Chicago where there are almost no children; regions where half the boys of juvenile-court age are recorded, at least once in the course of a year, as delinquents;[1] other regions where there are no divorces, and still others in which the percentage of divorces and desertions is larger, with one exception, than that of any other political unit in the United States.[2]

The proportion of age and sex groups shows extraordinary variations in different parts of the city, and these variations are dependable indices of other cultural and character differences in the population.

It does not follow, from what has been said, that the populations in the different natural areas of the city can be described as homogeneous. People live together on the whole, not because they are alike, but because they are useful to one another. This is particularly true of great cities, where social distances are maintained in spite of geographical proximity, and where every community is likely to be composed of people who live together in relations that can best be described as symbiotic rather than social.

On the other hand, every community is to some degree an independent cultural unit, has its own standards, its own conception of what is proper, decent, and worthy of respect. As individuals rise or sink in the struggle for status in the community they invariably move from one region to another; go up to the Gold Coast, or down to the slum, or perhaps occupy a tolerable position

---

[1] See Clifford R. Shaw, *Delinquency and Crime Areas of Chicago* (Chicago, 1929).

[2] Ernest R. Mowrer, *Family Disorganization*, pp. 116–23.

somewhere between the two. In any case, they learn to accommodate themselves more or less completely to the conditions and the code of the area into which they move. The case records of social agencies and institutions make it possible to follow the migrations of individuals and families and learn what has happened to them. It is often possible to carry these studies of individuals and families farther and to get information and insight in regard to their subjective experiences, their attitudes and states of mind, outlook on life, and above all their changing conceptions of themselves incident to their movements from one milieu to another. The numerous life-histories of immigrants that have been published in recent years furnish materials of this sort.

The more we understand the attitudes and personal histories of individuals, the more we can know the community in which these individuals live. On the other hand, the more knowledge we have of the milieu in which the individual lives, or has lived, the more intelligible his behavior becomes. This is true, because while temperament is inherited, character and habit are formed under the influence of environment.

As a matter of fact, most of our ordinary behavior problems are actually solved, if solved at all, by transferring the individual from an environment in which he behaves badly to one in which he behaves well. Here, again, social science has achieved something that approaches in character a laboratory experiment. For the purpose of these experiments the city, with its natural regions, becomes a "frame of reference," i.e., a device for controlling our observations of social conditions in their relation to human behavior.

IV. THE INDIVIDUAL

It is due to the intrinsic nature of society and of social relations that we ordinarily find our social problems embodied in the persons and in the behavior of individuals. It is because social problems so frequently terminate in problems of individual behavior and because social relations are finally and fundamentally personal relations that the attitude and behavior of individuals are the chief sources of our knowledge of society.

The city always has been a prolific source of clinical material for the study of human nature because it has always been the source and center of social change. In a perfectly stable society where man has achieved a complete biological and social equilibrium, social problems are not likely to arise, and the anxieties, mental conflicts, and ambitions which stimulate the energies of civilized man, and incidentally make him a problem to himself and to society, are lacking.

It was with what Simmel calls inner enemies—the poor, the criminal, and the insane—that personality studies seem to have had their origin. It is, however, within comparatively recent years that poverty and delinquency have come to be reckoned along with insanity as personality and behavior problems. At the present time this is so far true that social service has come to be recognized as a branch of medicine, and the so-called psychiatric social worker has come to replace, or at least supplement, the work of the friendly visitor. The probation officer, visiting teacher, and the public playground director have all achieved a new professional status as the notion has gained recognition that social problems are fundamentally behavior problems.

A new impetus was given to the study of personality

problems with the organization in 1899 in Chicago of the first juvenile court of the United States. Juvenile courts became at once, as far as was practicable under the circumstances under which they came into existence, behavior clinics. Putting the delinquent on probation was an invitation to him to participate in an experiment, under the direction of a probation officer, that had as its aim his own rehabilitation.

It was through the establishment of the Juvenile Psychopathic Institute[1] in connection with the Juvenile Court of Chicago that Healy began those systematic studies upon which that notable book, *The Individual Delinquent*, published in 1915, was based. It was followed by similar studies, under the Judge Baker Foundation, in Boston, and by the establishment of other institutes for child study and so-called behavior clinics in every part of the country, notably, the Child Welfare Research Station at the University of Iowa, the Institute of Child Welfare at the University of Minnesota, the Institute for Child Welfare Research at Teachers College, New York City, the Institute for Child Guidance, and locally supported child-guidance clinics established through demonstrations of the Commonwealth Fund Program for the Prevention of Delinquency in St. Louis, Dallas, Los Angeles, Minneapolis, St. Paul, Cleveland, and Philadelphia.[2]

The study of juvenile delinquency and of behavior problems in general was established on a firm basis in Chicago with the organization in May, 1926, by Dr. Herman M. Adler of the Behavior Research Fund. Dr. Adler has brought together a notable group of students and ex-

---

[1] Now the Institute for Juvenile Research.

[2] For a review and analysis of the child-study movement see W. I. Thomas and Dorothy S. Thomas, *The Child in America* (New York, 1928).

perts and has set up an administrative machinery for making accurate scientific records, both psychiatric and social, which as they have accumulated have created a fund of fact and information that is now being subjected to elaborate statistical analyses which are yielding surprising and important results.

Studies of the Institute of Juvenile Research and of the Behavior Research Fund are in certain respects unique. They are at once psychiatric and social studies, i.e., studies not merely of the individual and his behavior but of the environment and of the situation to which the behavior is a response. This realizes, in the form of a definite program, a conception which has been the subject of several conferences between the psychiatrists and representatives of the other social sciences, seeking to define the relation of psychiatric and social studies and to determine the rôle which psychiatry is likely to play in co-operation with the social sciences in the investigation and solution of social problems.

There is not now, if there ever was, any question that the individual's conception of himself, the rôle which he plays in any society, and the character which he eventually acquires are very largely determined by the associations which he makes and, in general, by the world in which he lives. The city is a complex of such worlds—worlds which touch but never completely penetrate.

The differences between urban areas in respect to the type and character of the social life which they support is undoubtedly as great as the standards of living that they maintain, or the price of land on which they are situated. One of the important series of local studies which the University of Chicago has undertaken is that which involves a delimitation and characterization of all the important areas of the city. This study is based on the assumption that more complete knowledge of the localities and of the peoples of the city will throw a new light upon the extraordinary variation, in the different areas of the city in the amount and extent of desertion, divorce, delinquency, crime, and other evidences of social disorganization. In doing this it will be of service to every social agency that is seeking to deal directly or indirectly with these problems. But in determining with more definiteness the conditions under which social experiments are actually being carried on, it will make the city in some more real sense than it has been hitherto a social laboratory.

v. institutions

The city has been made the subject of investigation from many different points of view. There is already a considerable literature on the geography of the city, and there is a vast body of research concerning the city as a physical object, including studies of housing, city planning, and municipal engineering. N. S. B. Gras, in his *Introduction to Economic History*, has made the city the central theme in the history of an economy that has evolved through the stages of village, town, and city to the metropolitan economy of the present day. As a matter of fact economic history assumes a new significance when it is written from the ecological and regional point of view, and when the city, with its market place, is conceived as the focal center of an area of ever widening boundaries over which it is constantly extending and consolidating its dominance and control.

The political and administrative problems of cities have come to occupy a place in political science that has steadily increased in importance as cities have increased in population, in influence, and in complexity.

The urban community is, finally, because it is now as it has always been the melting pot of races and cultures, the region in which new institutions emerge, as earlier ones decline, are modified, and disappear.

The family, in its origin at least, is probably not an institution. It is rather the first and most primitive form of society—a form which has been preserved, although continually modified under all the changing circumstances of man's eventful career. The family has, apparently, formed the basic pattern for every type of civilization except our own. Occidental civilization is based on the city, on the *polis*, as the Greeks called it, and is political rather than familial in origin. It was in the city states of Greece and Rome that society organized on kinship, custom, and the family was superseded by a society based on civil rights and a political organization.

The family is now in process of change and disintegration in every part of the civilized world, including the regions where it has persisted longest in its original form, Japan and China. Changes in the family, however, are taking place more rapidly in cities than elsewhere. Everything that is characteristic of city life, a mobile population, a wide division of labor, and the multiplication of municipal institutions and social conveniences of all sorts have contributed to bring about these changes. Schools, hospitals, and all the numerous agencies for personal service which have taken over, one by one, the functions once performed by the home and in the family have contributed indirectly to undermine that ancient institution and diminish its social importance.

As it is in the urban environment that the older forms of the family have declined, so it is in the city that most of the experiments in new forms of family life are taking place.

That is why the institution of the family can be studied to the best advantage in cities rather than elsewhere.

The city and the conditions of life that it imposes have greatly tended to the secularization of all aspects of social life, and this has had profound effect upon the organization of the church. Numerous local studies of city and rural churches have been made in recent years, but as yet no studies have been made to show the extent of changes which involve the structure and function of the church as a social institution.

There is, however, no doubt but that changes are taking place and that as the social sciences develop an interest in and methods for the study of civilized, as they have for primitive, man the changes taking place in contemporary religious institutions will assume an importance that they do not now seem to have.

In recent years, particularly in Chicago, under the inspiration and initiative of Professor Charles E. Merriam, a beginning has been made looking to more realistic studies of the actual workings of the political process as it takes place under the conditions of modern city life.[1]

The political process, broadly conceived, includes much more than the formulation of laws by legislatures and their interpretation by the courts. It includes a whole cycle of events that begins with some sort of general unrest, in which political issues arise, and concludes with the general acceptance into the mores and habits of the community of a new rule of conduct, and—to use an expression which W. I. Thomas has made familiar—a new definition of the situation.

[1] See Charles E. Merriam, *New Aspects of Politics* (Chicago, 1925); *Four American Party Leaders* (New York, 1926); *Chicago: A More Intimate View of Urban Politics* (New York, 1929).

The political process includes public discussion and a definition of issues; the formation and expression of public opinion; the election of legislators; the framing and enactment of legislation; the interpretation and enforcement of the law, and, finally, the general acceptance of and acquiescence in the enforcement of the law by the community. In this way the law eventually passes over into custom and becomes fixed in the habits of the community. The political process covers all the operations of government; and since society is essentially an organization for social control, it involves finally every aspect of social life.

The organization in New York City, Chicago, and elsewhere, of bureaus of municipal research and the more recent studies in Cleveland and St. Louis of the administration of criminal justice indicate the direction and progress of research in this field.

The studies of the political science group at the University of Chicago are indicative not only of the trend toward a more realistic perception of the political process but of the attempt to introduce scientific methods into the description and prediction of political behavior, as in the research projects already published of *Non-Voting* by Charles E. Merriam and Harold F. Gosnell, *Getting Out the Vote* by H. F. Gosnell, *The Chicago Primary of 1926: A Study in Election Methods* by Carroll H. Wooddy, *Carter H. Harrison I: A Study in Political Leadership* by C. O. Johnson, and *The City Manager* by Leonard D. White.

Sumner says that there are two kinds of institutions, (1) those which grow, and (2) those which are enacted. But institutions are not merely enacted. Rather, they are discovered and invented. The fact seems to be that institutions always grow, but they grow, ordinarily, by the addition and summation of specific inventions.[1]

One thing that makes the city a peculiarly advantageous place in which to study institutions and social life generally is the fact that under the conditions of urban life institutions grow rapidly. They grow under our very eyes, and the processes by which they grow are open to observation and so, eventually, to experimentation.

Another thing that makes the city an advantageous place to study social life and gives it the character of a social laboratory is the fact that in the city every characteristic of human nature is not only visible but is magnified.

In the freedom of the city every individual, no matter how eccentric, finds somewhere an environment in which he can expand and bring what is peculiar in his nature to some sort of expression. A smaller community sometimes tolerates eccentricity, but the city often rewards it. Certainly one of the attractions of a city is that somewhere every type of individual—the criminal and beggar, as well as the man of genius—may find congenial company and the vice or the talent which was suppressed in the more intimate circle of the family or in the narrow limits of a small community, discovers here a moral climate in which it flourishes.

The result is that in the city all the secret ambitions and all the suppressed desires find somewhere an expression. The city magnifies, spreads out, and advertises human nature in all its various manifestations. It is this that makes the city interesting, even fascinating. It is this, however, that makes it of all places the one in which to discover the secrets of human hearts, and to study human nature and society.

[1] Sumner, *Folkways*, pp. 48–50.

CHAPTER II

THE LOCAL COMMUNITY RESEARCH COM-
MITTEE AND THE SOCIAL SCIENCE
RESEARCH BUILDING

Faced with the fascinating complex of problems inherent in the modern city, the social science group at the
University of Chicago undertook in 1923 to focus their
efforts more definitely, and with a greater degree of co-
operation, on the processes of urban life. Stimulated by
the inspiring, but unhappily brief, leadership of Dr. E. D.
Burton, president of the University of Chicago, and by the
dynamic personality of A. W. Small, dean of the Graduate
School of Arts, many of the fundamental issues of urban-
ism, of maladjustment, of the growth and interaction of
institutions, of personality were realized more sharply than
ever before to spread themselves at our feet for inspection
and analysis, and even for diagnosis and prescription.

All agreed that the city and its region could not and
ought not to absorb the whole range of interests and activities of the social science group. The historian particularly cannot limit himself to so narrow a field, but the
phenomena of interest to the sociologist, the economist,
the political scientist, and the student of welfare institutions were abundantly present. To exploit them most
meaningfully, there was general agreement that the varying points of view of the various disciplines, so far as might
be feasible in a given case, should all be brought to bear.
This involved the abandonment of any remnants of the
idea of vested rights in any subject matter in the range

of the social sciences, and the immediate co-operation of any and all members of the faculty who possessed special interest in or knowledge of problems or methods.

I

Such a point of view implied a new administrative organization, and we wish in the present chapter to describe this organization and its new quarters, the Social Science Research Building dedicated on the campus of the University of Chicago at the close of 1929.

The departments and schools which became associated in the new enterprise included the Departments of Philosophy, Sociology and Anthropology,[1] History, Economics,[2] and Political Science, and the School of Social Service Administration. This by no means represents the whole range of the social sciences found in the University Faculties, for it takes no account of the Law School, the School of Education, the Graduate Library School, the Divinity School, or the Departments of Geography, Psychology, Hygiene and Bacteriology, or Home Economics, to say nothing of more remote but nevertheless real associations with the Medical School, and the Department of Physiology.

In 1929 other potential associations were set up by reason of the affiliation with the University of Chicago of the International City Managers' Association and the Bureau of Public Personnel Administration. Still another contact is opened up by the appointment of August Vollmer as Professor of Police Administration.

The Local Community Research Committee therefore is not a body fully representative of the whole range of the social sciences, but with its six members and executive secretary it serves for administrative purposes as such.

[1] In 1929 a separate Department of Anthropology was established.

[2] Which also represents the School of Commerce and Administration.

From the beginning its duties have been twofold: (1) to plan research, either independently or by approving projects submitted to it by members of the faculty, (2) to discharge the necessary administrative duties incident to an extensive research program.

In practice the initiative in proposing research has generally come from the departments and from individuals. In such cases the function of the Local Community Research Committee has been to evaluate the different projects brought to its attention and to approve, modify, or reject. An annual program is agreed upon in the spring of each year.

The Committee also exercises a general supervision over the research which it authorizes. The responsibility for each project is vested in a supervisor or a subcommittee; quarterly progress reports are received from them, and from time to time an oral report is presented by the supervisor to the Committee. The executive secretary is directed to keep in general touch with research; and without diminishing in any way the responsibility of the supervisor, he is able to be of assistance in many cases.

Subject to the general supervision of the executive secretary, a central stenographic pool is maintained under the immediate direction of an office manager; this office also supplies general clerical service. Such operations as mailing (en masse), photostating, blue printing, and mimeographing are performed in the appropriate University offices, or by commercial firms. Much of the drafting is performed by members of the office force.

Subject to the authority of the Committee a very extensive research program has developed. In Appendix I may be found a list of the publications and completed studies resulting from five years' activity, a list which will give some idea of the scope of the work. The bulk of the present volume is devoted to a brief summary of the more important lines of research.

One of the objectives of the organization has been from the outset to secure co-operation and criticism of research from varied points of view. Reference has already been made to subcommittees charged with the responsibility of carrying on research. These are a characteristic illustration of the interpenetration of the various disciplines in attacking a given problem. The Local Community Research Committee itself has been the seat of considerable self-education in different points of view; the subcommittees, which are fundamentally research rather than administrative committees, offer a more intensive opportunity for each discipline to react on others.

Two or three illustrations will make this clear. The Causes of War Subcommittee is presided over by Mr. Quincy Wright, of the Department of Political Science, and includes Messrs. Bernadotte Schmitt, of the Department of History; Jacob Viner, of the Department of Economics; Fay-Cooper Cole, of the Department of Anthropology; and Harold D. Lasswell, of the Department of Political Science. The Subcommittee holds meetings from time to time, and at less frequent intervals meetings with the research staff as a whole. Nineteen persons were co-operating on this study in 1929.

The Joint Committee on Registration of Social Statistics is directed by Mr. H. A. Millis, of the Economics Department, and includes on the University side Miss Edith Abbott and Messrs. Harry Lurie, of the School of Social Service Administration; Clarence R. Rorem, of the School of Commerce and Administration; and Leonard D. White, of the Department of Political Science. The Association of Community Chests and Councils is represented by William J. Norton, Detroit Community Fund; Fred C. Croxton, Community Fund of Columbus and Franklin County, Ohio; Pierce Atwater, Community Chest, Wichita, Kansas; and Raymond Clapp, the Welfare Federation of Cleveland, Ohio.

The Committee on Personality comprises Messrs. Ellsworth Faris, of the Department of Sociology, L. L. Thurstone, of the Department of Psychology, and Charles E. Merriam and Harold D. Lasswell, of the Department of Political Science.

The Committee on Public Finance consists of Messrs. S. E. Leland, chairman, (economics), C. E. Merriam (political science), A. H. Kent (law), H. A. Millis (economics), Paul H. Douglas (commerce and administration), Jacob Viner (economics), and Leonard D. White (political science).

Not every attempt to cross-fertilize by the device of a joint subcommittee works, but in most cases effective co-operation and interpenetration develop. The process will be materially accelerated in the quarters provided in the new Social Science Research Building.

II

The social sciences have not ordinarily been thought of as using or needing laboratory equipment, and it still remains true that much social science research is conducted with documentary material not lending itself to the experimental method. The community has often been described, in a broad sense of the word, as a laboratory for the social sciences, wherein proceed sequences of significant events which may be observed if not controlled. Social scientists regularly treat the community as a clinic, diagnosing on the basis of existing knowledge and insight, and prescribing with what wisdom they may possess for social ills.

In a more precise sense, however, the social sciences have now reached the point where it is open to them to use laboratory methods. Mr. Gosnell's experiment with a section of the Chicago electorate, applying a known stimulus under controlled conditions, reveals the social scientist at work in an out-of-door laboratory; the various analyses of personality, including the application of the technique of the psychologist and psychiatrist, involve laboratory technique and equipment provided in the new Social Science Building.

It may be more accurate to refer to this building, the erection and maintenance of which was made possible by the generous gift of the Laura Spelman Rockefeller Memorial, as a workshop, for not all the research enterprise which is taking place within its walls is experimental nor does it all require laboratory methods. A workshop par excellence it certainly is from basement to roof, and it includes specifically a laboratory for anthropometrics and archaeology, special rooms for linguistics, a psychological-psychiatric laboratory, and an extensive statistical laboratory.

The Social Science Building is contiguous to the Harper Memorial Library, extending eastward along the Midway for a distance of 158 feet, with a depth along the main axis of 52 feet, which increases by reason of a projection at the eastern end to a depth of 70 feet. It is thus immediately adjacent to the main stock of books, and provision is made for intercommunication on the basement, first, and third floors of the Harper Library. This in turn leads directly to the Law Library, to the modern-language collection in Wieboldt Hall, and to the Classics Library.

The design of the building is harmonious with Harper

Library and when completed will fill in the Midway front. Contrary to the arrangement in the Harper, Wieboldt, and Classics Buildings there will be only a single basement, which will have direct light from both sides and adequate cross-ventilation. The basement will be used principally for storage, but one room with excellent southern exposure has been designed to care for the punch card and electric sorting-machines. Above the basement are five stories, each of standard 13-foot height.

In many respects the Social Science Building is unique. In the first place, it is devoted exclusively to the *research and graduate school* activities of the social science group. The non-research and undergraduate activities of these departments and schools are not housed in this building. Departmental offices, conference rooms for instructors, reading rooms, and the like are provided elsewhere. Instructors whose primary interest is in under-graduate teaching will not be housed here.

Second, it is the center of the co-operative research enterprises of this large group. In harmony with the intention of the grant to the Local Community Research Committee, this building gives primary consideration to the provision of facilities for projects which tend to cross departmental lines, which require borderland exploration, and which combine various techniques. Thus, by way of illustration, a series of rooms has been set aside for the investigation of the causes of war, a project which combines forces in the Departments of Political Science, History, Economics, Sociology, and Anthropology. In the assignment of studies to members of the staff little attention has been given to departmental groupings; a historian may hobnob with a sociologist to the left and with a political scientist to the right.

Third, with the exception of four graduate seminar rooms and a lecture-room seating about two hundred persons, there are no classrooms in the building. The plant is not intended for instructional purposes, except as instruction may be related to research.

Fourth, with the exception of a small data room connected with the statistical laboratory, there are no stacks and no provision for collection of books. This may seem at first thought an amazing oversight, but is explained by two considerations. The main collection of books is immediately at hand in the Harper Library and is easily accessible. More than this, a very great deal of the research conducted by the social science group at the University of Chicago involves the collection of fresh material from the field rather than the distillation of new conclusions from documentary sources. We are as much in need of a galvanometer, a calculating machine, an electric sorting- and counting-machine and a planimeter as we are in need of books, although naturally an extensive collection of documentary material is indispensable.

Fifth, the allocation of space in the building is in part flexible, being subject to reallocation as one project is finished and another appears. Much of the building will necessarily and properly be regularly occupied; thus professors' studies and the three laboratories will be substantially settled allocations. Other space, however, will be allocated to a project as such, and will provide space for research assistants, clerical help, and field-workers. This space, which is chiefly on the south side of the building, will be subject to frequent readjustment as projects are completed.

The Social Science Building is in fact a workshop where perhaps two hundred scholars and workers combine their efforts in a comprehensive research program. The layout of the rooms reflects the workshop spirit. The following diagram of the third floor, which is typical of the other floors, makes this clear.

A brief explanation of the floor plan is needed. The main axis of the building (which was fixed by its relation to Harper Library) was both too wide and too narrow to be most effectively used. It was too wide because the city building code made it impossible to carry the outside rooms back to the corridor, the rooms in that event being relatively narrow; it was too narrow because a court could not be introduced to give light from the center of the building. The arrangement worked out by the architects provides a series of inner rooms, artificially lighted but with good ventilation, which in turn give access to the studies and workrooms. They will be used for a variety of purposes, including the housing of books, filing of papers, display of maps, occasional clerical or statistical work, and the like. They will have another incidental but highly valued use to the harassed professor—they make him doubly inaccessible!

With these general observations on the character and plan of the building, a few words may be said concerning the particular uses to which each floor will be put.

The first floor contains the offices of the executive secretary of the Local Community Research Committee, the office manager, and the central clerical pool. These are arranged in a suite, conveniently placed off the main lobby. These offices will provide the general "control" of the building, where information can be had, where appointments can be made, and where various services can be supplied.

On this floor also are four seminar rooms, each seating

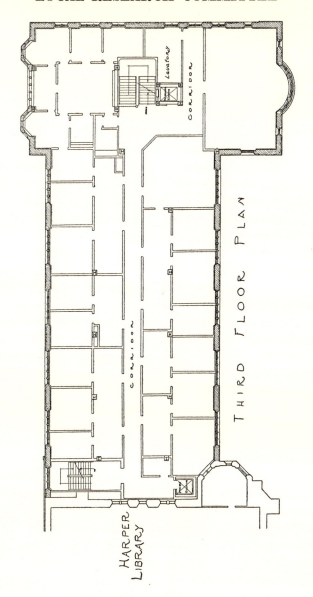

from twenty to thirty persons. One at least will be equipped with a microphone, and the lecture hall will be wired for this purpose. The primary use of these rooms will be in connection with advanced research courses given to supplement research projects. Thus Mr. Jernegan is now giving a seminar on the early history of immigration in connection with his project in this field; Mr. Quincy Wright is conducting a seminar on the causes of war, and Mr. Merriam on leadership. The seminar-rooms will also be available for other advanced work in the departments concerned.

The large lecture hall on the first floor is designed to provide opportunity for distinguished lecturers from this and other countries to present to the University group their contributions to the social sciences. The room is carefully finished to present a dignified aspect in keeping with the significance of its use.

The remaining rooms on the first floor are typical studies and workrooms. Definite understandings exist that each professor normally is entitled to a private study; research assistants will join in the use of workrooms, two or more being assigned to a room.

On the second floor is found the Commons Room, an attractive lounging place with a southern exposure, with a fireplace and kitchenette. This room is open at all hours and is the convenient meeting-place of the whole group. Here it is expected that the various disciplines in the social sciences will cross-fertilize each other in easy conversation over a cup of tea, or in fruitful silences at the close of day.

The second floor is also the home of the archaeological group which, under the direction of Professor Fay-Cooper Cole, is exploring the prehistory of the neighboring region.

The anthropometric laboratory is adjacent to the archaeological laboratory and is bordered by a special sound-proof room for the study of linguistics. These rooms, like the lecture hall on the first floor, are equipped with stereopticon and motion-picture cameras. The remaining rooms on this floor are typical studies or workrooms.

The third floor contains drafting-rooms with drafting tables and equipment, together with a special room for map display and a room for map storage. Further provision for map storage is made in the basement.

The third floor also contains the psychological-psychiatric laboratory, a suite of nine rooms including a small chemical laboratory and special speech reproduction apparatus.

The fourth floor is dedicated to the statistical method in the social sciences. Here is the statistical laboratory, a suite of four rooms containing a substantial array of calculating machines. In addition to the usual equipment there is a specially constructed planimeter and a harmonic analyzer, both built by Coradi in Switzerland. Here also will be housed the projects based on the statistical method, such as the registration of social statistics, the studies in taxation and finance, the determination of prices, and the index of real wages.

The fifth floor, apart from studies and workrooms, is of interest because it is the home of the six social science journals published by the University of Chicago Press. These are the *International Journal of Ethics*, the *American Journal of Sociology*, the *Journal of Political Economy*, the *University Journal of Business*, the *Social Service Review*, and the *Journal of Modern History*. Each journal will have its own quarters and in addition may call upon a central stenographic office.

This brief survey of the plans for each floor of the Social Science Building gives some idea of the nature and purposes of the structure. To the fullest possible degree the facilities of the building are at the disposal of the whole University and in a genuine sense of the word of the whole community. The building and its equipment are tools in the hands of an earnest group of social scientists who are patiently seeking better ways of life for the city and for the state. It is a significant symbol of one of the most characteristic developments of the twentieth century, organized co-operative research on human problems.

CHAPTER III

CO-OPERATION WITH CIVIC AND SOCIAL AGENCIES

The extent to which the research group known as the Local Community Research Committee has already been of service to the city is a fair indication that the facilities and equipment described in the preceding chapter will be of continuing advantage. Indeed long before the grant which brought into existence this organization, members of the University in their individual capacity had rendered notable service in solving political, economic, and social problems of the city and state. The new organization established in 1923, and the new quarters provided in 1929, have made it possible to develop this university-community contact on a richer and more complete scale.

I

The character of the grant made to the University of Chicago presupposed an intimate relationship with the city. A part of the funds was put immediately at our disposal for the study of local problems, broadly construed. Another part of the funds was released to the extent that it was matched dollar for dollar by other contributors. The expectation was that individuals or groups perplexed by some specific problem of social adjustment would turn to the University as an impartial, disinterested fact-finding agency, and would be able to secure not only expert advice or expert assistance in securing the facts, but also some financial aid. The sincerity of these persons and the significance of their problems were to be attested by a willingness on their part to contribute a portion of the expense of discovering the essential facts.

The program of the Local Community Research Committee therefore from the outset has comprised two sections, each bearing a more or less close relation to the other. On the one hand are those projects initiated by the Committee in furtherance of the research program in which different members of the University, or the Committee collectively, are interested; on the other hand are projects brought to our attention with a request for help by outside groups.

In order to present the entire situation, it must be added that the Local Community Research Committee has never absorbed all, or nearly all, the research interest or activities of the social science departments at the University of Chicago. For several years, the jurisdiction of the Committee was limited to local problems; and although these were often liberally construed, it remained true that much research could not qualify under this description. Later a special fund was established, to be used in the discretion of the president of the University either for local or "outside" projects; but it remains true today that a substantial proportion of the total research energy of the social science group is expended beyond the supervision of the Local Community Research Committee.

Illustrations of this situation may seem invidious, but to call to mind only such projects as Thompson's *History of Mediaeval Germany*, Hutchinson's forthcoming *Life of Cyrus McCormick*, Schmitts' analysis of the causes of the Great War, Merriam's extensive study of civic education, Clark's *Theory of Overhead Costs*, and Smith's *Democratic Way of Life* will suffice to demonstrate the point.

In discussing our co-operation with civic and social agencies, it is important to remember that, in this phase of our work, the initiative rests with the community. We have never taken the view that all of our matched funds should be used, irrespective of a real community desire for our services. We have not engaged in a sales campaign to match funds with any group in order to provide research opportunities. In fact, members of the Local Community Research Committee have sometimes expressed regret that that part of the research program which we initiate and which represents borderland inquiries which we believe particularly significant, have at times been delayed by the necessity for giving thought to co-operative research which is of primary importance to other groups.

The community has in fact been eager to take advantage of the research facilities of the University. As a rule, substantially all of the matched funds have been absorbed in co-operative projects; and in the fiscal year 1928–29 they proved inadequate. There follows a list of these projects showing (a) the project, (b) the co-operating group, and (c) the amount of their contribution. The total amount expended in the five-year period under review is twice the amount here indicated, as these funds were matched dollar for dollar.

Analysis of this tabulation shows that funds have been received from three official sources, the Children's Bureau, the City of Chicago, and the Smithsonian Institution; from six foundations and institutes, including the Wieboldt Foundation, the Rosenwald Foundation, the Commonwealth Fund, the Helen Crittenden Memorial, the Institute of Economics, and the Chicago Historical Society; from six clubs, including the City Club of Chicago, the Commonwealth Club, the Union League Club, the Chicago

CO-OPERATIVE RESEARCH PROJECTS

Year	Project	Co-operating Agency	Annual Amount	Total
1924–25....	Truck Garden project	U.S. Children's Bureau	$........	$ 450.00
1924–25....	Recreation Facilities	City Club	....	172.52
1924–25....	Morale of City Employees	City of Chicago	....	947.03
1924–25....	Study of Begging	Wieboldt Foundation	....	500.00
1924–25....	Rehabilitation of Physically Handicapped	Wieboldt Foundation	....	50.00
1924–25....	Regional Planning	Commonwealth Club	5,000.00	....
1925–26....	(Map, Miss Jeter's and Mr. Fryxell's studies)	Commonwealth Club	1,000.00	....
				6,000.00
1925–26....	Regional Planning (Publication of *The Geographic Background of Chicago*)	Chicago Real Estate Board	....	2,500.00
1925–26		Commonwealth Club	10,000.00	....
1926–27	Regional Planning (Industry Studies)	A Friend	1,000.00	....
1927–28		A Friend	1,000.00	....
1928–29		A Friend	1,000.00	....
				13,000.00
1924–25		Commonwealth Fund	4,500.00	....
1924–25	Type Studies of Commodities and Services	A Friend	1,000.00	....
1925–26		Commonwealth Fund	4,000.00	....
				9,500.00
1924–25	Social Service Exchange	Helen Crittenden Memorial	307.15	....
1925–26		Helen Crittenden Memorial	82.91	....
				390.06
1924–25		Wieboldt Foundation	500.00	....
1924–25	Social Forces in Settlement Areas	Federation of Settlements	500.00	....
1927–28		Henry Booth Settlement House	50.00	....
				1,050.00
1924–25	Railroad Labor Board	Institute of Economics	500.00	....
1925–26		Institute of Economics	500.00	....
				1,000.00
1924–25....	Publishing Studies of Family Welfare and Immigration	Rosenwald Publication Fund	....	5,000.00
1924–25	Incomes and Standards of Living of Unskilled Laborers	Council of Social Agencies	850.00	....
1925–26		Council of Social Agencies	500.00	....
1925–26		Leila Houghteling	500.00	....
				1,850.00
1924–25	Survey of Chicago Civic Agencies	Union League Club	500.00	....
1926–27		Union League Club	1,107.44	....
				1,607.44

CO-OPERATIVE RESEARCH PROJECTS—*Continued*

Year	Project	Co-operating Agency	Annual Amount	Total
1924–25		Chicago Woman's Club	$ 600.00	....
1925–26		Chicago Woman's Club	875.00	....
1926–27		Chicago Woman's Club	525.00	....
1926–27		Lower North Child Guidance Center	50.00	....
1927–28		Lower North Child Guidance Center	200.00	....
1927–28	Behavior Problems of Delinquent Boys	South Side Child Guidance Center	250.00	....
1927–28		Chicago Woman's Club	450.00	....
1928–29		South Side Child Guidance Center	375.00	....
1928–29		Lower North Child Guidance Center	125.00	....
1928–29		Chicago Woman's Club	302.00	....
				$3,752.00
1925–26	Leisure Time Activities of Young People in the Northwestern University Settlement Areas	Northwestern University Settlement	350.00	....
1926–27		Northwestern University Settlement	350.00	....
				700.00
1925–26....	Study of Chicago Commons Neighborhood Conditions	Chicago Commons Association	....	350.00
1925–26....	Mental Hygiene Clinic	Sidney Schwartz	....	1,000.00
1925–26....	Life History of an Icelander	Wieboldt Foundation	....	50.00
1925–26....	Publication of *The City*	Mr. Park and Mr. Burgess	....	1,200.00
1925–26....	The Immigrant in Chicago	Chicago Immigrant Protective League	....	4,000.00
1925–26....	The Administration of the Aid to Mothers' Law in Illinois, 1917–25	U.S. Children's Bureau	....	50.00
1925–26....	Issuance of Home Employment Permits to Children in Chicago	U.S. Children's Bureau	....	50.00
1926–27....	Chicago Family Study	American Home Economics Association	....	2,500.00
1926–27....	Publication of Governmental Reporting in Chicago	John Beyle	....	1,000.00
1926–27....	Certain Aspects of Illinois Tax Situation	Chicago Real Estate Board	....	1,000.00
1926–27....	Juvenile Delinquency	Illinois Association for Criminal Justice	....	3,500.00
1926–27....	Public Recreation in Chicago	Frederick L. Olmsted	....	442.00
1926–27....	Public Welfare Administration	Caroline Perkins	....	150.00
1928–29		Joint Service Bureau	550.00	....
1928–29	Children's Institutions (connected with public welfare project)	Chicago Foundlings Home	150.00	....
1928–29		Evangelical Orphanage and Old People's Home	100.00	....
				800.00
1926–27....	Survey for Vocational Guidance, Training, and Placement of Crippled Children	Rotary Club	....	750.00
1926–27....	Immigrant Groups in Chicago	Union League Club	....	500.00

CO-OPERATIVE RESEARCH PROJECTS—*Continued*

Year	Project	Co-operating Agency	Annual Amount	Total
1927–28 1928–29 1928–29	Local Communities of Chicago	Chicago Historical Society Chicago Historical Society Chicago Council of Social Agencies Otto L. Schmidt E. L. Glasser	$1,500.00 500.00 250.00 100.00 150.00	....
				$2,500.00
1926–27....	Jewish Scholarship Children of Chicago	Scholarship Association for Jewish Children	....	425.00
1926–27....	Publication of *Carter Henry Harrison I*	C. O. Johnson	....	500.00
1927–28 1928–29	Registration of Social Statistics	Association of Community Chests and Councils Association of Community Chests and Councils	7,036.95 9,468.31	....
				16,505.26
1927–28 1928–29	Registration of Social Statistics in Chicago	Chicago Council of Social Agencies	1,044.67 1,705.98	....
				2,750.65
1927–28....	Census of Market Research Agencies for the Chicago Region	International Advertising Association	....	750.00
1927–28....	Vital Statistics of Heart Disease in Chicago	Chicago Heart Association	....	500.00
1927–28 1928–29	Archaeological Survey of Illinois	Frank Logan Frank Logan	250.00 500.00	....
				750.00
1927–28....	Living Problems of Young People in the Rooming House District	Mrs. Douglas Smith	....	1,200.00
1927–28 1928–29	The Negro in Chicago	Chicago Urban League Chicago Urban League	101.66 2,572.59	....
				2,674.25
1927–28....	Legal Status of Women in Illinois	National League of Women Voters	....	2,000.00
1927–28....	Meat Packing Industry	Institute of Meat Packing	....	12,000.00
1928–29....	Placement of Negro Children	Julius Rosenwald	....	5,000.00
1928–29....	The Negro in Business	Julius Rosenwald	....	750.00
1928–29....	Study of Basic Causes of Organized Crime	American Institute of Criminal Law and Criminology	....	2,695.40
1928–29....	Police Department Survey	Julius Rosenwald	....	2,500.00
1928–29....	Publication of the *History of Illinois State Federation of Labor*	Illinois State Federation of Labor	....	1,200.00
			Total	$120,511.61

Woman's Club, the Rotary Club, and the National League of Women Voters.

Special interest groups have been active in seeking our assistance in their problems. They include the Chicago

Real Estate Board, Federation of Settlements, Henry Booth Settlement House, Council of Social Agencies, Child Guidance Centers, Northwestern University Settlement, Chicago Commons Association, Chicago Immigrant Protective League, American Home Economics Association, Illinois Association for Criminal Justice, Joint Service Bureau, Chicago Foundlings Home, Scholarship Association for Jewish Children, Association of Community Chests and Councils, International Advertising Association, Chicago Heart Association, Chicago Urban League, and Institute of Meat Packing.

The larger matched fund gifts include (a) studies in the economics of the meat packing industry ($12,000); registration of social statistics ($16,505 to date); regional planning ($21,500); type studies ($9,500); behavior problems of delinquent boys ($3,325); the immigrant in Chicago ($4,000); juvenile delinquency ($3,500); and the placement of Negro children ($5,000).

II

These co-operative research projects are organized on different bases but always in such a way that the Local Community Research Committee has control of the expenditure of funds and management of the project. In many cases the co-operating body does not desire to be represented in the actual conduct of research. In these cases the usual method of procedure with a supervisor and perhaps an Advisory Committee is followed.

In other cases the co-operating group desires to follow the research more closely. In such cases a Joint Committee is established in which is vested control of the research, the majority of the committee comprising university representatives. The Committee becomes the supervisor, and its chairman ordinarily is designated to approve expenditures.

By way of illustration, the Committee on Registration of Social Statistics is a body of ten persons of whom six are university delegates and four are representatives of the Association of Community Chests and Councils. The project, which was initiated by this association, and which is intended to improve the reporting and statistical operations of welfare agencies, requires an annual budget of over $20,000. Meetings are held ordinarily once a quarter. The research is conducted by a director, Mr. A. W. McMillen, and by a staff under the general guidance of the University group in accordance with plans agreed upon by the Joint Committee. Other Joint Committees are composed of three or five persons.

It may be of some interest to colleagues in other universities to know that the money in a matched fund project is paid in to the University comptroller, and is administered by him.

Several problems have arisen with regard to community co-operation in our research activities. Occasionally it happens that an appeal is made to conduct an investigation for which the University has not the qualified personnel. A study of some engineering phases of city or regional planning illustrates the point. In such cases, we are obliged to say that we cannot undertake the project unless sufficient funds are available from outside sources to enable the University to make a temporary appointment for the purpose. A limited number of such appointments are in fact made. Thus Professor J. H. Cover, of Pittsburgh University, was invited to assist for a period of one year on certain studies of the packing industry. Mr. Bruce Smith, the police expert of the National Institute of Public Administration, was likewise retained to survey the Chicago Police Department for a period of one year. Broadly speaking, however, it is not the policy of the Local Community Research Committee to conduct research which falls outside the interests or special techniques of the members of the University Faculty.

A similar problem arises also when a request is made for co-operative studies which, although falling within the scope of our activities, comes at a time when the available personnel cannot be freed from outstanding obligations. Contrary to a prevalent belief, "professors" do not, at least at the University of Chicago, belong to the leisure class. They are heavily burdened with various types of duties, teaching, lecturing, consulting, administering university and extra-university affairs, serving on countless committees, writing, researching, and sometimes even reflecting. The twenty-four hours of the day will stand only so much stuffing, and eventually a point is reached when no more research can be undertaken. Our experience indicates that a much larger staff in the social science departments is necessary if the legitimate demands of the community for our help are to be satisfied.

A generous gift from the Spelman Memorial in 1927 has permitted the appointment of a number of research professors. These included in 1929 Mr. L. L. Thurstone in psychometrics, Mr. Henry L. Schultz in statistics, Mr. S. E. Leland in public finance, Mr. Clarence E. Ridley in measurement of governmental processes, Miss Bessie L. Pierce in social history, and Chief August Vollmer in police administration.

An easier problem arises when requests are made for help on what are not essentially research problems. Such requests are occasionally brought forward, usually informally, but are readily withdrawn when the purposes of the Local Community Research Committee are explained.

The time element has given difficulty in a few cases. Research preliminary to an administrative program or a campaign to secure legislation is frequently geared up to an exacting time schedule. The academic mind is accustomed to lectures recurring at stated intervals, but has not been and perhaps cannot well be habituated in research to the precise time schedules on which a manufacturer or a builder proceeds. Research often properly develops new leads which were not foreseen, difficulties in securing materials are often encountered, and research assistants sometimes fail to meet the demands put upon them, to say nothing of overoptimistic predictions ventured by the supervisor when the project is commenced. All this means nothing to a business man's organization which needs the results of a piece of research in order to enable a course of action to be taken. Two things have to be watched with the greatest care in these matched fund projects: first, that adequate time be agreed upon at the outset; second, that definite progress be made week by week so that engagements entered upon can be honored. The confidence of the community cannot be won by dilatory and uncontrolled methods.

Research invited by outside agencies sometimes deflects attention from our own research projects. There are within the social science departments many systematic research programs, developed by individuals, groups, or departments, and pursued both within and without the jurisdiction of the Local Community Research Committee. Each is the "first love" of some member of the faculty, who may be pardoned a sigh of regret when a sense of obligation to the community pulls him away to a venture in which he is interested, but perhaps to a less degree than in his own. At times his obligation is clear to continue his own program, but the Local Community Research Committee believes that to the greatest extent possible it should meet the requests of the city.

An interesting extension of the grants made to the University by the different organizations listed on an earlier page in this chapter for research on a matched fund basis is the series of grants which are made from time to time in which the total cost of carrying on a piece of work is met from outside. These contributions come to all universities, but it is thought they have been stimulated by the considerable extension of our local research activity along the lines of matched fund procedure. Such, by way of illustration, are the study of prohibition referendum votes which Mr. Carroll H. Wooddy made at the request of a member of Congress, the forthcoming study of the Frank L. Smith campaign for Senator of Illinois upon which Mr. Wooddy is now engaged, and the *Life of Cyrus McCormick* by Mr. William T. Hutchinson.

III

Five years' experience with community co-operation in social science research has thus thrown up its problems; but on the other hand it has amply justified the matched fund arrangement. The social science departments stand today in a relation to the city so removed in degree from its position five years ago as to constitute almost a difference in kind. In a practical way the University and the city had had contacts, notably those of Mr. Merriam in the governmental field, but only on a very limited scale had the research activity of the social science departments made effective contact with problems encountered by the many groups and organizations which work in the city.

The Local Community Research Committee has now marshaled the research interests of the University and by a demonstration of the way in which it can be helpful has gone far to become recognized by the city as a fact-finding staff agency of competence, characterized by impartiality and an objective point of view. Its position in the community is being won by the service it renders, not by persistence in bringing itself to the notice of interested parties. The invitation to co-operate comes from without; and it is of much significance to watch year by year the steadily increasing number of requests which come to the Committee. They have now doubled the available resources at our disposal, and in the spring of 1929 we were obliged to say in many cases that we could not undertake to deal with problems brought to us for solution.

The University and the community are thus more and more intimately related, to the undoubted advantage of both. If the community profits by the special information and detached point of view of the University, the latter benefits greatly by the opportunity to come into close contact with specific social problems, by the necessity of dealing with men and women of varied types, by the pressure for usable results, and the general extension of horizons. The University professor who accompanies a police squad on a series of midnight raids, or who advises the sanitary board how to extricate itself from financial embarrassments, or who comes to know by personal contact a large proportion of the precinct captains of the city is a more intelligent and a more useful instructor than one who reads of these things in books.

To the extent that graduate students, in the rôle of research assistants, also participate in these contacts, the same process of stimulation and intensification takes place. The Local Community Research Committee from the outset has conceived a part of its obligation to train effectively the next generation of research men and women. To deal with these concrete situations and to be expected to discover workable solutions for real problems puts the graduate student in a novel but important position.

The results are clear. They appear in part in the range of present positions now held by former research assistants, shown in Appendix II. They also appear in the eagerness with which, to take a single case, the research assistants in archaeology are sought by other institutions. In the summer of 1929 investigations sent out by the American Museum of National History, the Bishop Museum, the Logan Museum, the Pennsylvania and the Indiana State Archaeological Surveys were directed by men who had received their training with Mr. Cole in connection with the work of the Local Community Research Committee.

Reverting to the results of these community contacts from the point of view of the members of the staff, it may be pointed out in conclusion that to a steadily increasing degree, the faculty is represented on "downtown" committees of a civic or public nature. Committees to advise on public finance, on ballot revision, on the extension of the merit system, on traction problems, on industrial arbitration, on the method of taking the census, on the extension of recreational facilities, on health problems, on the location of housing experiments, and on many other topics have found University representation.

The aloofness which used to be represented by the Town and Gown tradition has therefore disappeared so far as the social science departments of the University of Chicago are concerned. They are vitally concerned in the problems and needs of the community and in the deeper understanding of the conditions of life in the community, an attitude significantly strengthened by the influence of the Local Community Research Committee.

CHAPTER IV

BASIC SOCIAL DATA

There is at least one important difference between the laboratory of the physical scientist and that of the social scientist. In chemistry, physics, and even biology the subjects of study can be brought into the laboratory and studied under controlled conditions. This as yet, except on a small scale as with institutes of child research, is not feasible in the social sciences. The objects of social science research, as persons, groups, and institutions, must be studied if at all in the laboratory of community life.

Yet it is quite as necessary in the social as in the physical sciences to make observations and comparisons of behavior under controlled conditions. One method of obtaining control in the social science laboratory is, first, to determine the significant factors, or variables, which influence behavior, and then to find out for each its quantitative value in extent or degree. In this way, where it is possible, the social sciences obtain what is an approximation of the controlled experiment in the method of the physical sciences.

If, then, the city is to become a suitable and adequate laboratory for the social sciences there must be assembled and organized the basic social data upon the chief factors determining behavior under the conditions of urban life. Accordingly six years ago when the Local Community Research Committee of the University of Chicago was first organized, the question was at once raised, "What basic social data are necessary and available for social science research?"

I. FUNDING CURRENT RESEARCH DATA

Before engaging in research, it seemed the part of wisdom for the Local Community Research Committee to undertake a survey of studies and investigations completed or then in progress. Local social agencies, civic organizations, commercial organizations, and departments of the city government had been making maps and gathering information and data. No one knew just how much material valuable for research was preserved in the files of these organizations. Mr. Erle F. Young, then an instructor in the Graduate School of Social Service Administration, undertook this survey.

The findings of this survey, while necessarily far from complete, were illuminating, and led to significant conclusions. The chief points issuing from the inquiry may be briefly summarized as follows:

1. The materials in the files of the agencies, such as maps, original data, were often more valuable from the standpoint of future research than the printed report in which appeared only tabulations from the material.
2. These original materials were, in general, poorly cared for and in danger of destruction; indeed valuable data from earlier studies had disappeared.
3. Studies then in progress by certain agencies were being conducted with little or no reference to previous or current studies.
4. The studies already made had seldom taken advantage of data already collected in previous studies, and had not infrequently expended much time in gathering material already accessible from other studies.

The central conclusion from the study, summarizing and integrating the preceding points into a major premise of social research, was the need for a central depository in which there could be filed the original materials and the printed reports of research and studies. The need of such a clearing house or central depository of social investigations and research had already been perceived by the community. Under the leadership of Mr. Willoughby Walling, then president of the Executive Committee of the Chicago Council of Social Agencies, a Committee on Community Studies and Surveys was organized, consisting of representatives of the chief agencies of the city more or less continuously engaged in conducting or sponsoring studies and research. This Committee carefully considered the report of the survey of studies completed or in progress and designated the Local Community Research Committee of the University of Chicago as the central depository for research materials.

Representative of the original materials that have been filed with the Local Community Research Committee in this central depository are the following:

Complete original data of the Survey of the Illinois Health Insurance Commission, 1918.

Original data of the Cook County Jail Survey, 1920.

Newspaper clippings of the Chicago Citizens' Association, 1887–1912.

Files of the Committee of Fifteen from 1911 to 1920.

Original data of the Illinois Crime Survey made by the Illinois Association for Criminal Justice, 1927–28.

The bringing together of these data in a central depository is not the end but the beginning of the task. It is necessary to organize this material, to classify it, and to place it in a form available for further research. A brief statement of the work of the Local Community Research Committee in working over and utilizing certain collections of these materials will carry its own point.

The original materials of the Health Insurance Study

included the findings of a survey of over 3,000 working-men's families secured by a house-to-house canvass of forty blocks selected as representative of the distribution of wage-earners in the city. These materials were the basis of a recanvass of these same forty blocks five years later, in 1923, in a study, "Living Conditions Among Wage-Earning Families in Forty-one Blocks in Chicago," by Mr. Franc L. McCluer.[1] It was only by the preservation of the original data that exact comparisons were possible of changes in the composition of population, duration of residence, and changes in economic status.

The newspaper clippings compiled for a thirty-year period by the Chicago Citizens' Association were an invaluable source of records of past events. Although classified by subject matter when turned over to the central depository, these materials were not in condition to be used advantageously and were in imminent danger of destruction. Under the supervision of Mr. Marcus W. Jernegan, great headway has been made in arranging these materials in scrapbook form and in rendering them accessible for use. This valuable collection of clippings has been used or is now in use in studies of industrial trends, elections, crime and vice, and other investigations.

The complete files of the Committee of Fifteen up to the year 1921 would have been destroyed in order to provide office space if it had not been for the existence of a central depository. These materials have now been reclassified and fill five large filing-cases and four library shelves. A preliminary survey of these materials has been made to determine the best research uses to which they may be put.

[1] Manuscript in University of Chicago Libraries.

II. THE FUNDING OF RESEARCH MATERIALS

The program of a continuous series of studies undertaken by the Local Community Research Committee soon raised the question not merely of preserving but of funding these research materials. By funding research data is meant its organization in accordance with a plan that will make it readily available in the most advantageous way for future studies. The funding of research materials raises two fundamental questions: (1) What are the basic data indispensable for social science studies? (2) What are the units for the organization of these materials?

It was early recognized that the statistics compiled by the Census Bureau were important at least as background material for practically every local community study.

III. CENSUS STATISTICS AS BASIC DATA

In the different reports of the United States Census Bureau a great amount of statistical information is published covering a wide range of subject matter. Composition of population is given with great detail as by age and sex groups, race and nationality, mother tongue, marital status, citizenship, literacy, school attendance. Other valuable figures for local community studies include number of families, home-ownership or tenancy, occupation of males and females gainfully employed, statistics of manufacturing, religious bodies, prisoners, and juvenile delinquents.

In general these materials are published for the city as a whole although some items in abbreviated form are given by wards. While for villages, towns, and small cities figures for the municipality have great value, their importance rapidly decreases with the size of the community, so that for a city the size of Chicago figures for the entire area have little or no value except for general comparisons with other large cities. Even in cases in which statistics on a few items are given by wards for the large cities, their value is lessened because of two facts. The first is the large size of these wards. In 1920 the thirty-five wards into which the city was then divided contained an average of over 77,000 population. The second is that before any *Census* volumes had been published, but on the preliminary reports of population, the city council created fifty wards with boundaries entirely different from the alignment under the thirty-five ward plan. And this action was only a repetition of what had happened after every previous census. It is not feasible under the plan of publishing statistics by wards to make satisfactory comparisons by census periods of changes in number and composition of population.

It was clear that it was highly desirable to have census data tabulated by some permanent area so that comparisons could be made over a period of years. It was also agreed that this permanent area should be smaller than the ward. But here agreement ended. There was marked disagreement about what kind of small permanent unit should be selected.

The interest in a small permanent area as a unit for census enumeration and publication of population findings was not new nor confined to Chicago. Indeed, the liveliest and at first almost the only interest in it was manifested in New York City.

Although in 1910 the United States Census Bureau divided all cities of 500,000 population and over into census tracts for the tabulation of certain population data, New York was the only city that made use of this material on any extensive scale. In 1920 the Census Bureau again performed this service for New York, Chicago, Philadelphia, Boston, Cleveland, St. Louis, Pittsburgh, and Baltimore, but only New York, Chicago, and Cleveland made use of these materials to any great extent for local community studies.[1] There is, however, a widespread interest in many cities for securing tract tabulation of the 1930 population data.

When the census tracts were first established for Chicago in 1910 they were laid out on the basis of square miles and of subdivisions of square miles with increasing density of population with the smallest unit one-eighth of a square mile, or eighty acres. In the central part of the city the majority of the census tracts were one-eighth of a mile, around these were tracts of one-quarter square mile, still farther out tracts of one-half square mile area, and at the outskirts the tracts were one square mile or even larger. It would have been a great boon if this systematic plan of divisions by tracts had been retained intact for the 1920 census. Unfortunately, there were several rather serious departures from it so that comparisons between the two censuses involve many technical difficulties. In not a few cases tracts were combined. In the outlying areas where there was little population in 1910 but an unexpected increase by 1920 the census tracts for the latter census did not follow mile lines but were irregularly laid out. The greatest source of complications, however, was the change in ward lines in 1911, a change made because of the legal requirement that compilations be published by wards. The 1911 ward boundaries with marked irregularities were determined not so much by rhyme and reason as by the exigencies of the political situation.

[1] "Methods of Securing the 1930 Census by Sanitary Areas for Cities," in *American Journal of Public Health*, XIX (February, 1929), 199–202.

The vital interest in planning for the 1930 census among commercial, governmental, and social agencies was shown by the organization under the initiative of the commissioner of health, at first Dr. Herman N. Bundesen and then Dr. Arnold H. Kegel, of the Chicago Census Committee. The members of this Committee represented the following organizations: Chicago Association of Commerce; Chicago Church Federation, department of research; Chicago Community Trust; Chicago Council of Social Agencies; Chicago Department of Public Health; Chicago Plan Commission; Chicago Real Estate Board; Commonwealth Edison Company; *Chicago Daily News*, survey department; *Chicago Evening Post*, survey department; *Chicago Herald and Examiner*, survey department; *Chicago Tribune*, survey department; Illinois Bell Telephone Company; Local Community Research Committee, University of Chicago; Northwestern University; Peoples Gas, Light and Coke Company; and the Wieboldt Foundation.

All the members of this Committee were in complete agreement upon the value of census material by small permanent tracts for the surveys and studies upon which they were engaged. There was, however, a difference of opinion upon the question of what lines the boundaries of these tracts should follow. There were governmental bodies which desired the tracts to fall within ward lines. Others believed that for their work the division by square miles and subdivisions of square miles would be preferable. Still others were convinced that the tracts should fall within the boundaries of the eighty local communities of the city as worked out by the Local Community Research Committee.

The problem was solved by a plan of tracts designed to

meet the needs of all organizations. A plan of 935 tracts
was drawn up in which all the tract boundaries were made
in accordance with one or more of the following requirements:

1. That direct comparisons of population data be possible between the
   499 tracts of 1920 and the 935 tracts of 1930.
2. That all the 935 tracts for 1930 fall within the fifty ward boundaries
   as at present constituted.
3. That each of the 935 census tracts conform to the two hundred odd
   square miles which comprise the area of the city.
4. That the 935 census tracts be subdivisions of the eighty local communities of the city.

A working map based upon these requirements, drawn
up by the Local Community Research Committee of the
University of Chicago, was approved by the Chicago Census Committee and was accepted in principle by the director of the United States Census. With only a few minor
changes this map is now being used by the Census Bureau
as a basis for the plans of organizing the enumeration of
the 1930 census. The working out of this plan will give
Chicago the most flexible and comprehensive system of
census tracts of any city in the United States. If the present tentative proposal to code by city blocks all population
data, which is now being favorably considered by the
Census Bureau, is adopted, Chicago with all other census-
tract cities will possess a unit of basic social data suscepti-
ble to almost any possible combination and permutation
of city areas that could be desired for any enterprise of
social research.

IV. SOCIAL RESEARCH BASE MAP

Even before the organization of the Local Community
Research Committee, as early as 1916, the need of an adequate base map for research purposes was recognized by

local organizations in the city and by social science departments in the University. The maps prepared and published for commercial use had too much irrelevant detail to be serviceable as base maps for the plotting of social data. The Department of Sociology had found the best available base map to be one prepared by the Commonwealth Edison Company in the size of four inches to the mile. Through the courtesy of this organization reproductions of this map were provided at cost and made possible the preparation of a series of maps which were later turned over to the Local Community Research Committee upon its organization.

One of the first acts of the Local Community Research Committee was to authorize the making of a social research base map especially adapted for local community studies. For research purposes it seemed essential that such a map should represent certain basic uses of land that would serve as a background for the data which would be superimposed upon it in a more vivid form. Fortunately the completion of the exhaustive study of the Chicago Zoning Commission made possible the preparation of the social research map at small cost.[1] The use maps of the Zoning Commission made possible the showing of the basic present use of land in the following ways:

1. Railroad property was shown by solid shading.
2. Property devoted to industrial use was represented by cross lines.
3. Property utilized for retail business was denoted by heavy lines along street frontage.
4. Vacant property was indicated by giving the block outlines in broken lines.
5. Parks and boulevards were set off by stippling.
6. Elevated and surface lines were also shown.

[1] This map was prepared under the direction of Erle F. Young, now professor of sociology, University of Southern California. See article by him, "The Social Base Map," *Journal of Applied Sociology*, January–February, 1925.

The value of this social research base map at once became evident. In plotting cases of poverty or family desertion or juvenile delinquency, it was now perceived, as it had not been before, why certain strips of territory had no cases: there was no population there, as a result of their use for railroad lines or yards, or industry or commerce. Other districts had large areas of vacant property awaiting residential or industrial development. Often it was possible by this map to form hypotheses to explain the distribution of the phenomena plotted upon it. A uniform base map of this kind made feasible comparisons of a series of maps exhibiting different types of data. It was clear that the social research base map was one way, and a strikingly graphic way, of assembling and exhibiting basic social data. The Committee solved the problem of exhibiting these maps so that they might readily be compared, by securing a large map hanger of a size adapted for the social research base maps with space for the display of forty maps. The map exhibit room soon became a mecca for class and conference groups as well as for research students, social workers, and visitors interested in examining and studying the basic social data which they presented.

The social research map also gave the impetus to the further study of a question that has already been stated, but not answered in this article: What areas of the city should be selected as the unit for social science studies and for the organization of basic social data?

For the base map showed strikingly how the elevated railroad lines which crisscross the city and are generally flanked with industry, constitute barriers which divide the city into many separate districts. The industrial residential districts of Chicago when studied by this map are seen to be areas surrounded by a wall of elevated railroads and a ring of industrial establishments. In a similar fashion the better residential districts were typically surrounded by lake front, parks, and boulevards. The question at once arose: Do these obvious external physical separations correspond to actual differences in the economic and social life of the people of Chicago? Do these walled-in districts constitute local communities? If so, are these local community areas the most practical territorial units for the classification and organization of basic social data?

V. DETERMINING THE BOUNDARIES OF LOCAL COMMUNITIES

In 1924 the Local Community Research Committee authorized a project under the supervision of Miss Vivien M. Palmer to find out the correspondence, if any, between this physical formation of the city with its areas separated by river, elevated railroad walls, industrial belts, and parks and boulevards and the currents of the economic and social life of the city. There was devised a number of ingenious tests to check this relationship of which the following are perhaps sufficiently representative:

1. Well-recognized historical names and boundaries of local communities and the changes which these have undergone.
2. Dividing lines that are at present recognized by residents, as when on one side of a street persons state that they live in one community and persons on the other side of the street state that they live in another community.
3. Boundaries of areas claimed by local organizations as business men's associations, by local newspapers and by improvement associations, and in cases of dispute checking claims by plotting memberships of these groups.
4. Plotting membership or attendance or patronage of local community institutions or enterprises and noting the effect of barriers like parks and elevated railroad lines.
5. Plotting the distribution and movement of cultural groups like immigrant colonies and noting the effect of these barriers.

Without going into a detailed analysis of the findings of this study it will be sufficient to state only the general conclusion that indicated that the lines of physical separation, with some few exceptions, were also the dividing lines between local communities. It was also found that while these local communities were in a state of change, more or less rapid as the case might be, the changes taking place were more or less localized by the effects of these permanent physical barriers. These and other considerations led to the conclusion that the eighty local communities, as determined by this study, were basic social units in the present organization of the life of the city.

VI. SOCIAL FORCES AND TRENDS IN THE GROWTH OF LOCAL COMMUNITIES

But the question may be fairly raised, Why is it necessary or even desirable to subdivide the city into units for social science studies? Why not be content with statistical findings that apply to the city as a whole? The answer perhaps may be briefly made as follows. In scientific research an object is studied not as a whole but by breaking it up into its parts which are then described and analyzed in their interrelationships. The local communities of Chicago, like the Lower North Side, the Near West Side, Hyde Park, Bridgeport, Back of the Yards, and Uptown, are organic parts of the larger community whose organization and interaction determine the total course of the life and action of the entire city. Therefore, social science research should focus its magnifying glass of research upon these local communities, if for no other reason than to understand the life-processes of the larger community.

These local communities are widely different. The total statistics of social, economic, and political conditions for the city of Chicago obscure by canceling these marked variations which come out clearly when statistics are pre-

TABLE I

COMPARISON OF A BETTER RESIDENTIAL COMMUNITY WITH AN INDUSTRIAL COMMUNITY

Social Data	A Better Residential Community	An Industrial Community
Population, 1920....	37,159	37,806
Land values, 1920...	Range: $ 40–1,000 Commercial: 200–1,000 Residential: 40–1,000	Range: $ 20–3,000 Commercial: 175–3,000 Residential: 20–50
Chain stores, 1921..	10 Atlantic and Pacific 3 Piggly Wiggly 2 United Cigar Stores	1 Atlantic and Pacific 0 Piggly Wiggly 1 United Cigar Store
Banks, 1922........	3	3
Physicians, 1921....	247, or 66 per 10,000	28, or 7 per 10,000
Who's Who, 1921...	20 ecclesiastical 95 professional 45 educational 29 scientists 3 government officials 13 business	.... 1 professional ....
	205, or 55 per 10,000	1 per 37,000 1/200th of the better resi- dential community ratio
Politicians, 1922....	9 city administrators 4 state administrators 3 county administrators 1 city legislator	3 city administrators .... 1 city legislator
	17, or 5 per 10,000	4, or 1 per 10,000
Divorce, 1921......	35	8
Desertion, 1921.....	13	20
Suicides, 1922......	Men 1 Women 3	Men 3 Women 0
Poverty 　United Charities 　Jewish Social Serv- 　ice Bureau, 1921	20 families............	185 families
Delinquent girls, 1921	6	11
Delinquent boys, 1924	32	132

sented by local communities as shown by the accompanying table.

If the city was to be a working laboratory for social

science research, it was necessary to define, describe, and analyze the factors governing the differences which are so apparent between these local communities. To understand the present and to forecast the future required a study of the social factors and forces that had entered into the growth of each community. One mode of prediction is by establishing trends and continuing them into the future. The assumption is that unless some sudden change takes place, like war or disaster, a trend can be projected forward with some assurance, at least for a short time. The studies already made of local communities indicate that one powerful differential factor is that of neighborhood custom and tradition. The cultural heritages of an immigrant community,[1] the local traditions of gang life, or law and order, or criminality,[2] established customs or precedents have been found to play a significant rôle in conditioning behavior of groups and persons in the community.

It seemed therefore important to secure, as a part of the general fund of basic social data, material on the social forces and trends of local community life. A comprehensive plan of study was drawn up and the work is now well under way under the direct supervision of Miss Vivien M. Palmer.

While the specific and detailed techniques worked out for this study are given in full in Miss Palmer's book, *Manual of Field Studies in Sociology*, certain aspects of this inquiry may be briefly stated here. The different libraries of the city were visited and digests were made of

---

[1] R. E. Park and H. A. Miller, *Old World Traits Transplanted*, chap. i; chap. vii, "The Immigrant Community," pp. 145–224; chap. viii, "Immigrant Heritages," pp. 1–24; "Types of Community Influence," pp. 225–58.

[2] W. Healy and A. F. Bronner, *Delinquents and Criminals, Their Making and Unmaking*, pp. 190–98; C. R. Shaw, *Delinquency Areas in Chicago*.

all available material in print which pertained to any specific area of the city or to any events which affected the entire city or any large section of it. These materials were classified in three sets of files: (1) a series of files on every local community of the city, (2) a file of general data on Chicago by decades, and (3) a topical file of outstanding events. Through co-operation with other institutions additional valuable material was secured, as from the Chicago Historical Society, the departments of sociology of Northwestern University, of the Garrett Biblical Institute, of the Young Men's Christian Association College, the department of surveys and studies of the Congregational City Missionary Society and the Chicago Theological Seminary, and the department of surveys of the Board of Education.

Special reliance, however, was placed upon field work in the local communities, interviewing old residents and others, such as real estate men, who have much exact and complete knowledge about the community, its outstanding events, and the factors that are operating for social change. These interviews with old residents, real estate men, and others, excerpts from daily papers, and historical accounts were first subjected to an elaborate system of checks and then put in the form of documentary material. From these documents, aggregating from fifty to a hundred in number on each local community, an article or digest was prepared giving a descriptive and analytical account of community growth, and showing the different stages of social change through which each district had passed. Not least in significance was the subdivision of the eighty local communities into four hundred smaller areas or neighborhoods, which were in turn made the units for classifying much of the material.

ers of different agencies at work in the same field and for local community organization.

While this plan has not as yet been put completely into effect, progress has been made. In several organizations changes in boundaries have been made in accordance with it. The Committee of Fifteen is now recording all its statistics by the eighty communities.

The *Social Service Directory* for 1926, issued by the Chicago Council of Social Agencies, contains a classification of local social agencies according to this plan of local communities. Dr. Arnold H. Kegel, the commissioner of health, has adopted these communities as the units for working out the plan of health centers with the public schools.

VIII. THE CENTENNIAL HISTORY

In 1933 Chicago celebrates the centennial anniversary of its settlement. Members of the Local Community Research Committee are in touch with the plans now in process of formulation, and it is expected that the committee will participate in several phases of the centennial celebration.

Inter alia a centennial history of Chicago is planned. In the course of the many investigations already made by the social science group, whether under the guidance of the Local Community Research Committee or otherwise, a very considerable mass of material has already been compiled. A comprehensive history of Chicago, with broad reference to the economic, industrial, social, religious, and political experience of the city will both unify these studies already completed and suggest other types of studies required by a well-balanced program.

Such materials as those supplied by the social history of local communities (Mr. Burgess and Miss Palmer), the

location of industry (Mr. Wright and Miss Magee), the
life of Carter Henry Harrison I (Mr. C. O. Johnson), the
forthcoming life of Cyrus McCormick (Mr. Hutchinson),
the use of the referendum (Mr. Maynard), the history of
trade unions (Mr. Millis) are already abundantly at hand.
Miss Pierce is now organizing and supplementing these
studies in a large-scale effort.

IX. MASS DATA, SOCIAL RESEARCH, AND THE SOLUTION OF COMMUNITY PROBLEMS

The present interest in social science research is stimulated by and has its raison d'être in the great problems
of urban life that press for solution—problems of poverty,
crime, vice, and government. These problems cannot be
solved without wider and deeper knowledge of the forces
in human nature and in the community determining man's
behavior. Agencies dealing with these problems find rec-
ord-keeping essential; these records supply the indispensable mass data for social research. If these mass data are
to yield their full value both for science and human welfare
they must be collected upon vital and standardized units,
by uniform and permanent districts, and continuously
over long periods of time. Basic data so assembled and
organized for research purposes furnish one of the indispensable conditions for a social science research laboratory.

CHAPTER V

ANALYZING THE GROWTH OF THE CITY

Why is the student in the social sciences interested in analyzing the growth of the city? He is interested, in the first place, because growth brings in its wake a train of social, economic, psychological, and political consequences that are his chief concern. Growth may not be a prime cause but it is without doubt an attendant circumstance, very probably a contributing factor, and cannot therefore be overlooked. He is interested, in the second place, since for purely statistical reasons he must have a "base" to which he can relate his measurements of social problems. The number of deaths increases, but how much of the increase is significant from the point of view of new conditions to be investigated and controlled, how much due to the expected increase in the numbers of the population exposed to death? Crime likewise increases, but how much of it is due to the outcropping of new tendencies to lawlessness, or to new methods of treatment, how much to mere increase in numbers? These things he must know if he is to proceed carefully.

I

Among the consequences of growth itself is the economic question of the provision for transportation facilities. Growth of population, more elevated trains; more population, subways; more population, more subways. Which is cause and which effect? It perhaps no longer matters. Social engineers are convinced that there is an interrelationship. The phenomena of growth must be studied if the problems of transportation are to be solved.

Another consequence of growth is the complicated mechanism of marketing facilities.[1] By what devious routes do fresh fruit and vegetables, meat, and milk reach the kitchen of the city-dweller? In the hands of private enterprise is this marketing mechanism the most economical that could be devised? Is the matter of obtaining food a function of city life, a public function that should be taken over by the public authorities to be administered like the public-school system?

City growth may also bring in its wake bad housing conditions. Bad housing may, of course, also be found in a village, but the combination of bad housing with high cost of housing is peculiarly a city problem.[2] Other physical effects of growth which the social engineer must combat are the deficiencies in fresh air and in space for recreation. Smoke, dust, and overcrowding increase as the city grows.

Growth within the last century has been largely due to immigration from Europe. Hence the social fabric of the modern city is shot through with diverse strands against variegated cultural backgrounds. City life may present many difficulties to the newcomer from rural America, but how much keener is the distress of the European immigrant who may be exploited at every turn because of his double handicap of language and urban inexperience![3] Have the case-work facilities of the modern city kept pace with its growth?

The student interested in the problems of nervous wear and tear, in the increase in the number of psychiatric

---

[1] See several studies of marketing in the Chicago area by E. A. Duddy.

[2] See E. Abbott, *Population and Housing in Chicago* (in preparation).

[3] See E. Abbott, *Immigration: Select Documents and Case Records* (Chicago).

cases, in the phenomena of gang life, in the increase in crime, will find certain wellsprings in the rapidity and character of growth of the modern city. Impersonal relationships increase as the city grows. Machine politics thrive upon the inability of the average voter to judge adequately what is so remote from him, upon his acceptance of the judgment of his infallible friend, the ward politician.

Not all the effects of growth, however, must be viewed with so great concern. Increasing numbers bring increasing ability to support the opera, the civic orchestra, the theater, the art gallery. The arts flourish in the cities, not in the villages of the United States. In part this is due to concentration of wealth, but in greater part it is due to the fact that creative art springs from the tragedy, not the comfort, of life.

II

The second reason for interest in analyzing the growth of the city, the statistical need for a base, is a need for more precise measurements. A comparison between the absolute number of deaths in Chicago and in New York is meaningless because the population—or the number exposed to death—in the two cities is not the same. The number of deaths must be related to the population if they are to have significance. Even the total population, however, is too crude a measurement, since the death-rate quite normally varies with the age composition of the population. Moreover, since our only reliable count of population, the decennial federal census, gives us figures only once in ten years, there is a need for intercensal estimates of population to make it possible to compute annual death-rates. The United States Census Bureau provides these estimates for the city as a whole, but students are often interested in the variation in rates for certain local areas for which no official estimates are made.

The problem of determining a population base to which other measurements may be compared has become a matter of comparative simplicity in the computation of death-rates. The device of the "standardized" death-rate takes account of variations in age, which is the most important single factor affecting the death-rate. For birth-rates it is possible to use as a base the number of married women of childbearing age. But for the more complicated social problems of crime and poverty what factors must be allowed for in the population base? The crime rate undoubtedly varies with both age and sex and an allowance must be made for both factors. The juvenile delinquency rate may vary more significantly with economic factors, such as family income. Thus, as the social problem becomes more complicated, it becomes more and more difficult, but not less important, to determine an adequate population base.

III

When population growth itself becomes the object of study two questions confront the student: How and why does the city grow? It grows by a twofold process[1] of increase in numbers within the same area (aggregation) and by an overflow into adjoining areas that are eventually added to the main area (expansion). It is typical of American cities that they grow by annexation as well as by increasing density. Whenever a historical problem involves a comparison with population over a period of years a question as to what the city really was in past decades

---

[1] See *The City*, chap. ii, "The Growth of the City," by E. W. Burgess (Chicago: University of Chicago Press, 1925).

arises. Was it the legal city or was it in reality the legal city plus a fringe of villages at that time not even contiguous but now lost within the city?

Growth in numbers can come about in only two ways, by an excess of births over deaths or by an excess of immigration over emigration. In no other way can the city add to itself than by birth or immigration, and in no other way can it decline than by death or emigration. If it is possible to determine the balance between the birth-rate and the death-rate and between the rates of immigration and emigration, the problem of how fast the city is growing is solved.

The balance between births and deaths may in itself be a problem of interest to social students. From a statistical point of view a stationary population can be maintained quite as easily by a high birth-rate balanced by a correspondingly high death-rate as by a low birth-rate balanced by a low death-rate. But from a social point of view which is the more desirable situation?

It is undoubtedly true that the rapidity of growth of an American city depends to a larger extent upon excess of immigration than upon excess of births. This is certainly true of Chicago, which has trebled since 1890. This immigration includes influx from other parts of the United States as well as from abroad. But why do people move to the city, and why to Chicago rather than to some other city? The answer must be in the first place, geographical position, and, in the second place, industrial and commercial enterprises that make jobs.

The later streams of immigration which have contributed to Chicago's population are reasonably well known. Early immigration to the United States, however, has never been adequately described. In an effort to illuminate this unknown area, Mr. Jernegan has undertaken a three-year study of immigration into the United States from the close of the Revolutionary War to 1820. New materials have been discovered, and by extensive use of the photostat a very considerable volume of records is being assembled and studied.

A type of study which requires to be repeated for many national groups was completed under Mr. Jernegan's direction by Mr. A. J. Townsend, entitled *The Germans in Chicago*.

Most cities owe their birth to their location at a point at which trade and transportation routes find it convenient to pause. Thus medieval town life began in seaports (the beginning and end of great trade routes), at crossroads where markets were established, or at the junctions of tributaries and great rivers. So also Chicago began as an Indian trading-post at the mouth of the Chicago River, which empties into Lake Michigan. The little settlement might forever have remained a village had it not lain at a junction point between the Great Lakes transportation route and the Illinois-Michigan Canal which led to the Mississippi River, a continuous water way from the lakes to the Gulf of Mexico. With the decline of river and canal transportation Chicago might also have declined but again the town proved to be a strategic point for the beginning and end of railway systems. At present twenty-five railroads operating one-third of the total railroad mileage of the United States enter the city of Chicago.

Given adequate transportation facilities, the location of new industries is not unexpected. And when one of the industries, that of iron and steel manufacturing, is one of the basic factors in American industrial progress, when another is meat-packing, it is not surprising that the plants grow, that population is attracted by jobs, that the city increases rapidly.

The student confronted with the problem of deciding what the population of the city is at any time will turn first to the volumes of the *United States Census*. If the time is 1929, however, the *Census* is of little help for it is then nine years old. The number of persons receiving poor relief in 1929 cannot be compared with the population in 1920. One of the greatest defects in our knowledge of population is that we know its size with comparative certainty only once in ten years, and we can never be quite sure how it has behaved since the last complete count. In cases of practical necessity, therefore, an estimate must be made. In order to arrive at an estimate certain assumptions must be laid down. One of the most common assumptions is that the rate of growth has remained constant. But a constant rate of growth may mean either a constant arithmetic rate (addition of equal numbers) or a constant geometric rate (increase by equal percentages). The time and the place must determine which of these two assumptions is more likely to fit the case. In the days of Malthus the rate threatened to be geometric, but in more recent times the United States Census Bureau has relied upon the arithmetic assumption. Certainly for the city of Chicago there has been no departure from the arithmetic rate since the decade 1880 to 1890. For New York, Philadelphia, St. Louis, and Cleveland the geometric assumption is probably more correct.[1]

The assumption of a constant rate must be made, but constant over how long a period? The Census Bureau assumes the rate during the present decade to be equal to the

[1] See H. R. Jeter, *Trends of Population in the Region of Chicago*, p. 22, Chart IV.

rate during the one preceding decade regardless of the
history of population in earlier decades. For Chicago this
assumption does no violence to the facts but for Detroit
it probably departs far from the truth.[1]

These methods of estimate are arbitrary, but within a
period of ten years they are likely to produce no serious
error. For the practical purpose of computing death-rates
and other comparative measurements they are undoubtedly sufficiently accurate. For the purpose of predicting population for a longer period into the future, however, these
arbitrary mathematical methods may introduce a cumu-
lative error that becomes more and more serious as the
period of prediction becomes longer. The student in the
social sciences is anxious to find a "law" of population
growth that he can apply at any time and in any place, a
law that will yield a fairly reliable prediction of population
for any future date. This quest for a law of population is
not a new one. Malthus enunciated at the end of the
eighteenth century the principle that population unless it
is checked has a tendency to increase geometrically. It is
obvious, however, that certain checks are always more or
less in operation and that population never does at all times
and in all places grow at a geometric rate. The need is for
a "law" that will take into consideration the operation of
the checks as well as the maximum rate of growth. Such
a law has been formulated by Raymond Pearl and others
in terms of the logistic curve. If it be true that the population of any finite area grows according to the formula
$y = \dfrac{k}{1 + e^{ao + a \cdot x}}$ then the population of any city or region
can be predicted with comparative certainty. Unfortu-
nately, however, the mechanical aspects of applying the

[1] *Ibid.*, p. 22, Chart IV.

law are laborious, and the possible choices among methods of fitting the equation to the actual data leave some doubt as to which among several possible results is the best prediction. Ten trials[1] with population data for a region of twelve counties in the immediate vicinity of Chicago yielded maximum populations ranging from 3,800,000 to 6,300,000, with corresponding variation in the dates at which the maximum would be reached. For the year 1950 the prediction varied from 3,700,000 to 5,500,000. It is suggested[2] that for this particular area different parts of the region are growing at different rates and since the sum of two logistics is likely not to be a logistic, a better result would have been obtained by dividing the region into two parts, one Chicago, the other the area outside Chicago. A choice already had been made among five distinct methods of fitting and at least six different samplings of the data. If a choice must also be made among different combinations of various parts of an 'area the general applicability of the law of population growth to a city or a small region becomes even more doubtful.

IV

Fortunately the growth of the American city brings with it certain practical necessities for predicting the population. Whenever the question ceases to be an academic one and becomes a matter of dollars and cents, arbitrary mathematical formulas and theoretical laws of population growth give way before empirical methods. The student

[1] See Ardis I. Monk and Helen R. Jeter, "The Logistic Curve and the Prediction of the Population of the Chicago Region," in *Journal of the American Statistical Association* (December, 1928), pp. 361–86.

[2] See Raymond Pearl and Lowell J. Reed, "The Population of an Area Around Chicago and the Logistic Curve," in *Journal of the American Statistical Association*, March, 1929.

of the social sciences cannot afford to be scornful of the methods by which the public-service companies determine the necessary size of gas and water mains and telephone cables.[1] Failure to predict accurately the future use of these instruments of public utility may require enormous outlays for reconstruction in the future. While the error is likely to be on the side of predicting too large a population the error is not likely to be great.

Empirical methods of population prediction, unlike the arbitrary mathematical ones, involve the compilation of all available data that will throw light upon the probable trend of the population curve during the period since the last report of the census. Such facts as the increase in number of telephone subscribers, gas meters installed, children enrolled in school, and persons employed in various manufacturing and commercial establishments, throw some light upon the probable slope of the population curve.[2] No one set of data is infallible, but, taken together, they probably form a more reliable basis for estimate than the straight line or the geometric assumption.

Among these indications of population change may be the data collected by the factory inspector's office. Unfortunately the purposes of factory inspection do not coincide with academic interest in population growth. Hence the use of such material involves special labor, including extensive classification and tabulation.[3] But even after

[1] For use of public service company estimates see H. R. Jeter, *Trends of Population in the Region of Chicago*, pp. 36 ff.

[2] Care must be taken to distinguish between rates of increase which indicate population growth and rates of increase which indicate increasing mobility of the population. See E. W. Burgess, *op. cit.*, p. 60. It may in some cases be impossible to make this distinction.

[3] See Mabel Magee, *Trends of Industry in the Region of Chicago* (in preparation).

they are laboriously tabulated it seems apparent that no great reliance can be placed upon the data as indications of change in population since changing technique of industry may produce trends in number of wage-earners that are quite different from the trend of population.

Reliance upon the empirical method of population prediction involves a weighing and balancing of conflicting evidence that calls for careful study and sound judgment. In the hands of persons with a bias toward rapid increase in numbers the method is totally unreliable. Confidence in the method becomes largely a matter of confidence in the persons applying the method. Hence in many cities it will be necessary to fall back upon arbitrary mathematical assumptions of straight line or of geometric increase until a small army of social science students carefully amass the data which indicate in which direction and at what rate the population is changing.

CHAPTER VI

THE METROPOLITAN REGION OF CHICAGO

A metropolitan district is defined by the United States Census Bureau as "the city proper and the urban portion of the territory lying within ten miles of the city limits." The Census Bureau also takes account under another head of the whole region within ten miles, whether urban or not. In 1920 there were seven metropolitan regions each having a population of over a million and a total population of nineteen million. There were ten others each having a population of over 500,000 with a total of seven and one-half million. Together these comprise a total of seventeen regions each having a population of over 500,000 and a total population of twenty-six and one-half million. By way of comparison it may be pointed out that there are seventeen states of the American Union with a population of less than 1,000,000 and nine states with a population of less than 500,000.

I. THE COMPLEXITY OF THE SITUATION

These regions of the type of New York, Chicago, Boston, Philadelphia, like London, Paris, Berlin, are unities in the economic sense of the term and they also represent types of social and cultural unities. From the governmental point of view, however, their organization is highly decentralized. Each of these regions contains a large number of independent governments, often overlapping and often conflicting and without any central administrative control or supervision. In the Chicago region, for

example, which we construe as fifty miles from State and
Madison Streets, there are almost 1,700 independent governing agencies undertaking to carry on the governmental
functions incidental to the life of a community of three
and a half million people. Metropolitan Chicago extends
into four different states, Illinois, Wisconsin, Indiana, and
a corner of Michigan; it includes sixteen counties and an
innumerable array of cities, villages, towns, townships,
school districts, park districts, drainage districts. New
York extends into three states, New York, New Jersey,
and Connecticut, with a wide variety of county and local
governments within her borders. There are already ten
million people in the New York region, and it is estimated,
somewhat optimistically, that there will be twenty-five
million in the New York area within another generation.
It is conservatively estimated that the population of the
Chicago area in 1950 will approach eight million. Problems of regional organization are presented not only in
American cities such as Boston, Philadelphia, Pittsburgh,
Cincinnati, San Francisco, but in the great cities all over
the world.

It is obvious that some more compact form of organization is necessary in order to enable these groups to carry
on their governmental functions effectively. This is at
once evident in fields like those of city-planning, public
health, recreation, police, finance, transportation—in fact,
in almost the whole range of public activities. The health
of Chicago, for example, is cared for by at least four
states, to say nothing of the United States government and
350 local health organizations of varying size and importance. City-planning soon reaches its limit in the corporate sense of the term, and under modern conditions planning must enter the larger field of the region far beyond

the confines and jurisdiction of any one municipal corporation. A modern recreation plan involves almost immediately a projection of interest and activity far beyond the limits of any one city. In the policing of the community, our local Cicero is only a term for a type of similar area found in every metropolitan region under some other name, multiplying the difficulties in the local administration of the law. Again the development of water supply, of sewage systems, of garbage and waste disposal raises questions which no one city can begin to answer, but which can be met only by the concerted action of a considerable group of municipalities. From the financial point of view, the haphazard dealing with revenues, expenditures, budgets, and indebtedness in an overlapping series of great and small communities presents insuperable difficulties and leads inevitably to shocking forms of waste. From the point of view of political responsibility and control, the presence of a series of conflicting and competing local loyalties makes the problem of government increasingly difficult, for in the concentration of interests and responsibility is found the key to that intelligent and discriminating public opinion which the democratic experiment presupposes.

Equally serious is the loss of citizens drifting from the central city to its environs. Many persons profess to find the cause of urban ills in immigration from foreign shores. An impartial observer might conclude that the problem of the emigration from the city to the suburbs is a more important factor. There are more Bostonians outside of Boston than inside the corporate limits, in the ratio of 750,000 within to 1,000,000 without. There are 205,000 Cincinnatians outside the city and 400,000 inside. There are more than 600,000 Pittsburghers outside the city.

There are two and a quarter million New Yorkers who are outside the town. Chicago has half a million Chicagoans who are not in the city and three million who are.

II. SIGNS OF AMELIORATION

So obvious have been the difficulties of urban integration and independence that everywhere in urban areas there has been evident a tendency toward an amelioration of this situation. In recent times we have witnessed the creation of the Greater Berlin in Germany, and of the Greater Prague in Czechoslovakia. On a smaller scale there are many other instances of the development of larger urban areas by the annexation of adjacent territory as in the case of Chicago in the World's Fair time. In other cases there has been developed a combination between city and county, eliminating one independent jurisdiction, as in San Francisco, St. Louis, Philadelphia. A similar plan was proposed for Chicago and Cook County many years ago by the Chicago Bureau of Public Efficiency. In still other cases there have been special combinations ad hoc for purposes of parks, or waters, or sewers—notably in the region of Boston where boards and commissions have been established to undertake special local functions in larger than urban areas.

It goes without saying that there have been many instances, more or less successful, of voluntary co-operation between local governments. The Regional Planning Association of the Chicago area has undertaken the task of effecting co-operation in specific directions and has been notably successful in vehicular traffic and in zoning ordinances. It is important to explore still more fully the possibilities of this form of voluntary integration.

The problem of metropolitan organization is particularly acute in the vicinity of Chicago, and a study has therefore been instituted of the metropolitan region. This is the unit assumed by the Regional Planning Association; the territory includes the commuting area of Chicago, and a population of some 4,000,000, with 1,673 independent governments. These complicated social, economic, and political structures are a challenge to the powers of observation, analysis, and reconstructive ability of workers in the field of social research, and the problem is a long time one.

It was realized from the beginning that a many-sided approach must be made to the situation, and accordingly varied but converging types of study have been undertaken. The forms of inquiry thus far launched include a basic study of the geographical background of Chicago, an examination of the trends of population in the region, the regional growth and development of agriculture and of industry, the analysis of the governmental functions and agencies in the metropolitan zone, and an inquiry into the public welfare administration in that part of the area included in Cook County.

The mere enumeration of these types of inquiry is sufficient to show the magnitude and complexity of the problem, while the actual attempt to carry through such an investigation multiplies the difficulties in many unforeseen ways. The necessity, however, for careful analysis of what is going on in the region, and of constructive suggestions of possibilities of reorganization and readjustment, is very great, and fully warrants thorough and patient study of the whole situation in its many ramifications and aspects. At no point in the social process of the community is there greater opportunity to replace a policy of drift and chance with one of intelligent foresight and planning, based upon careful analysis of the social forces involved.

III. CONCRETE STUDIES AND PROJECTS

The first step in the metropolitan analysis was the study of the physical basis of the region. The hinterland of Chicago was studied in the broadest outline by Goode and the region itself was examined closely by Fryxell.[1]

In addition to these studies, a much needed base map of the region was prepared by Goode.[2]

This painstaking effort laid a precise cartographical foundation on which the various types of local areas might be traced and plotted as the regional movement developed, on a larger or smaller scale.

The trends of population in the region have been subjected to acute analysis by Jeter,[3] who traced the growth of population in Chicago and the various units of the area from 1840 to 1920. In this study there was also prepared and compiled a series of tentative estimates of the probable growth of population down to 1950, in Chicago, in the various units of the region and in the region as a whole. These estimates indicate a probable population of 8,000,000 in the area within the next twenty years, if present tend-

---

[1] Goode made a broad sweeping survey of the geological origins and geographical features conditioning the area of which Chicago is the commercial center, and gave thoughtful consideration to the bearing of these geographical facts upon the status and probable development of the urban area. A much more detailed analysis of the geographical features of the Chicago region was prepared by Fryxell. In this the special topographical and geographical elements of the urban community were carefully analyzed, and important data made available for a fundamental study of the basic characteristics of the area. See J. P. Goode, *The Geographic Background of Chicago* (Chicago: University of Chicago Press, 1927); and F. M. Fryxell, *The Physiography of the Region of Chicago* (Chicago: University of Chicago Press, 1927).

[2] In co-operation with the Chicago Regional Planning Association and with the aid of the Commonwealth Club of Chicago and the United States Engineer.

[3] Helen R. Jeter, *Trends of Population in the Region of Chicago* (Chicago: University of Chicago Press, 1927). See also Monk and Jeter, "The Logistic Curve and the Prediction of the Population of the Chicago Region," *American Statistical Association*, December, 1928.

encies continue without serious modification. Incidentally they show the growth of extra-Chicago in a ratio far surpassing that of the corporate Chicago, and suggest thereby the rapid governmental disintegration of the Chicago area by the emigration of population to the extra-corporate sections of the metropolitan region.

From another point of view, a beginning has been made in the study of the trends of economic development, both agricultural and industrial in the region. An analysis of agriculture in the Chicago area has been completed by Duddy.[1]

While the balance of interest in the Chicago area long ago shifted from agriculture to manufacturing and industry of other types, the nature and tendencies of the remaining agricultural activities are of very great importance in any careful or adequate analysis of regional forces and future regional organization; for it is precisely the failure to reconcile these rural and agrarian survivals in the area to the new urban-industrial forces that creates some of the most acute problems of regional growth and readjustment. The great city has an agricultural setting not only in the economic sense of the term but also in the governmental.

The analysis of the industrial forces and trends in the region is of course basic in any study of what is actually occurring, however difficult it may be to make a comprehensive or accurate investigation of the essential factors in the situation. A study of the trends in the major in-

[1] E. A. Duddy, *Agriculture in the Chicago Region* (Chicago: University of Chicago Press, 1929). This volume includes a discussion of the uses of land, the types of farms, the crops produced in the area, and other features in what is essentially a disappearing occupation in a great metropolitan territory. The trends of agriculture are also being traced historically. These studies are related to other inquiries into the Chicago grain market and the Chicago warehousing industry now in progress.

dustries of the area has been instituted and the preliminary phases of the work are practically completed.[1] The large industries examined are iron and steel, printing and publishing, clothing, railroad cars and repair shops, slaughtering and meat-packing, electrical machinery, apparatus, supplies, and furniture, together with a few other leading types. In addition to this, a general survey of the industrial development of the region has been made. Among the features included are the towns and industry in the rural counties of the area,[2] the development of the northern lake ports of Racine, Kenosha, Waukegan, and North Chicago, and manufacturing in the inland towns of Elgin, Aurora, and Joliet. There is also a survey of the very important industrial development in the Calumet region[3] and its relation to the Chicago region as a whole. Important summaries and conclusions are drawn as a result of this analysis of the economic forces operating in the territory.

A careful survey has been made of the independent units of government in the metropolitan region, which reach the surprising number of 1,673 distributed as follows:

Cities	203
Counties	16
States	4
Park districts	59
Sanitary districts	10
Townships	166
School districts	987
Drainage districts	188
Miscellaneous	40
Total	1,673

[1] Marshall and Magee, *Manufacturing in the Chicago Region.*

[2] Kendall, Grundy, Porter, Walworth, McHenry, Kankakee.

[3] Including Gary, Michigan City, LaPorte, Hammond, Whiting, East Chicago.

These, it should be observed, are not merely administrative units, subdivisions of some larger unit, but in each of the 1,673 cases independent, governing agencies, endowed with independent taxing powers and various forms of rule making authority. Taken together they constitute the world's greatest jungle of governing agencies.[1]

There is also under way a study of the personnel of the governing agencies in the region, their number, classification, distribution by types of agencies, and other important facts regarding the army of officials who administer the affairs of the metropolitan area of Chicago.[2]

The study of the governments of the Chicago region has been approached primarily from the point of view of a study of the special functions of the political agencies in the area. Thus the function of public health has been traced through the 350 health agencies scattered through the region by which the health powers are exercised. The police function is examined in the light of the many police agencies, municipal, county, and others through which the police function is administered. In the same way the judicial function is scrutinized. Likewise the function of education, and eventually finance, recreation, and other principal functions will be studied.[3]

The various types of functional agencies are scrutinized, types of personnel and equipment are noted, practices of co-operation and co-ordination or the opposite are observed, and the relation between the functional area and the metropolitan area carefully studied. This is a novel approach to the regional problem, but it is believed that it

---

[1] S. D. Parratt, *The Governments of the Metropolitan Region of Chicago.*

[2] R. F. Steadman, *Personnel of the Governments of the Metropolitan Area of Chicago.*

[3] R. F. Steadman, *The Function of Public Health in the Chicago Region.*

will be helpful in fixing attention on the specifically regional services and types of regional co-operation likely
to be most helpful, if adequately organized either under
voluntary or under governmental auspices as the case may
be. Important as they are, the structural organizations
are subordinate to the purposes they serve, or impede,
and the readjustment should be in terms of the structure
most useful for the functional purpose.

Further, a specific study of various administrative activities has been undertaken within the limits of Cook
County only and in the field of public welfare administration. While these studies do not focus directly upon the
regional problem, they are closely related to it. They illustrate in this smaller field the lack of planning and foresight
which is so conspicuous a feature of regional development
in other sections of the area—a situation which grows
worse as the entire area is gradually brought into view.
Among the many phases of the subject which were canvassed thus far are the history and operation of the almshouse at Forest Park, Oak Forest, the thirty methods of
administering poor relief in Cook County, the public subsidies to private institutions for the care of dependent
children, the pension fund for the blind, and the county
doctor. The special attention given to the historical development of these situations and to the extent of co-ordination of effort or its lack makes the material of great
value to the student of regional activity and planning.[1]

When the important data regarding the social and
economic basis of the region and its governmental ar-
rangements have been assembled and analyzed, the various
possibilities of reorganization of the governments of the region will be carefully studied in the light of local experience

[1] See chap. xi.

and that of other great metropolitan communities in this country and elsewhere. It is expected that a constructive program will be developed or at least that the alternative possibilities will be presented, canvassed, and appraised. The main purpose of the study will be to present the important facts to the regional community or communities, with the expectation that these facts will stimulate the production of important and feasible plans for better co-operation and reorganization, but the report of our research men will contain such findings and recommendations as may seem to them most useful in the situation, in no sense dogmatic, but representing their best judgment in the light of their studies of the facts and the outstanding possibilities.

Among the important possibilities thus far tentatively canvassed have been voluntary co-operation of independent governing agencies, as in the field of health; provision for various functional agencies in the region, as for example a metropolitan police district; annexation of outlying territories to Chicago; adoption of some form of borough government for the Illinois part of the region preserving some degree of local autonomy; the setting up of an independent state of Chicago covering the Illinois parts of the region. These are put forward at this time only as illustrations of the type of suggestion which has been brought under consideration down to this time. Other alternatives may of course develop in the course of inquiry and discussion.

The readjustment of the regional governmental services in the metropolitan area of Chicago is obviously not the task of a day or a year, but will require a long stretch of time for its completion. During this protracted period of reorganization, continuing research in this field will be necessary, and should lead to very substantial advantages, both from the point of view of expenditures and of services, as well as of popular control over government, and the prestige and satisfaction arising from the development of an actual regional loyalty through common public service and the recognition of common regional interests. It is hoped that the research already undertaken and likely to be later attempted, together with that of other local groups, will prove to be materially useful in substituting mastery for drift in this important phase of local affairs.

CHAPTER VII

TECHNIQUE OF MEASUREMENT

In business, government, and social work, plans for the future must be based upon past experience. Experience can be recorded in the form of a historical narrative, which emphasizes single unique events, or it can be recorded in statistical form, which emphasizes the grouping of events through the adoption of units of measurement. Quantitative data lend themselves to analysis more readily than narrative material and are more likely to be free from personal bias. In connection with studies made under the Local Community Research Committee a constant effort has been made to use quantitative methods wherever possible. Human society is so complex that the tasks of defining units of measurement, of ruling out disturbing factors, and of predicting future behavior seem almost insuperable. Work in this field requires vision, courage, and untiring patience. It frequently happens that many months of patient toil are required to obtain a single result. The brief descriptions that follow of some of the contributions made at the University of Chicago to the technique of measurement in the social sciences are designed to give a broad survey view of the possibilities in this field.

I

A continuous effort has been made by research workers at the University of Chicago to improve the existing methods for collecting social data. Notable advances have been made in this direction during the last few years. Among them should be mentioned the study on the vital statistics of heart disease in Chicago, which is being carried on under the supervision of Dr. I. S. Falk. One of the principal objects of this study is to improve the registration of heart-disease mortality. The first step was the transcription of all pertinent information concerning heart-disease decedents from the records of the Chicago Department of Health. The editing of these data was done in accordance with an internationally standard system of nosology. The accuracy of the data was evaluated in part from a priori considerations and in part from evidence internal to the data. The procedure was as follows:

1. Separation of records in which heart disease appears as a primary and as a secondary cause of death.
2. Calculation of rates of mortality for each major form of heart disease against variously estimated populations.
3. The study, by methods of correlation, of the apparent relations between heart-disease mortality and the race, nativity, age, sex, occupation, economic and social status, etc., of the decedents.
4. Computations of probable physicians' diagnostic practices and errors in heart-disease cases by distribution of the records according to reporting physicians and their education, years of practice, size of practice, etc.
5. The study, from internal evidences, of misuse of heart-disease diagnosis by certain recording-agencies to cover official lack of interest or incompetence in ascertaining the cause of death in homicide cases, in cases of certain types of indigent persons, etc.

These methods for studying the vital statistics of heart disease have revealed a number of improvements that could be made in official mortality records.

Considerable progress has also been made in perfecting methods for the registration of social statistics. An experiment conducted by Mr. McMillen and Miss Jeter in gathering statistics from agencies operating in the field of family welfare work showed that the existing data in this field are not reliable because of a lack of standard terminology.[1] Family welfare agencies in all sections of the country are accustomed to use the terms "major care case" and "minor care case." A questionnaire was devised to discover the actual policies followed in the field and to see whether any one policy was sufficiently widespread and sufficiently objective to recommend itself for permanent use. This questionnaire listed briefly a series of case-work situations and some ninety-four family welfare agencies in twenty-nine cities checked the cases under columns headed "Not a Case," "Minor Care," "Major Care," and "Doubtful." The situations presented were chosen so as to fall in the twilight zones between the different classes. The case summaries, while necessarily terse, were made sufficiently detailed to enable most agencies to make clear-cut decisions. The replies showed considerable variability, reflecting unmistakable variations in practice. The evidence obtained from the tabulation of the replies was not sufficiently uniform to justify the formulation of definitions. Similar discrepancies between definition and interpretation were subsequently discovered in medical-social service, in psychiatric social service, and in several other case-working specialties. It was suggested that some of the units of service in social work will not yield to verbal definition and that statistical comparability can be given such units only by means of descriptive summaries or illustrative charts.

A further significant step was taken during 1928–29 to improve the original entry from which all the statistics of social work derive. Joint Committees with the three following national societies have been organized: (1) American Association for Organizing Family Social Work, (2)

[1] A. W. McMillen and Helen R. Jeter, "Terminology in Family Welfare Field," *Social Service Review*, II (September, 1928), 357–84.

American Association of Hospital Social Workers, (3) National Organization for Public Health Nursing. These three national societies have entered into an agreement to work out a manual on records and statistics in their respective fields. These manuals will lay emphasis on the records of original entry and will show how statistics should be kept from the very first step up to the final preparation of the consolidated report. The completion of these manuals may require a considerable period of time, but it does not seem an exaggeration to say that it is an accomplishment to have got a piece of work under way that should result in standard statistical systems from which figures that are really comparable may be expected to result.

It sometimes happens that research workers come upon interesting discoveries which are incidental to the main line of inquiry. The task of predicting the population of the Chicago region was one of the problems undertaken by the Local Community Research Committee.[1] In working on this problem Miss Jeter and Mrs. Monk discovered that the logistic curve which had been used with apparent success in the prediction of the population for the New York region did not fit the Chicago conditions.[2] Extrapolations from one first order equation led to the surprising conclusion that the total increase in population during the one hundred and thirty years following 1920 would be less than the increase during the preceding period of only thirty years. Predictions from another curve placed the population of the region in 1920 below the actual census

[1] See chap. v.

[2] Ardis T. Monk and Helen R. Jeter, "The Logistic Curve and the Prediction of the Population of the Chicago Region," *Journal of the American Statistical Association*, December, 1928.

figures for that year. In short, the study showed that the history of growth of population in the Chicago region has not exhibited the necessary characteristics of a logistic. Several reasons were discovered for the failure of the general law to apply to this region. The period of observation is too short to draw sound conclusions. Only nine censuses, beginning with 1840, furnish figures for the greater part of the area studied. It was also found that the rate of growth has been so rapid that a symmetrical curve would exhibit an equally rapid falling off in the rate of increase. The facts do not show any such falling off. Lastly, it was demonstrated that the Chicago percentage of growth is probably not a linear function of the population itself. The linearity of this relationship is one of the assumptions of the logistic. The study showed the need for new methods to predict the growth of population in regions like the Chicago region.

II

A number of the studies made by the Local Community Research Committee involved new methods for collecting and analyzing social data. Notable among these is Mr. Ogburn's study of the influence of order of birth on personality. A comparison of percentages of children who were famous, failures, radicals, or insane was made according to order of birth. The essential problem was to make the comparisons with data which were similar in almost all other respects than that of order of birth. It was necessary, therefore, to hold the factors of size of family, age of birth, social class, responsiveness to questionnaires, etc., constant. This was done by ingenious selective methods. In the first part of this study questionnaires were sent out to one thousand artists, one thousand scientists, and one thousand business men selected at random from *Who's Who*. The 1,785 schedules returned were classified according to size of family, position in family, and age. A control sample of the normal population was obtained to see whether the oldest in a family returned cards more frequently than those in the middle. This sample was so selected that the age factor was eliminated. A comparison of normal expectancy and the actual rates found in the first part of this study showed that the first born were more successful. This conclusion could be relied upon because of the care taken to eliminate disturbing factors.

Mr. Ogburn also has a number of studies under way which involve careful and discriminating use of available data. One on social changes in recent years in the United States deals with a variety of topics. The method involved is largely the utilization of published data, chiefly from the census, but in order to make the year-by-year comparisons it is necessary to refine and analyze the data quite carefully and to eliminate various disturbing factors. All the best methods for making time series studies are being employed. Another one of his studies throws some interesting light upon the Malthusian population theory. Assuming that conditions in Iceland are similar to those which were found among primitive peoples, he analyzed the Icelandic death-rates from 1750 on. After putting a trend line through the data he computed the standard deviations. He did the same for the death-rates in twenty Massachusetts counties since 1820. The variability of the death-rate in Iceland was five times as great as that for the Massachusetts counties, thus showing that the hazards of life in Iceland were relatively great. Another study is being made on birth-rates of social classes in which correlations were made between the birth statistics showing the number of children born to mothers of 1925 with the birth-rates of the occupational classes for 1926. It was found that the census figures are substantially the same as the birth-rate figures. This makes it possible to compute the birth-rate for each occupational class.

A very suggestive use that can be made of census material and other data on different aspects of urban life has been pointed out by Mr. Burgess.[1] One of the most evident processes of urban development is that of radial expansion from the center. Mr. Burgess has been working on methods of measuring this process and its effects upon community life. Defining a gradient as the rate of change of a variable condition like poverty, or home ownership, or births, or divorce, from the standpoint of its distribution over a given area, he has worked out a number of gradients in the growth of Chicago. Four of these gradients have been based upon census material. Taking advantage of the fact that Chicago is one of the eleven so-called "tract cities," he obtained data for the 500 census tracts of the city. These data include, among other facts, home ownership, country of birth of the foreign-born, sex, and age groups. The census tracts are small enough in size to be satisfactory as unit districts. The gradients of home ownership were found to be particularly significant, since home ownership is both one of the most significant negative indices of mobility and one of the positive indications of the stability not only of the family but also of community life. In a similar way the data for poverty, divorce, and juvenile delinquency rates were worked out from spot maps prepared by research assistants.

In the study of factors making for success or failure on

[1] Ernest W. Burgess, "The Determination of Gradients in the Growth of the City," *Publications of the American Sociological Society*, XXI (1927), 178–84.

parole, Mr. Burgess, with the assistance of Clark Tibbitts, developed a technique for predicting success on parole.[1] This method grew out of a detailed analysis of the records of 3,000 men paroled from three penal institutions in Illinois. Twenty-one relevant facts were obtained regarding each of the men studied. This part of the work involved some difficult problems of classification. These facts were then related in turn to non-violation or violation of parole. Non-violation of parole means that the person has observed at least the letter of his parole obligations and has not been apprehended for a new offense. The strict application of this definition to the records revealed a large margin of error in the official reports of the Division of Pardons and Paroles. Using the actual records as a basis, the parole violation rates were worked out for a large number of subclassifications. Significant variations were found in the violation rates of the different subgroups. For example, although the violation rate for 1,000 youths from Pontiac is 22.1 per cent, it is less than half that among those with a regular work record prior to imprisonment (8.8 per cent); among those with very superior intelligence (9.5 per cent); among those who served less than one year (10.7 per cent); and among boys from farms (11.0 per cent). It is double this average rate for those who had lived in the criminal underworld and for certain other subgroups. In order to study the combined influence of these factors on the violation rate, each man was graded, in comparison with the average for the 1,000 cases from his institution, upon the probabilities of making good or of failing upon parole. Since there were twenty-one factors it was theoretically possible for a man

[1] A. A. Bruce, E. W. Burgess, and A. J. Harno, *Parole and the Indeterminate Sentence: A Report to the Honorable Hinton G. Clabaugh, Chairman, Parole Board of Illinois* (1928).

to be in a more favorable group than the average on all twenty-one factors, or upon twenty factors, and so on down the scale to having a better position than the average upon three factors, upon two factors, upon one factor, and upon no factors. The men who were in from sixteen to twenty-one subgroups with low violation rates showed only a violation rate of 1.5 per cent, while those who were in from but two to four of the favorable subgroups showed a violation rate of 76 per cent. This method not only constitutes a striking improvement over earlier methods of predicting success on parole, but it also represents in a remarkable way the successful application of statistical methods to the solution of a practical problem. When applied on a larger scale and taken into consideration with other data, expectancy rates of violation should be invaluable to parole boards.

III

Of considerable theoretical and practical significance have been the studies made on the basis of available records and statistics. Some pronounced improvements in the methods of mathematical and statistical economics have been made by Mr. Schultz. In trying to obtain fuller *quantitative* knowledge of price phenomena, he has been endeavoring to derive empirical supply and demand curves for the more important commodities, to show the shifting of these curves as a result of dynamic conditions, to supplement our existing knowledge of profit-making forces and of the relation of cost to output, and to reconstruct the accepted theories of price determination in the light of the empirical results obtained.

In his study of the law of demand and supply for sugar,[1]

---

[1] Henry Schultz, *Statistical Laws of Demand and Supply with Special Application to Sugar* (Chicago, 1928).

he shows how the accepted theory of demand and supply has to be restated in order to make it amenable to the quantitative approach. The most general formulation of the dynamic law of demand is that the quantity of any commodity consumed is a function not only of its price but also of all other prices and of time. To obtain the form of this law observations must be made of the market behavior of purchasers.

A great variety of statistical techniques were employed by Mr. Schultz in deducing for the first time the demand and supply curves for sugar. By adopting the operational point of view, he succeeded in restating the hypothetical, statical law of demand in a form admitting of concrete, inductive treatment. In order to handle the time variable, the ratio of the given year's value to that of the preceding year (link relative) and also the ratio of the absolute price to its trend were taken. Both of these methods were applied to the observed or unadjusted data for prices and consumption of sugar in the United States, as well as to data which were first corrected for changes in the general level of prices and for population growth. Great ingenuity was shown in selecting trend lines which were most fitted to the purpose of the problem in hand and also in choosing the type of equations which were most suitable for the purpose of deriving the best value of the coefficient of elasticity. The accepted methods of curve fitting, it was found, lead to equivocal results in demand and supply studies. Ways to overcome this difficulty through the use of better methods of curve-fitting were suggested. In his search for the law of supply for sugar new methods of multiple correlation were also introduced.

The results are of general and practical importance. They show that based on the experience of 1890–1913 the demand for sugar is inelastic; that is, an increase of 1 per cent in the price will reduce consumption by less than 1 per cent—normally by only 0.5 of 1 per cent. The United States' demand for sugar has shown a marked shift in the period studied. For example, a rise or fall in the price of sugar (in terms of the 1913 dollar) of 1 cent per pound would have affected per capita consumption by 5.2 pounds in 1894; by 6.8 pounds in 1904; and by 9.7 pounds in 1914. The supply of sugar from domestic and insular sources is also inelastic, though relatively less so than the demand. An increase of 1 per cent in price will increase production between 0.6 and 1.0 per cent under normal conditions. Finally, for the first time, a scientific determination of the effect of the tariff on the price of sugar is presented. During the period of 1903–13 an increase in the duty of 1 cent per pound would have increased the domestic price by 0.86 of 1 per cent. To obtain this result it was necessary to deduce the world, as well as the domestic, demand and supply curves for sugar.

In connection with further studies along the same lines, which he is now making, Mr. Schultz has made a number of valuable methodological discoveries. In analyzing the demand and supply for corn, potatoes, and other commodities, he found that the same data sometimes yield demand and supply curves of different shapes, depending on the method employed. Thus, when the method of trend ratios leads to the conclusion that the demand function for a commodity is a negatively sloping *straight line*, the method of link relatives applied to the same data may lead to the conclusion that it is a negatively sloping *curve*. It was also found that statisticians use misleading, if not definitely erroneous, formulas for the probable error of a trend.

Detailed studies of price determination can yield very

useful results. The business man in planning a production or sales program, the legislator in considering a tariff policy, and the economist in his study of the price-making forces find it necessary or at least highly desirable to be able to arrive at some quantitative measure of the elasticities of demand and supply. Intelligent action or a correct appraisal of the probable effect of a given course can be arrived at only by knowing the intensity of the price-making forces.

IV

In the field of labor statistics, Mr. Douglas has been making some important contributions to the study of real wages in the United States. Following the lines of an earlier study,[1] he has been making significant comparisons between the relative movement of the cost of living and the relative movement of money wages and earnings. His cost of living index is based primarily upon the statistics collected semiannually by the United States Bureau of Labor Statistics of changes in the cost of living for thirty-three cities. In securing a country-wide index, he weighted the percentage change for each city by the relative population of that city instead of using the less exact method employed by the Bureau of Labor Statistics.[2] In order to obtain monthly cost of living indices, interpolations were made on the basis of the figures furnished by the National Industrial Conference Board. The basic assumption made was that the Bureau of Labor Statistics index would show the same relative fluctuations from its normal trend as would that of the Conference Board, and that any differ-

[1] P. H. Douglas, *Real Earnings in the United States 1890–1926*.

[2] The Bureau of Labor Statistics computes an unweighted arithmetic average of the increases for each main group by its proportionate importance in 1918 in working-class budgets.

ence in the rate of change between the two over the period in question would be evenly divided as between the months.

In computing money earnings, series were computed for the three main methods by which wages may be measured, namely, wage rates, average earnings of employed persons, and average earnings of the wage-earning class as a whole. The computing of each of these series involves special problems. Wage rates are amounts which are paid for specified periods of work. They make no allowance for short time or overtime, nor do they include fines, bonuses, or premiums. The statistics for hourly and full-time weekly wage rates were gathered from (a) collections of union wage rates made by the United States Bureau of Labor Statistics for the building trades, book and job printing, newspaper printing, baking, and stonecutting; (b) the wage rates of hourly earnings and full-time weekly earnings derived from periodical surveys of pay-rolls in slaughtering and meat-packing, foundries and machine shops, iron and steel mills, cotton manufacturing, woolen manufacturing, hosiery and knit goods, sawmills, men's clothing establishments; (c) farm labor rates; (d) unskilled labor rates; (e) wage rates in bituminous and anthracite coal mines; (f) average daily salaries of teachers; (g) average weekly salaries of government employees in Washington.

The average earnings of employed persons were obtained by dividing the actual amount paid out in wages or salaries during a period, whether a week or a year, by the average number of persons employed. While this figure makes allowance for short time and overtime and for bonuses and fines, it does not make allowance for the relative amount of unemployment which prevails. Average earnings are shown by the biennial censuses of manufacturing. Monthly indices during the census years were computed on the assumption that the monthly variations of the average census earnings above their yearly average would be equal to the average deviations of the average earnings of wage-earners in these industries as shown by the monthly pay-roll studies on employment and earnings made by the United States Bureau of Labor Statistics. Interpolations for the non-census years were made on the same two sets of data. Figures were also obtained from various government reports and from private sources regarding the annual earnings of manual and clerical workers on the railways, of farm-laborers, of coal-miners, of street railway employees, of teachers, of ministers, of government employees, and of other workers.

The average earnings of the wage-earning class as a whole were obtained by multiplying the average annual earnings of employed workers by that percentage of the labor supply which is employed. The index of unemployment was obtained by computing (a) the labor supply for manufacturing, transportation, and mining, and other lines of work, and deducting from this the numbers employed in these occupations; (b) for the building trades, the percentages of unemployed have been computed from trade-union statistics for Massachusetts and Ohio. Curves of labor supply were built up from an assumption of population growth and net immigration and emigration, and from these were subtracted the numbers employed in the various industries.

The absolute figures obtained for each industry in these three series were combined into groups by weighting the average for each industry by the relative number of persons employed in it during each year. Composite averages were also secured for all industry as a whole. These were in turn reduced to relatives, with the averages for 1914 serving as a point of reference. Indices of real wage rates and real average earnings were then obtained by dividing these relatives of money earnings by the relatives of the cost of living. It is of interest to note that the real annual earnings of the employed workers in industry as a whole were, in 1926, 28 per cent higher than during 1914. There was little change during 1927, but the average for the employed workers, at least, rose during 1928 by approximately 5 per cent.

V

In analyzing the prestige value of public employment, Mr. White applied to the study of public opinion some interesting and novel devices.[1] Briefly stated, the problem was to discover and to state with as great precision as possible the degree of prestige attached to the Chicago public service by the mass of people living in Chicago. It was assumed that a high prestige would tend to attract suitable candidates for city positions and to encourage the efficient conduct of city business, while a low prestige was assumed to depress the standards of entrants and to discourage good work in the city hall. This problem was therefore primarily one of analysis of opinion. Several methods were employed. The method of choice between paired occupations, one being public, the other private but otherwise equivalent, was the principal method. Twenty such pairs were constructed, and 4,680 subjects asked to check the occupation in each pair for which they had the higher esteem. Over 90,000 expressions of opinion were thus secured, which were analyzed to show the differentials of sex, age, education, occupation, years' residence in

[1] Leonard D. White, *The Prestige Value of Municipal Employment in Chicago* (Chicago: University of Chicago Press, 1929).

Chicago, race and nationality, and economic status. Significant variations were discovered by each of these criteria, excepting years' residence in Chicago. A second method involved the use of an association test, in which thirty words were read at the rate of about five per minute to 690 persons who were instructed to write the first word which came into their mind. Among the thirty words were ten or twelve relating to the subject of city employment. The reactions to these words proved to have significance for the purpose of the study. A third method involved a completion test. The subjects were requested to select one of the nine possible completions. Similar completions were constructed for courtesy and honesty.

In order to translate the results of the paired occupation test into prestige indices, it was assumed that if one hundred persons all indicated a higher prestige for each of the twenty city occupations, the prestige value of city employment for the group would be plus one hundred; if they indicated the private occupations without exception, minus one hundred; if they divided evenly, the prestige value would be at the neutral point, or zero. These assumptions enable any division of opinion to be recorded on a scale ranging from plus one hundred to minus one hundred.

The actual prestige value discovered for the representative sample of 4,680 persons was minus 14.03. Women revealed a higher prestige index than men, young persons a higher prestige index than elderly, the poorly educated a higher index than the well educated, foreign-born a higher index than the natives, with native-born persons of foreign fathers occupying a midway position, unskilled labor a strikingly higher index than that of the executive-proprietor group, and persons of low economic status a higher index than persons of a high economic status. The word association test showed a preponderance of unfavorable reaction words. The completion test showed a decided weighting of opinion against city-hall employment.

One of the voting studies made under the auspices of the Local Community Research Committee was an attempt to measure the influence of a nonpartisan mail canvass to get out the vote.[1] It was based upon observation of the voting behavior of 6,000 persons in Chicago during the presidential election of 1924 and the aldermanic election of 1925. In order to set up this experiment it was necessary to keep constant within reasonable limits all the factors that enter into the electoral process except the particular stimuli which were to be tested. The factors known to have some relation to non-voting are: sex, the dramatic quality of the election, the convenience of the voting system, mobility, foreign language training, and the nature of the local party organization. The method of random sampling was used to control these factors during the testing of the particular stimuli used in the experiment. A thorough canvass was made of all the adult citizens in twelve selected districts in the city. Extraordinary efforts were made to list all the eligible voters living in these areas. The second step in the experiment was the division of the citizens in each of the districts canvassed into two groups, one of which was to be stimulated while the other was not. The assumption was made that if a larger proportion of the stimulated citizens registered and voted than of the non-stimulated citizens, then the particular stimuli used had had some effect. Since the stimulated and non-stimulated citizens were selected from the same precincts, there was no reason to suppose that the strength of the local party organizations would vary much as between the

[1] H. F. Gosnell, *Getting Out the Vote* (Chicago, 1927).

two groups. Furthermore, the percentage distributions of the stimulated and non-stimulated by sex, color, country of birth, length of residence in the district, rent paid, knowledge of government, and schooling were practically the same. It can therefore be said that as far as possible these variables were kept constant during the experiment.

The citizens in the experimental group were sent postcard notices regarding the importance of registration and voting upon four different occasions. On each occasion it was discovered that 9 per cent more of the experimental than of the control group responded, except in the matter of registration for the aldermanic election, in which 6 per cent of the experimental group registered as against 1 per cent of the control group. The results of the experiment were then analyzed by party preferences, citizenship status, country of birth, term of residence in the district, economic status, schooling, and knowledge of American government. In this study an attempt was made to conform to the scientific requirements of exact observation, statistical measurement, and isolation and variation of the conditioning factors.

VI

One of the outstanding contributions to methodology in the social sciences has been the work of Mr. Thurstone in the measurement of attitudes. The object of his work has been to devise a method whereby the distribution of attitude of a group on a specified issue may be represented in the form of a frequency distribution.[1] He has devised a base line to represent the range of opinions from those at one end who are most strongly in favor of the issue to

[1] L. L. Thurstone, "Attitudes Can Be Measured," *American Journal of Sociology*, XXXIII (January, 1928), 529–54.

those at the other end of the scale who are as strongly against it. Somewhere between the two extremes on the base line is a neutral zone representing indifferent attitudes on the issue in question. The ordinates of the frequency distribution represent the relative popularity of each attitude. As in other measurement problems, the attributes can be measured only when they are represented upon a linear continuum. Using psychophysical methods which have heretofore been employed largely in the study of discrimination of physical stimuli, he has ingeniously worked out this continuum. Those aspects of attitudes are studied for which one can compare individuals by the "more-or-less" type of judgment. It can be said understandingly that one man is more in favor of prohibition than another, more strongly in favor of the League of Nations than another, more militaristic than another, more religious than another. The measurement is effected by the indorsement or rejection of statements of opinion. The center of the whole problem was in the definition of a unit of measurement for the base line.

In making a scale, a group of three hundred persons are asked to sort a number of statements into an imaginary scale representing the attitude variable. Thus, in the construction of a scale on prohibition the subjects are asked to arrange the statements in rank order according to their "wetness."[1] It is assumed that two statements on a prohibition scale will be as easy or as difficult to discriminate for people who are "wet" as for those who are "dry." In other words, the assumption is that the proportion of "wets" who will say that statement a is wetter than statement b will be substantially the same as the corresponding

[1] L. L. Thurstone, "The Measurement of Opinion," *Journal of Abnormal and Social Psychology*, XXII (January, 1928), 415–30.

proportion for the same statements obtained from a group of "drys." This assumption is now being verified on an empirical basis. It is also assumed that if it is difficult to discriminate between statements a and b either one of them may more or less readily be perceived in the same stimulus.[1] The distance between the two statements on the imaginary scale depends upon the extent to which they are likely to be associated together by the same person. It was found sufficient for purposes of making the scale that the judgments behaved as though their respective probabilities of association with a given stimulus were a normal frequency distribution. The unit of measurement is the standard deviation of the frequency distribution for a specified stimulus. For example, the proportion of times that statement a is declared "wetter" than statement b represents an area under the normal probability curve. The scale distance between these two statements in terms of the standard deviation of one of them may be read from tables of the normal probability integral.[2] This unit of measurement is called the standard discriminal error for the specified stimulus. It is based on the principle that equally often noticed differences are equal. It is a valid unit of measurement even when the objective stimulus, in this case a statement on prohibition, cannot itself be quantitatively measured. The computing of the final scale is based upon all the available stimulus comparisons. This method of obtaining an attitude scale enables one to compare several groups as to distribution, central tendency, and dispersion of opinion on any stated opinion variable,

[1] L. L. Thurstone, "A Mental Unit of Measurement," *Psychological Review*, XXXIV (November, 1927), 415.

[2] L. L. Thurstone, "The Unit of Measurement in Educational Scales," *Journal of Educational Psychology*, November, 1927.

irrespective of the shape of that distribution or the amount and direction of bias in each of the groups.

At the present time Mr. Thurstone and his associates have prepared or are preparing scales to measure attitudes toward prohibition, the church, the negro, militarism, and pacifism. In preparing these scales the method of equal-appearing intervals was used instead of the one described in the foregoing. Under this method, several hundred persons are asked to sort a hundred or so statements of opinion into ten piles that range from the most favorable to the most unfavorable opinions. The subjects are instructed to make the steps in attitude as nearly equal as possible so that the ten piles may be regarded as an equally graduated series. The series of ten piles is then regarded as a series of ten class-intervals in a continuous scale and each opinion is assigned a scale-value which is the median point on the scale at which it has been allocated by the several hundred judges. The final scale by which attitude is measured consists of a series of forty opinions selected so as to constitute an evenly graduated series of scale-values. The subject whose attitude is to be measured is asked to check those statements the sentiment of which he agrees with. His attitude is assigned a numerical value equal to the average scale-value of all the opinions that he has indorsed. These scales could be used to measure shifts of opinion within a given group or to measure the differences between a number of groups on the questions specified.

Another of Mr. Thurstone's experiments was intended to measure the national and racial attitudes of a group of students. Instead of asking the subject to judge, as in the classical psychophysical experiments, which of two weights is the heavier or which of two straight lines is the longer, he was asked to tell us which of two given nationalities he would rather associate with. A list of twenty nationalities was prepared and every one of these twenty nationalities or races was compared with every other one in the entire list so that the total number of comparisons was 190. For each pair the subject merely underlined that one of the two nations or races which he would in general rather associate with. The result is a series of 190 scale separations by psychophysical procedures that are discussed in the published articles.[1] It was found that each of the twenty nationalities could be assigned to a point on a straight line so that all of the 190 experimentally determined scale separations agree well with the linear separations on the postulated scale of attitudes. One end of this scale represents attitudes strongly favorable while the other end represents attitudes strongly unfavorable. With our group of several hundred students the Americans were of course at the top of the list, followed by the English-speaking nationalities such as the English, the Scotch, the Irish, while at the bottom of the scale was found the Negro.

It should be noticed that such a scale constitutes a description of our group of students. If another group of subjects was asked to fill in the schedules, we should, of course, expect a different set of scale-values for the different nationalities. Now, if such a study were made on university students or on other occupational groups in different countries, it would be possible to make quantitative comparisons of the prejudices and the preferences of the different countries for or against each other. Furthermore, the spread of the whole scale is a quantitative measure of the discrimination or prejudice in the group studied. If they have strong likes and dislikes about foreign countries,

---

[1] L. L. Thurstone, "An Experimental Study of Nationality Preferences," *Journal of General Psychology*, I (October, 1928), 405–25.

that will show by a wide spread of scale-values while a more uniformly tolerant attitude toward different countries and races will be indicated by a relatively smaller linear spread of the whole values. The degree of similarity or dissimilarity in international attitudes between any two countries can also be quantitatively expressed in terms of the coefficient of correlation of the two sets of scale-values. These remarks serve to illustrate the type of problem to which the method of paired comparison lends itself.

VII

A number of other contributions to the technique of measurement in the social sciences have been made in connection with the work of the Local Community Research Committee. Among these might be mentioned Mr. Beeley's study of the bail system in Chicago, Miss McKinney's study of certain characteristics of citizenship, Miss Houghteling's study of family budgets, and Mr. Cowley's analysis of leadership traits.

The aim of the brief descriptions given in this chapter has been to show some of the applications of quantitative methods to the study of human relationships. Such problems have been attacked as the testing of the reliability of social statistics, the measurement of urban growth gradients, the prediction of success on parole, the derivation of empirical supply and demand curves, the trend of real wages, the prestige value of public employment, the measurement of the influence of a nonpartisan mail canvass to get out the vote, and the measurement of attitudes on specified questions. A number of novel statistical devices have been employed in solving these problems. The methods have in each case been adapted to the problem in hand. The results indicate that there is hope for establishing social studies upon a sound scientific basis.

CHAPTER VIII

URBAN AREAS

A human community, like a biological organism, grows by the process of subdivision. As a city grows, its structure becomes more complex and its areas more specialized. Increasing differentiation, however, involves more rather than less co-operation and interdependence. The specialized areas of the city, as the central retail business district, the industrial community, the residential neighborhood, and suburban towns and villages are all organic parts of the city, because of rather than in spite of their differentiated functions.

It was, therefore, from the standpoint of the growth of the city, and their organic relation to it, that studies of individual urban areas were oriented. Accordingly, an analysis of the factors and forces in the growth of the city was first made[1] in order to understand the general pattern of the formation of urban areas.

Out of the many factors affecting the pattern of city formation, three may be selected as, perhaps, decisive:

1. The radial character of city growth, or the tendency of a community to outward expansion from its center.
2. Natural or artificial variations in the topographical features of the city, including elevation, site on coast, lake, or river, barriers like river, elevated railroad lines, and parks.
3. The general features of the street plan of the city, including the structure of the local transportation system.

[1] See E. W. Burgess in R. E. Park, *The City*, chap. II, "The Growth of the City"; and R. E. Park, "The Spacial Pattern and the Moral Order," in "Proceedings of the American Sociological Society," *Urban Community*.

Of these factors in city growth, that of radial expansion seems to leave its deepest impress upon the structure of the city. The various studies of urban areas in Chicago have traced out the factors in city growth, movement of population, and community organization.

I. RADIAL EXPANSION AND THE FIVE URBAN ZONES

As any community increases in numbers of inhabitants, expansion naturally takes place by movement of residents beyond the outskirts of the already settled territory. The expansion of the urban business district may be in the air, via the skyscraper; but it also presses outward into the surrounding residential district. This outward expansion in all directions from the center toward the peripheries of the community may be called the force of radial extension. In the absence of counteracting factors, the assumption is advanced that the modern American city would take the form of five concentric urban zones as represented in the chart on the opposite page.

Zone I: The Central Business District.—At the center of the city as the focus of its commercial, social, and civic life is situated the Central Business District. The heart of this district is the downtown retail district with its department stores, its smart shops, its office buildings, its clubs, its banks, its hotels, its theaters, its museums, and its headquarters of economic, social, civic, and political life. Encircling this area of work and play is the less well-known Wholesale Business District with its "market," its warehouses, and storage buildings.

Zone II: The Zone in Transition.—Surrounding the Central Business District are areas of residential deterioration caused by the encroaching of business and industry from Zone I. This may therefore be called a Zone in Transition, with a factory district for its inner belt and an outer ring of retrogressing neighborhoods, of first-settlement im-

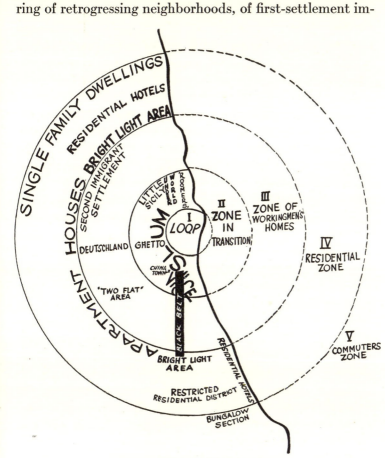

URBAN ZONES AND AREAS

migrant colonies, of rooming-house districts, of homeless-men areas, of resorts of gambling, bootlegging, sexual vice, and of breeding-places of crime. In this area of physical deterioration and social disorganization our studies show the greatest concentration of cases of poverty, bad housing, juvenile delinquency, family disintegration, physical and mental disease. As families and individuals prosper, they escape from this area into Zone III beyond, leaving behind as marooned a residuum of the defeated, leaderless, and helpless.

Zone III: The Zone of Independent Workingmen's Homes.—This third broad urban ring is in Chicago, as well as in other northern industrial cities, largely constituted by neighborhoods of second immigrant settlement. Its residents are those who desire to live near but not too close to their work. In Chicago it is a housing area neither of tenements, apartments, nor of single dwellings; its boundaries have been roughly determined by the plotting of the two-flat dwelling, generally of frame construction, with the owner living on the lower floor with a tenant on the other. While the father works in the factory the son and daughter typically have jobs in the Loop, attend dance halls and motion pictures in the bright-light areas, and plan upon marriage to set up homes in Zone IV.

Zone IV: The Zone of Better Residences.—Extending beyond the neighborhoods of second immigrant settlements, we come to the Zone of Better Residences in which the great middle-classes of native-born Americans live, small business men, professional people, clerks, and salesmen. Once communities of single homes, these are becoming in Chicago apartment-house and residential-hotel areas. Within these areas at strategic points are found local business centers of such growing importance that they have been called "satellite Loops." The typical constellation of business and recreational units includes a bank, one or more United Cigar Stores, a drug store, a high class restaurant, an automobile display row, and a so-called "wonder" motion-picture theater. With the addition of a dancing palace, a cabaret, and a smart hotel, the satellite Loop also becomes a "bright-light area" attracting a city-wide attendance. In this zone men are outnumbered by women, independence in voting is frequent, newspapers and books have wide circulation, and women are elected to the state legislature.

Zone V: The Commuters' Zone.—Out beyond the areas of better residence is a ring of encircling small cities, towns, and hamlets, which, taken together, constitute the Commuters' Zone. These are also, in the main, dormitory suburbs, because the majority of men residing there spend the day at work in the Loop (Central Business District), returning only for the night. Thus the mother and the wife become the center of family life. If the Central Business District is predominately a homeless-men's region; the rooming-house district, the habitat of the emancipated family; the area of first-immigrant settlement, the natural soil of the patriarchal family transplanted from Europe; the Zone of Better Residences with its apartment houses and residential hotels, the favorable environment for the equalitarian family; then the Commuters' Zone is without question the domain of the matricentric family.[1] The communities in this Commuters' Zone are probably the most highly segregated of any in the entire metropolitan region, including in their range the entire gamut from an incorporated village run in the interests of crime and vice, such as Burnham, to Lake Forest, with its wealth, culture, and public spirit.

The pattern of concentric zones may be carried even beyond the Commuters' Zone, whose outer boundary is ordinarily understood to be coterminous with that of the

[1] See E. R. Mowrer, *Family Disorganization*, p. 113.

metropolitan region. But beyond the metropolitan region of Chicago, with a radius of sixty miles and including sixteen counties in three states, lies the great hinterland which looks to the metropolis as its market and its jobbing center. This larger Chicagoland includes all or practically all of the five states of Illinois, Michigan, Indiana, Iowa, and Wisconsin. Its leadership in certain activities extends over all the North Central States.

If the principle of radial extension outward from the center of the city were the only factor operating to determine urban growth, then we might expect Chicago and every other rapidly growing American city to exhibit perfect examples of the five-zone pattern. Even with the complications caused by lake front location and the Chicago River with its north and south branch, the studies made by the Local Community Research Committee, the Institute of Juvenile Research, and the Department of Survey of the Chicago Church Federation, and the Congregational City Missionary Society show how phenomena of poverty, delinquency, crime, boys' gangs, home ownership, increase or decrease in population, increase or decrease in church membership rise or fall as the case may be, with only slight irregularities from zone to zone as one proceeds from the center of the city to the Commuters' Zone.[1] This distribution of these phenomena would seem to indicate the predominance of this factor of urban extension in city growth over counteracting forces. Nevertheless, it is important to explain differences as well as uniformities by defining and analyzing the rôle of these other factors.

[1] E. W. Burgess, "The Measurement of Gradients in City Growth," in *Proceedings of the American Sociological Society* (1927); C. R. Shaw, *Delinquency and Crime Areas in Chicago* (Chicago, 1929); S. C. Kincheloe, "Major Reactions of City Churches," *Religious Education*, XXXIII, 172–76.

II. DISTORTIONS OF THE ZONAL PATTERN
BY VARIATIONS IN TOPOGRAPHY

Elevation, which is a chief factor in complicating the zonal pattern of urban formation just outlined, is absent in Chicago. In cities of hills and valleys like Montreal or Seattle, which have been examined for comparative purposes, it is interesting to note that elevation introduces another dimension into the zonal pattern. In a plains city the favored residential sections are farthest out; in a hills city, farthest up. The zonal pattern still holds in Montreal and Seattle, but with the poor in the valleys, the well-to-do on the hillsides, and the wealthy on the hilltops. The mountain tops in the Los Angeles area have become the commanding sites for the magnificent homes of millionaires.

Elevation is almost a negligible factor in Chicago, which explains why in this city the zonal pattern is so little deranged in its actual manifestation. Yet even slight elevations like "the Ridge" in Beverly Hills are at once seized upon as more favorable for residence.

The one factor which for Chicago, and also for Toronto and Cleveland, to name only two other cities, profoundly alters the general theoretical pattern is their site on a lake front. The scheme of concentric circles is at once modified to a plan of semicircles. For Chicago alone of these cities the preservation of the lake front very largely as a favorable site for residence has served to maintain its residential character and to prevent the encroachment of business and industry or of groups of lower economic status.

Natural barriers like rivers and artificial barriers like elevated railroads have profoundly influenced community organization in Chicago and have prevented to a greater or less degree the free movement of business, industry, and population in accordance with the principle of radial extension outward to the peripheries from the Central Business District. The north and south branches of the Chicago River divide the city into three parts, the North Side, the West Side, and the South Side. These parts of the city have developed to a considerable extent independently, have specialized functions, are the habitat of more or less divergent racial and cultural groups, and possess a certain degree of sectional consciousness as in part indicated by the South Park Board, the West Park Board, and the Lincoln Park Board, and by the customary territorial recognition of these sections in political action.[1]

An even greater effect of the Chicago River and its two branches has been established in a recent study which shows that their banks were not only the location of early industrial establishments but consequently the place of residence of the first immigrants, Irish, German, and Scandinavian.[2] These river wards, as they were abandoned by their first inhabitants, became in succession the ports of first entry of Bohemians, Poles, Russian Jews, Lithuanians, Italians, Negroes, and Mexicans.[3] The Americans of native birth held to the lake front, north and south, and to the somewhat higher land running straight west along Washington Boulevard.

The elevation of the complicated system of railroad lines in Chicago has had the effect of dividing large areas by artificial barriers into more or less isolated and self-sufficient local communities. These "walled-in" communities in consequence of this derived economic and social

[1] In selecting political slates and in the organization of the city council.

[2] Marvin R. Shafer, *The Catholic Church in Chicago: Its Growth and Administration* (manuscript in the University of Chicago Libraries, 1929).

[3] See study by Paul F. Cressey, *The Process of Succession in Chicago.*

solidarity tend to resist the changes involved in the pressure of radial extension outward from the center. Change, when it succeeds in overcoming this resistance, takes place rapidly and affects the entire local community as a single unit.

III. THE CHECKERBOARD STREET PLAN

Chicago, like almost all American cities, possesses nearly all the advantages and disadvantages of the checkerboard street plan. If this factor were operating alone, community growth would not be radial but at right angles outward from the center of the city. When this street plan is laid out by the points of the compass it makes most accessible to the center of the city, and therefore most desirable for residence, those districts lying directly north, east, south, and west, and correspondingly undesirable residentially those sections in between located along the diagonal angles. A natural tendency under the checkerboard plan has been to lay out the local system of street railroads and rapid transportation on or near the main arterial streets running north and south, east and west.

The result has been to accelerate the force of radial expansion on arterial streets running at right angles to the Central Business District, but to retard and even impede the tendency to radial expansion on the oblique angles which ran across rather than with the checkerboard street formation. The total effect of the superimposition of the square pattern of the checkerboard street plan upon the circular pattern of urban zones is to give the typical American city, like Columbus, Ohio, or Fort Worth, Texas, (i.e., a city located on a plain and away from a lake or large river front), the form of a Maltese cross.

In Chicago the effect of the Chicago River was to make

more inaccessible and unfavorable for residence the sectors situated along the oblique angles. The river wards are and have remained the location of heavy industry and of neighborhoods of poverty and of bad housing. A few diagonal streets following old plank roads, which were formerly Indian trails, are to be found in Chicago and have had some effect in mitigating the tendencies inhering in the checkerboard street plan. But, on the whole, their influence has been slight because only one of them, Milwaukee Avenue, has the genuine character of an arterial street proceeding definitely at an oblique angle and traversing a wide territory. And Milwaukee Avenue suffers the handicap of all other diagonal streets in Chicago, namely, the fact that it does not proceed directly out from the Central Business District as do North Clark Street, West Madison Street, and South State Street.

The combination of the circular plan of radial extension and the north and south, east and west arterial highways of the checkerboard street scheme has been to concentrate the pressure of population movement outward from the center of the city in these four major directions. In Chicago, with its site on the lake front, the main trunk lines of population movement, to use Professor A. E. Holt's expressive term, have been north along the lake shore, south along the Illinois Central, and west, following West Madison Street and Washington Boulevard. These three major movements of native-born American population have resulted in the development of a succession of high-grade residential suburbs.

Between the three fingers of the most rapid movement of population there remain two sectors, the northwestern and the southwestern, of slower moving groups of immigrant colonies from the Old World and the Southern Negro and Mexican from the New World. It is significant to note, as shown in the map on the following page, how the movement of all these groups follows in the wake of important thoroughfares.

IV. TYPES OF COMMUNITY FORMATION

Up to this point, the findings of studies bearing upon the growth of the city and the movement of population groups have been presented. These are the forces making for community change and they must always be reckoned with. At the same time it is possible and desirable to study the play of these and other forces tending toward equilibrium and adjustment. This brings us to an analysis of the different types of community formation, namely, the economic, cultural, and political forces and forms of organization.[1]

Basic to an analysis of these three major types of community organization is an understanding of the physical formation of the city. The physical formation of Chicago includes not only its division into different areas by rivers, elevated railroad lines, parks, and boulevards but it also includes its system of local transportation, its street pattern, its existing layout in industrial and business plants, and its different types of dwellings. In addition, it comprises all the public utilities indispensable for the existence of civilized man, as water supply, sewage disposal, gas, electricity. These utilities represent, and in a sense symbolize, the great co-operative mechanism of impersonal services which underlies the essential solidarity of human

---

[1] E. W. Burgess, "Can Neighborhood Work Have a Scientific Basis?" in *Proceedings of the National Conference for Social Work* (1924), pp. 406–11; E. W. Burgess, "The Natural Area as the Unit for Social Work in the Large City"; Helen I. Clarke, "Uniform Area for Chicago City-Wide Agencies," in *Proceedings of the National Conference for Social Work* (1926), pp. 504–14.

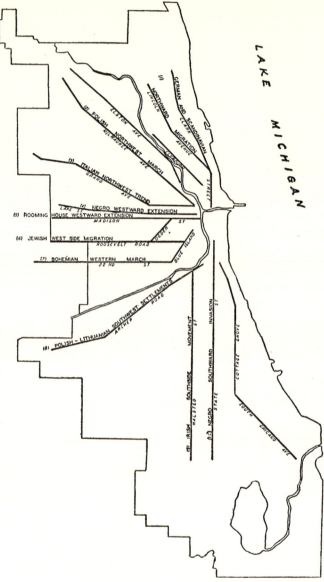

MAP OF CHICAGO SHOWING RADIAL EXPANSION OF
IMMIGRANT GROUPS

life in the urban environment, a solidarity that rests upon the communal use of public utilities and the division of labor, rather than upon any vital cultural unity.

The physical formation of the city provides a frame in which develop the different forms of community organization, and within which, therefore, they may advantageously be studied. In addition, the physical formation of the city provides a permanent grouping of areas for the continuous collection and organization of statistical and case-study data.

Three chief forms of community organization have been differentiated: (1) the economic organization, which includes the distribution of business and industry within an urban area; (2) the cultural organization, which includes the voluntary forms of community association, as schools, churches, social clubs, social centers, and settlements; and (3) the political organization, which covers not only the formal agencies of government but all other groups in so far as they attempt to affect legislation and social policy. The plotting of these enterprises and organizations and their patronage or attendance upon maps indicate both the way and the extent to which they are or are not conditioned by the physical formation of the city.

In working out the retail business organization of the city, the highest points of land values were first entered upon the map. These gave the location of the centers of retail trade throughout the city. This was then checked by plotting the location of banks and drug stores on the assumption that the banks would show the centers of trade in local communities and that distribution of drug stores would disclose the scatter of neighborhood trade. When these were placed together upon one map the pattern of the business organization falling within the physi-

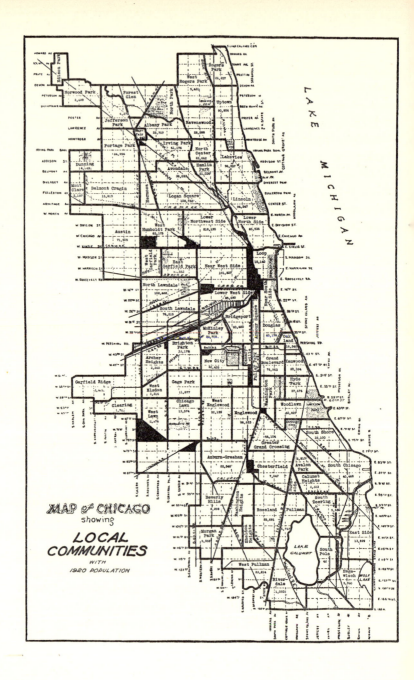

MAP of CHICAGO
showing
LOCAL COMMUNITIES
WITH
1920 POPULATION

cal formation of local communities became apparent. In studies of selected communities, the distribution of bank depositors, the patronage of local stores, and the membership of business men's organizations were studied in order to secure verification or disproof of this theoretical expectation.

These special studies indicated that a process of community integration was at work by which a number of previously economically independent local communities were being coalesced into a larger retail trading area. This was particularly evident in the rise on the North Side of the Wilson Avenue trade center and the creation of the larger community of Uptown out of the smaller neighborhoods, and of the growth on the South Side of Sixty-third Street and Cottage Grove Avenue as the business center not only of Woodlawn but of the wider area sometimes called Midsouth Town that comprised in addition several larger communities like Hyde Park, Washington Park, and Grand Crossing.

The development of these outlying business centers, "satellite Loops" as they have been called, represents from one point of view a movement of decentralization from the earlier retail dominance of the Loop. It also indicates the economic significance of the rise of "wonder" motion-picture theaters and the dancing palaces, which are located at strategic centers to insure patronage over wider areas than the neighborhood "movies," and cheap dance halls, which have rapidly declined in the last twenty years. The automobile, as well as the general system of rapid transportation, has been found to play a significant rôle in giving many of these amusement centers, located outside the Loop, something like a city-wide attendance.[1]

[1] Series of maps prepared by Daniel C. Russell and others.

If the intersection of two main business streets indicates the center of the local community as a trading area, it at the same time divides the district into its component neighborhoods. And the neighborhood seems to be, in general, the unit area for the life and growth of social institutions like the school, the church, and the social center. The cultural life of persons, families, and groups seems still in the city to depend largely upon the intimate face-to-face contacts and association.

The study of the chain store by Ernest H. Shideler[1] described and analyzed the development of the retail business organization in its interrelations with community growth through the stages of the general store of the village, the stores and shops of the town, the department stores of the large city, and the centralized decentralized system of chain stores of the metropolis. He showed how this new system of standardized, impersonal, and unified retail selling is at once the index and cause of profound changes taking place in the life of the local community. Local communities can be graded according to the proportion of the local business conducted by chain stores, lowest in immigrant neighborhoods and highest in the apartment-house districts.

The neighborhood with its institutional center appears to be the territorial unit of the larger cultural area of the city. Individual studies have blocked out and characterized these diverse cultural areas of a modern American city. The boundaries of Hobohemia were found by Nels Anderson in his study of *The Hobo* by plotting its characteristic institutions, cheap lodging-houses, pawnshops, missions, burlesque shows, barber colleges, lady barbers.

---

[1] *The Chain Store—A Study of the Ecological Organization of the Modern City* (dissertation, University of Chicago Library).

Its three areas thus differentiated extended out from the Loop along its three main thoroughfares, West Madison Street, "the Slave Market" district; South State Street, "The Home Guard" section; and North Clark Street, or "Bug House Square" center. Hobohemia, like every other cultural area, constitutes a social world with its own traditions, code of living, customs, and manners. Although the most mobile residential area of the city, it carries on a cultural life that is intense and fascinating to its shifting and changing participants.

The rooming-house area, extending around and beyond Hobohemia, has been defined and described by Harvey W. Zorbaugh.[1] It is not a homogeneous district culturally but a Babel of individuals, who have lost or are losing their diverse cultural backgrounds and are seeking some new center of cultural orientation whether it be religious fundamentalism of the Moody Bible Institute type, or the new psychology, or Bohemian or pseudo-Bohemian philosophy, or some esoteric cult of the hygienic, eugenic, erotic, or metaphysical variety. The problems of young people, temporary residents of rooming-houses, attracted to the big city as the center of education and opportunity, are now being studied by Mr. W. R. P. Ireland.

Hobohemia and the Rooming-house Region form the central core of that larger area, the Zone of Transition, already described in this chapter as encircling the Central Business District. This zone of physical deterioration and social disorganization has often been denominated "the slum" because the total drift of community life was toward neighborhood, family, and personal disorganization. Nels Anderson points out that since the slum is a natural re-

---

[1] Harvey W. Zorbaugh, *The Gold Coast and the Slum* (Chicago: The University of Chicago Press, 1929).

sultant of the forces of rapid city growth, it will continue despite the mitigating effects of housing reform, zoning laws, and social welfare agencies.[1] Anderson divides the slum into the following districts, homeless-men's areas like Hobohemia, Chinatown, and Greektown; rooming-house areas like Bohemia, "the world of furnished rooms," and vice-resort streets; and immigrant and racial areas like the Ghetto, the Black Belt, Little Sicily, and Little Poland.

Nearly all the areas within the Zone of Transition have been subjects of special descriptive studies. The most exhaustive and continuous of these are the series of housing studies, carried forward under the direction of Sophonisba P. Breckinridge and Edith Abbott.[2] The units of these studies are groups of blocks so selected as to be representative not only of the different industrial residential neighborhoods of the city but also of the nationality and racial composition. The recanvassing of these blocks at different intervals provides an unusual basis of comparison of trends in housing conditions, rents, and movement of population.

Each special study makes its contribution to an understanding of the segregation and movement of the cultural groups within the city. In a study of the social forces and trends in those industrial residential neighborhoods in which settlements are located Clark Tibbitts showed that no settlements in Chicago have survived outside the Zone of Deterioration which appears to be the habitat favorable for their planting and growth. He pointed out how the movements of immigrant and other population groups may be predicted so that neighborhood institutions may take account of impending changes in planning their work. The area over which a settlement or social center exerts an

---

[1] Nels Anderson, "Slum Endures," *Survey*, LVII (1927), 799.

[2] See chap. i, pp. 4–5.

influence is limited to a half-mile radius with the exception for the most part of the members of mother clubs, who continue to attend although they may now live many miles away, outside of the Zone of Transition.

This process of movement outward from the center to the peripheries of the cultural groups has been most intensively studied by Louis Wirth[1] for the Jewish community, which has the highest tempo of residential change. Mr. Wirth makes a vivid contrast between the ghetto of the Old World where separation from the gentile community was enforced by law, and the ghetto of the American city where segregation was the natural result of accommodation to the American environment. He graphically analyzes the different factors that are at present destroying the ghettos of American cities and dispersing their former residents by an almost regular succession of stages among the inhabitants of the urbanized sections of the city.

If the Jewish ghetto is in process of disintegration, the Chinatowns of Chicago and other American cities still constitute ghettos self-contained in themselves, isolated and maintaining a life of their own. The entire history of Chinese life in the United States, the social organization of the Chinese community, their relations with the environing American culture, the problem of racial relations, intermarriage, and of the American-born generation are fascinatingly described in a volume shortly to be published entitled *Chinatowns*, by C. C. Wu.

Another type of "segregated district" was that once officially set apart for commercialized prostitution. In the work, *The Natural History of Vice Areas*, Walter C. Reckless breaks new ground when he shows that both the location of recognized "segregated districts" and of outlawed

[1] Louis Wirth, *The Ghetto* (Chicago: University of Chicago Press, 1928).

and proscribed vice resorts are determined by the same factors and forces that determine the growth of the city. Vice areas tend to be situated close to the center of the city in homeless-men's regions and rooming-house districts, where demand is greatest, where mobility is high, where community control is lax, and where anonymity prevails. When formal control is exerted, as by the police and other law-enforcing agencies, the tendency is for vice to concentrate outside the political boundaries of the area particularly in the municipally unorganized rural districts or in vice-controlled villages and towns like Burnham and River Forest. Within residential neighborhoods, even of low economic status, vice fails to find a foothold because of community opposition. For this reason the absence or presence of vice resorts may be taken as an index of the degree of community organization or disorganization.

Beyond the boundaries of the municipality lie not only suburban villages controlled in the interests of organized vice and crime but also those that select out of the emigrants from the metropolis those of the highest culture, refinement, and social vision. A preliminary study of one such model suburban community has recently been completed by Clarence E. Glick,[1] working under the supervision of Robert E. Park.

The political organization, while it still rests upon territorial areas, no longer conforms, in most American cities, to the boundaries of the economic and cultural organization of the city. Its unit is the ward organization, but ward boundaries shift from census to census with lines drawn with reference to political expediency. Under these circumstances the ward organization, constituted by job-holding precinct captains, is able to maintain its hold upon

[1] C. E. Glick, *Winnetka, A Study of a Residential Suburban Community.*

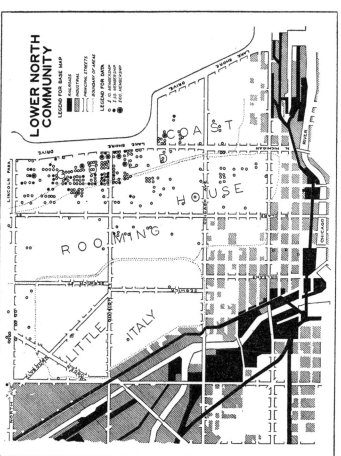

THE LOWER NORTH COMMUNITY.—"East of State Street lies the Gold Coast, Chicago's most exclusive residential district. West of State Street lies a nondescript area of furnished rooms; Clark Street, the Rialto of the half-world; 'Little Sicily,' the slum. This map of the membership of the Lower North Community Council shows it to be a local social agency supported by the Gold Coast."—Zorbaugh, *The Gold Coast and the Slum*, pp. 7, 218.

the voter by political favors and assistance in ways that are being studied by Harold F. Gosnell.[1]

The underlying problems of community and political action were dramatically revealed in the study of the Lower North Side district in Chicago made by Harvey W. Zorbaugh and published under the title, *The Gold Coast and the Slum*. This is a compact district with well-defined natural boundaries. The greater part of this area of more than eighty thousand inhabitants comprises the Forty-second Ward, and the district as a whole forms the territory of the Lower North Community Council and the Lower North District of the United Charities of Chicago.

While a compact territorial area, it is made up of widely different cultural communities having little or nothing in common. First, south of Lincoln Park and along Lake Michigan is found the Gold Coast where reside the best families with memories of the history of Chicago, who see the interests of the city as a whole, and who are active in the promotion of movements and agencies for the cultural, civic, and social welfare of the city. Next, comes Towertown, with its Latin Quarter with its geniuses of sculpture, painting, music, and writing, with its struggling and aspiring students, and with its hangers-on of pseudo-Bohemians. In the center of the district is the region of rooming-houses and its deteriorating mansion-houses of an older period, and their lonely inhabitants of the present. Still farther west is Little Sicily, with its peasant inhabitants with their Old World traditions and their New World problems.

The Lower North Side is the area of greatest contrasts in the city. It has the highest residential land values and the

[1] H. F. Gosnell, *The Precinct Captain* (in progress).

lowest; more professional men, more politicians, and more persons in *Who's Who* than any other community in the city. Within a stone's throw of the greatest concentration of wealth in the city, along Lake Shore Drive, is to be found the largest accumulation of poverty in what has been called "Little Hell."

The findings of this study explain, while they do not solve, the problems of community and political action. The heterogeneity of community life, the rapidity of social change, and the high rate of mobility found on the Lower North Side give the reader a vivid and concrete picture of the complexities of the processes of life of the modern city with its polyglot population, its thousand and one occupational and cultural groupings, its specialized and diversified social types, and the acute conflicts of Old World sentiments and prejudices, divergent habits and standards of conduct, and conflicts of purposes and interests. Out of this chaos of habits and attitudes there crystallizes, so far as political action is concerned, the so-called bilateral organization of the city of which the river wards within the Zone of Transition constitute the nucleus of the political machine bent on the exploitation of public service for personal profit, and of which the Lake Front wards of the Zone of Better Residences form the central core of the reformers' band with its emphasis upon good government and the safeguarding of civil service. This duality in the cultural organization explains why the gangster and the politician, on the one side, and the good citizen and the reformer, on the other side, fail so signally to understand one another. As yet, no adequate medium of mutual social interpretation between these two great elements in city life has been found.

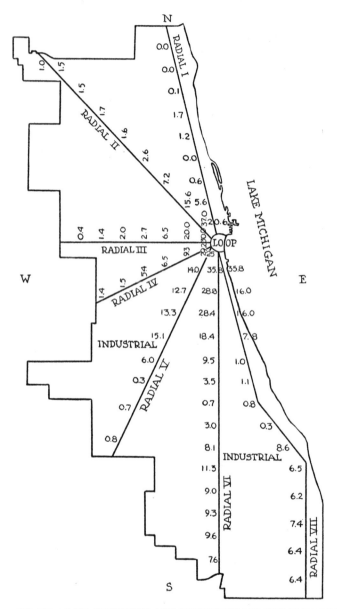

RATE OF MALE JUVENILE DELINQUENCY BY SQUARE-MILE
AREAS ALONG LINES RADIATING FROM LOOP

V. THE SCIENTIFIC STUDY OF URBAN AREAS

So far the study of urban areas has been largely descriptive. The first step in social research was to explore this *terra incognita* of urban life, to determine and define its regions, to trace the main directions of population movements, and to discover, if possible, the processes of city growth and community formation. With this task largely accomplished, attention is now being turned to an analysis of these processes and to a comparison, so far as possible statistically, of the play of social forces and trends in the different local communities of the city. Already Clifford R. Shaw and his associates, sociologists of the Institute of Juvenile Research, have determined quantitatively over a thirty-year period the regularly declining rate of juvenile delinquency from the center of the city to the periphery. Their calculations show a similar rate of change for many other phenomena of urban life like family disintegration, adult crime, increase and decrease of population, proportion of foreign-born, etc. Trends of juvenile delinquency and family disintegration for individual communities can be worked out which would be of immediate practical value to social agencies dealing with these problems.

These studies of urban areas, in so far as they have to do with the location and movement of individuals, groups, and institutions in space and time, open up a new field of social science research, namely that of human ecology.[1] Ecological studies seek to define the processes determining social organization which result from the distribution and

[1] See chapter on "The Ecological Approach," by R. S. McKenzie in R. E. Park, *The City*, pp. 63–79, and chapter on "The Concepts of Human Ecology," in *The Urban Community*, edited by E. W. Burgess, and article by R. E. Park, "The Moral Order and the Spacial Pattern," in the same volume.

movement of individuals over a given area, uncomplicated so far as it is possible to determine by the effects of communication and culture. Once these processes are defined, it is then possible to apply statistical procedures to the measurement of these processes and to establish quantitative indices of the type and degree of social organization of the different local communities of the city. When this is done civic and social agencies will not only possess an objective criterion of community conditions but also, what has hitherto been almost entirely lacking, an objective standard for the measurement of the efficiency of their own work. Thereafter civic and social effort may be less romantic but perhaps more effective.

CHAPTER IX

STUDIES OF INSTITUTIONS

If a community may be regarded as "a constellation of institutions,"[1] then the community and its life may perhaps best be described and analyzed through studies of its component institutions. For many purposes of social science research the unit for the study of the community may well be the institution inasmuch as the family, the church, the school, industry, the market, financial institutions, the playground, the motion-picture theater, the welfare agency, and the state form not merely the social structure of the community that defines, directs, and limits the activities of their members but also formulates the ideals, objectives, and policies of communal action. For any enterprise or agency in the process of becoming an institution achieves for itself recognition as performing a community function with the rights and the obligations thereby necessarily incurred.

The institutions enumerated in the foregoing differ widely from each other in the degree to which they have achieved public recognition and, it might be added, in the acceptance of their responsibility in the performance of their communal functions. Certain of these institutions are ancient and well established; others are new and their status in the ranks of the institutions of the community is still open to question. All of these institutions, however, even those which formerly, like the family and the church, were most securely intrenched in custom and tradition,

[1] A definition of the community by Robert E. Park.

are confronted with the necessity of adjustment to the rapidly changing situations of urban life. That is why these institutions, which for so long a time were reverently protected from what would have been regarded as the sacrilegious scrutiny of research, are now themselves demanding to become the subjects of social studies. For their progressive leaders recognize that in a time of change the findings of research, rather than the authority of tradition, will be of service in mediating the crises of readjustment.

Accordingly, the studies of institutions undertaken by the Local Community Research Committee have been made partly from its own interest in social science exploration of community life and partly at the request of institutions alive to the necessity of readjustment to meet the changing conditions of city life.

As studies of individual institutions proceeded, distinctions between different types of institutions began to emerge and gradually their distinctive functions in community life became quite clear. There were, first of all, those basic cultural institutions, like the family, the church, and the school, with the function of transmitting the heritage of the past and remolding it to meet the present situation. Then there is the great group of economic institutions organized for services of utility rather than sentiment like industrial and commercial enterprises, labor unions, and real estate boards. Next to be considered are the recreational institutions which satisfy the human desire for entertainment, amusement, and play, and which, under conditions of city life, are playing an increasing rôle. Finally, there are the institutions of formal social control, including both governmental and social service agencies, which are dealing, in ways often different but frequently alike, with the problems of society and personality.

This fourfold classification of institutions is not presented here as final, but as tentative, and as serviceable for a review of the studies of social institutions in Chicago. These studies have naturally brought out the fact that any institution defies too rigid a classification under any of these heads. Certain churches, whose distinctive function would be classified as cultural or spiritual inasmuch as the function of religion is concerned with the inner life of members, are active in the Better Government Association and in the Anti-Saloon League, organizations that have frankly political programs even if these do embody moral issues. Labor unions have cultural and political, as well as economic, functions as evidenced by the establishment of labor colleges and by the participation of the Chicago Federation of Labor in political campaigns, municipal and national. Indeed, these studies have indicated the value not only of defining and of analyzing the specific social function of an institution, but also of describing and, if possible, of explaining its interaction with other institutions and with the environing community. For in its interaction with the community the true rôle of an institution is most clearly seen, and in the interaction of its component institutions is to be discovered the secrets of community action.

Taking up then the detailed analysis of institutions suggested in the preceding paragraphs, the main body of this chapter will be devoted to a survey of studies made under the auspices of the Local Community Research Committee, dealing respectively with (a) the family and the church, (b) economic institutions, (c) recreational institutions, (d) institutions of formal social control.

I. THE FAMILY AND THE CHURCH

Social science studies of cultural institutions in Chicago have included the family and the church. No systematic inquiry has been undertaken on the school as a social institution, although one authoritative and exhaustive study was made several years ago of truancy and non-attendance in the Chicago schools by Edith Abbott and S. P. Breckinridge.[1]

Since the eighties, if not before, there has been an increasing realization by everyone, common people and intelligentsia alike, of changes taking place in family life in the cities that threatened, if continued, to destroy or at least profoundly to modify this institution which seemed to many the very basis and source of American culture. The United States Bureau of the Census published two huge volumes giving in detail annual statistics of marriage and divorce for the period 1867 to 1906. These have been supplemented by annual reports for 1916, 1922–27.[2] Several careful studies of desertion have also been made. But none of these or other investigations attempted to define the family in its interrelations with changing conditions of community life. This failure to study the American family as a living organism in interaction with its environment, the community, was emphasized by Mr. Burgess in an article in which he defined the family as a "unit of interacting personalities" with each of its members assuming familial rôles and interacting individually and collectively with the community. He called attention to the study of

[1] *Truancy and Non-Attendance in the Chicago Schools* (Chicago, 1916).

[2] United States Bureau of the Census, *Marriage and Divorce, 1867–86; Marriage and Divorce, 1887–1906; Marriage and Divorce, 1916; Marriage and Divorce, 1922, 1923, 1924, 1925, 1926, 1927.*

the Polish family by W. I. Thomas as a model for a similar study of the family in the United States.[1]

As yet, no such study has been essayed in Chicago or in any large city. The study of family disorganization by Ernest R. Mowrer[2] is, however, an introduction to a research program in the field of the family, and in its own right a highly significant inquiry into the problems of the family in the urban situation. His findings on the variation of divorce and desertion, according to local neighborhoods of the city, tend to establish the dependence of the family for its stability upon the degree of community organization in the various areas of the city. His classification of city areas by type of family life opens up most promising fields of research upon family life in non-family areas, emancipated family areas, paternal family areas, equalitarian family areas, and maternal family areas.

More significant than Mowrer's findings is his keen analysis of methods of research in the field of family relationships. He points out that statistical method, based upon an atomistic conception of social phenomena, had had and could have but little value for an understanding of family life, but that proceeding from an organic analysis of the processes of family life in its community setting, it would unquestionably yield new and significant results. He, likewise, critically surveys current case study procedure and works out with exhibits the different steps in case-study technique of family disorganization as follows: the classification of family tensions, the logic of behavior sequences in family disorganization, and the method of

[1] Ernest W. Burgess, "The Family as a Unity of Interacting Personalities," *The Family*, VII (March, 1926), 3–9.

[2] Ernest R. Mowrer, *Family Disorganization: An Introduction to a Sociological Analysis* (Chicago, 1927).

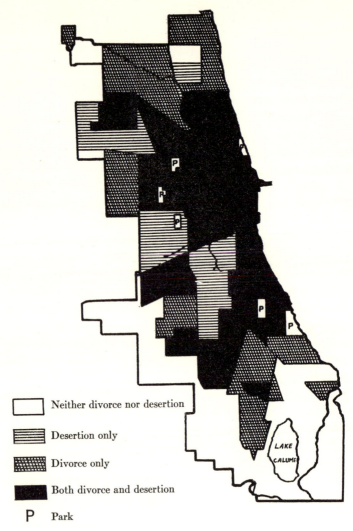

Neither divorce nor desertion

Desertion only

Divorce only

Both divorce and desertion

P   Park

AREAS OF FAMILY DISINTEGRATION IN CHICAGO, 1920

socio-analysis of individual cases. Not least in value is one of the Appendixes in the volume entitled *Factors in Family Disorganization* in which are listed certain selected representative factors that should be taken into account in case studies in this field. The value of this analysis for other studies is, in part, seen in the recent inquiry of Dr. Mowrer's *Family Discord* which was brought to completion by the support of the Social Science Research Council and the Wieboldt Foundation of Chicago, and by the penetrating and sympathetic studies of Harriet R. Mowrer in the delicate and tangled problems of domestic difficulty of families who are under the supervision of a family welfare agency.

This study of family disorganization has gone a long way in developing the technique required for a continuous study of the cultural aspects of the family in the urban environment. Other aspects of family life have been made the subjects of special studies, such as family composition, by Hazel Kyrk; incomes and rent of wage-earning families, by Franc L. McCluer; the housing of immigrant families, by S. P. Breckinridge and Edith Abbott; family backgrounds of juvenile delinquency, by Clifford R. Shaw; family budgets and the cost of living of the families of unskilled laborers, by Leila Houghteling; and the problems and the treatment of family problems by social agencies, by S. P. Breckinridge. All these studies, which are discussed in more detail elsewhere in this book, are referred to here to show at how many points the life of the family in a metropolitan city like Chicago has been examined by our local community studies.

The most intensive cultural study of the family in the urban community is that of *The Negro Family in Chicago*, by E. Franklin Frazier, undertaken under the joint auspices of the Local Community Research Committee and the Urban League of Chicago. The cultural backgrounds of the Negro family in a metropolitan city like Chicago are sought in the comparison, with its far-reaching implications, of the well-developed family life of the free Negro and the more or less loosely integrated family group of the slave. Since emancipation, and particularly under the freer conditions of northern cities, the Negro family has become highly differentiated so that at present there are as many, and probably more, gradations within the Negro family than in any other racial or cultural group within our American cities. This differentiation of the Negro family into cultural types ranging from the family of the laborer recently arrived from the Southern plantation and likely to disintegrate in the city to the stable family of the professional man, highly organized around familial traditions and sentiments, provides the framework for isolating and explaining the factors making for family organization and disorganization, in general. For in the Negro family, with its recent social origin and its almost entire lack of institutional characteristics in certain situations in slavery, is afforded a unique laboratory situation for the comparative study of all the aspects of the processes of family formation.

Then, too, the distribution of these different cultural levels of family life permits perhaps the most basic characterization of the various and varying neighborhoods of Negro settlement within the city. The distribution of Negroes in small tracts by occupation and family composition for 1920 was secured from the Census Bureau and when tabulated showed wide local variations. With each small area thus defined and characterized, the ensemble was available for use as a laboratory device by which the original data secured in the study could be measured and analyzed. The rates of incidence of certain social phenomena which had been selected as indices of family instability or disorganization, like divorce, separation, illegitimacy, and juvenile delinquency, were then found to vary widely but with general regularity from the highest rates in the tracts near the center of the city characterized by large numbers of unskilled workers recently from the South to the lowest rates in the settlements farther out, which had the largest proportion of families of professional and business men. This study, so far as it has progressed, seems to show with graphic convincingness that these and other social problems, which have been found in large proportion among Negroes, are entirely relative, as with whites, to the cultural level of family and community life.

The most important contribution of this study is, however, not its bearing upon the definition and solution of the Negro problem, significant as that is, but the light which it throws upon the forces creating and maintaining family life and the rôle of familial culture upon personality development and community organization. Its findings portray clearly both the workings of non-institutional factors, like affection and personal sentiment, and of cultural factors, such as familial tradition, community status, and public opinion in family formation. They also reveal the subtle processes by which a person's ideals and ambitions are largely formed within the intimate and stimulating circle of family life. Finally, it gives a picture and analysis of the interaction of the family with other institutions by reason of which the family finds its place in the community and so participates in community organization and action.

Historically, and in the rural community, the church is "a family of families." For the church is peculiarly the institution in the community that maintains the common cultural heritage which has its concrete expression in familial and personal ideals. In the rural community of the past the church was typically the social, as well as the cultural, center.

In the city the church faces a new situation, complex and complicated. It finds itself in competition with other institutions and agencies for the leisure time of people. In the larger churches increasing membership diminishes in number and intensity the intimacy of association which made the rural church a vital social and spiritual influence. In certain areas of the city, as the slum, the rooming-house districts, immigrant colonies, and apartment-house sections, the conventional American Protestant church faces the problem of readjustment or extinction.

The studies made under the auspices of the Local Community Research Committee of the church in the urban environment have been mainly preliminary and exploratory. In the last two years this field has been occupied by a notably comprehensive and continuous program of interrelated studies directed by Arthur E. Holt and Samuel C. Kincheloe, of the Chicago Theological Seminary, under the joint auspices of the Congregational City Missionary Society and Chicago Church Federation. Recently a plan has been worked out by which several theological seminaries, the Chicago Theological Seminary, the Disciples Divinity House, the Divinity School of the University of Chicago, the Garrett Biblical Institute, the McCormick Theological Seminary, and the Western Theological Seminary have united under the leadership of the Chicago Church Federation for a religious survey of Chicago. The studies already made or in progress, while without official connection with the work of the Local Community Research Committee, have been carried on with a large degree of informal co-operation and interchange of research materials so that reference to them is quite natural in the following discussion.

The mission, as an adaptation of the church to meet the religious needs and personal problems of the homeless man, had been briefly described by Nels Anderson in *The Hobo*.[1] The historical development of the mission and the origin and elaboration of its technique of soul-saving were the object of a more intensive study begun by Lawrence Guy Brown.[2] As a part of the Chicago Church Survey, a further study of the mission is in progress which purposes to inquire more deeply into the religious experiences and inner life of the homeless man, and also to determine the extent to which the mission as now functioning succeeds or fails in the spiritual and material rehabilitation of men who are down and out.

A study now going forward of the personal experiences and problems of young people in rooming-house areas has as one of its purposes the sounding of the religious experiences of youth adrift in the city.[3] It also essays to determine the nature and vitality of the appeal of the church to young people and the effectiveness of its guidance in assisting in the solution of their problems. The study has already disclosed, by means of a series of maps and a group of life-histories, that the rooming-house district on the Lower North Side harbors thousands of young people, largely of native American stock drawn from the small cities and towns of the Middle West, preparing as students for careers in business, art, music, or the professions, or

[1] Chap. xvii, "The Mission," pp. 250–62.

[2] In manuscript.

[3] W. R. P. Ireland, material in manuscript.

just entering the commercial world, detached from the influences of home and community, eager for experience and impatient of tradition. The study is now seeking to find out both the ways in which young people themselves attempt to solve the problems that arise out of their loneliness and quest for adventure.[1] Special attention will be paid to successful outcomes and to those unconscious experiments which are always going on but seldom systematically observed and reported upon of agencies and of groups which are appealing to intellectual or aesthetic or spiritual needs of rooming-house residents. In fact, as the study has developed two or three experiments have been consciously undertaken in order to test out the validity of certain hypotheses which have developed from this inquiry.

A second study[2] of the rooming-house situation has its setting in a nondescript rooming-house region in drab contrast to the picturesque and colorful Lower North Side. The center of its attack has been the problem not only of the church but of all social organizations to survive in an area of physical deterioration and cultural retrogression. This study clearly brings out the helplessness of social institutions and community enterprises against the adverse tide of forces of mobility and demoralization. Not only do the conventional church, the business men's associations, and social clubs fight an uphill battle, but families tend to disintegrate and persons to become disorganized. The respectable people who are marooned there look forward to escaping from the area as the intrusion of beer flats, vice resorts, disorderly houses, and rendezvous of drug addicts becomes evident. Just as in a new suburb all the factors of community life are favorable to wholesome family life

[1] See H. W. Zorbaugh, *The Gold Coast and the Slum.*

[2] Raymond Gibbs, material in manuscript.

and to the growth and vitality of the church and other institutions and enterprises, so in a community on the down grade the trend of economic and cultural factors is adverse to the normal development of personality and of the family and severely handicaps the work of religious and social institutions.

The continuous program of research,[1] directed by Arthur E. Holt and Samuel C. Kincheloe, includes not only intensive studies of local church situations and special studies of the religious life of certain immigrant and racial groups, as the Mexican and the Negro, but also a basic study of the church in the changing community. This study, upon which Mr. Kincheloe has been engaged for several years, seeks to define and analyze the process by which, in areas undergoing a population turnover, the traditional Protestant church makes a readjustment, or fails to adjust and becomes extinct and is perhaps supplanted by a radically different type of institution. Through the techniques of mapping these churches and their movements, of making statistical studies of changes in church membership over a long period of years, and of making intensive studies of the life-histories of individual churches, he finds certain events or behavior sequences that may happen to the historical, or conventional, Protestant church when it is faced with the crisis of readjustment.[2] Only occasionally does it become a down-town

[1] See for general point of view of method, A. E. Holt, "Ecological Approach to the Church," *American Journal of Sociology*, XXXIII (1927–28), 72–79; "Case Records as Data for Studying the Conditioning of Religious Experience by Social Factors," *ibid.*, XXXII (1926–27), 227–28; "Religion," *ibid.*, XXXIV (1928–29), 172–76.

[2] See Samuel C. Kincheloe, "Major Reactions of City Churches," *Religious Education*, XXXIII (1928), 868–74; "The Behavior Sequence of a Dying Church," *ibid.*, XXXIV (1929), 329–45.

church with an appeal that is city-wide and even national. It may move, or it may federate with a church in a similar predicament, or it may become an institutional church, or it may die, or it may be succeeded by some type of primitive religious church like the Salvation Army or the mission.

Exploratory inquiries have also been made of the rôle of the church and the type of religious experiences of persons in industrial residential communities[1] and in apartment-house regions.[2] These inquiries have uncovered the peculiar situations which the church faces in these areas not only because of the mobility of population and the consequent changes in its composition but also because of significant changes in attitudes toward religion and life. All these studies indicate that to secure significant findings the churches should be studied in their adjustment to the particular type of community in which they are located, and raise serious problems for any uniform program for all communities, at least for the Protestant churches.

One outstanding conclusion from these studies of the church in the metropolitan community is the necessity for a continuous research program in this field, an objective that happily promises to be realized in what seems to be functionally the most promising set-up, namely, the union of the research departments of the theological seminaries. In addition to the obvious advantage to research, this new plan means the introduction of students in training for the ministry to active participation in the study of the problems confronting religious leaders.

[1] Raymond Nelson, "The Study of an Isolated Industrial Community by the Participant Observer Method" (Master's thesis, University of Chicago Library).

[2] E. L. Setterlund, "The Church in the Apartment House Community" (material in manuscript).

II. ECONOMIC INSTITUTIONS

Within the highly evolved economic system of modern society are highly specialized institutions, such as transportation, marketing, industrial organization, industrial relations and trade unions, retail business and business men's organizations, real estate, local improvement and protective associations and real estate boards, insurance, credit, and banking. Many of these institutions, as for example industry itself, rest upon or have created complicated physical mechanisms; other institutions, like banking, develop complex and intricate devices of accounting, credit, and security; and still other institutions, like labor unions, are conflict groups ever on the alert to maintain and raise their status, and are on their guard against unfriendly and unsympathetic investigation. All these and other factors, combined with the enormous number of individual units of many of these institutions, make any adequate and complete study of the economic institutions of a metropolitan city a difficult task.

As it is, the studies undertaken under the auspices of the Local Community Research Committee, and in certain instances with the co-operation of outside organizations, have not as yet, even in preliminary fashion, covered this whole field. For instance, no thoroughgoing studies have been made of the highly important institutions of insurance and credit, although inquiries here would lead to the crux of the social as well as of the financial organization of modern society. Studies in most of the other economic fields have been avowedly partial and preliminary.

Quite extensive studies have been undertaken in the fields of manufacturing, marketing, banking, labor unions and industrial relations, retail business organization, and the real estate board.

The study by L. C. Marshall and Mabel Magee, *Manufacturing in the Chicago Region*, has already been referred to because of its significance in showing the trends in plant location within the Chicago region. But it also makes a signal contribution to our knowledge of a vital factor in the economic development of the Chicago region through the emphasis which it places upon the history of the growth of manufacturing in this region from its early beginnings to the present time. The stress in the statistical part of the study has been placed on the period since 1900 in the attempt to show in greater detail the trends in the larger industries, not only in location within the region but also in expansion of production and in the number of people employed. Growing out of this and related with it are the detailed studies of several of the more important industries made possible not only through a painstaking analysis of factory inspectors' reports in Illinois and Wisconsin but also through an enormous amount of personal investigation and correspondence with different manufacturing concerns.

The market is one of the most important, although one of the least known and understood, of the economic institutions of the city. The great mass of the statistical material basic to the study of the market as an institution of rural-urban relationships is being gathered and organized by E. A. Duddy. This research is of necessity not confined to Chicago or to the Chicago region but reaches out into and includes the investigation of the regional areas of the country with their network of central metropolises and dependent smaller urban centers. In *A Study of the Supply and Distribution Areas of the Chicago Grain Market*, he is making a detailed analysis of the different grain receipts (wheat, corn, oats, barley, and rye), tracing their flow into the Chicago market from the different counties of the twelve surrounding states of Illinois, Indiana, Iowa, Kansas, Michigan, Minnesota, Missouri, North Dakota, Oklahoma, South Dakota, and Wisconsin.

The movement of grain shipment out of Chicago to other points has also been analyzed in order to segregate the volume distributed to the various freight-rate territories for domestic use from that which finds its way to seaports for export.

In a companion inquiry, Mr. Duddy has made a comparative study of storage space and its utilization in Chicago and the other cities of the country. In Chicago and the north central region the trend in refrigeration space and warehousing is toward centralization in the metropolis, but in the other regions of the country the trend is toward decentralization. A study of total storage holdings showed a general tendency away from centralization. Ratios of high, low, and average holdings to the net available storage space were worked out for public cold-storage plants.

In the field of banking, several studies are under way. Among these are the history of banking in Illinois since the Civil War, the history of state banking in Chicago, the influence of Chicago bankers on the passage of the Federal Reserve Bank Act, and the market for short-term funds. This latter inquiry, carried on by Lloyd W. Mints, focuses upon the description and analysis of the function of commercial banks in the financial organization of modern urban society.

Under the direction of H. A. Millis a notable series of studies in the field of labor unions and industrial relations is under way which has so far progressed that the significance of the individual studies in relation to each other has emerged. The projects planned or completed include studies of selected trades and trade unions; the history of federations of labor in Chicago and Illinois; two racial studies, the Negro in industry and the Negro in business; strikes and the policing of industry; the labor market; the labor manager and personnel relations in industry; and the actual workings of workmen's compensation. When completed this series of projects will present both a description and an explanation of the industrial situations and economic processes that have produced the existing different systems of organization of the relationships of industry and labor.

Of the several studies of trades and trade unions four are selected as representative for discussion of the methods of investigation and findings. As three of these studies involve an interesting comparison of two allied trades with divergent economic situations, something like the observation of a controlled experiment was offered to the investigator. The first of these to be considered are *The History of Industrial Relations in the Book and Job Printing Industry* in comparison with *The History of Industrial Relations in the Newspaper Industry*. The history of both organized and unorganized book and job printing plants begins with their first establishment in Chicago and traces the course of industrial relations up to the present, while the study of the newspaper industry covers the period 1850–1929.

In these two industries, the technical operations of the workingmen are approximately, although not quite exactly, the same. Yet the studies find a well-nigh universal organization in unions of the workers in newspaper offices, but in the book and job trades less than one-half of the shops are organized. What is the explanation of this striking difference? It lies in their differential relationship to the labor market. The competitive struggle, which still continues unabated in book and jobbing plants, has been largely eliminated in the case of the newspaper because of its dependence upon regularity of publication. Inter-market competition, which is practically absent in the case of the newspaper, prevents thoroughgoing organization of workers in the book and job trades. Consequently, in striking contrast with the uniformity of wages and working conditions enforced by the union in different news-papers of the city, is the divergence in the book and job-bing industry between union shops working forty-four hours a week under union working rules, or rules jointly agreed upon, competing with non-union shops working forty-eight hours a week under their own wage scale and with freedom to adopt their own working rules.

A study involving equally interesting comparisons of the economic conditions in the situations that determine the growth and the success of the union is *The Garment-Making Trades of Chicago*, by Mabel Magee. A general comparison of the situation in New York, Chicago, and other places, in terms of wages and the other items that enter into labor costs, indicates the decided limitations upon what a labor union may secure in a highly competi-tive industry. Where there is intermarket competition, wages will in the long run adjust themselves to the neces-sities of the situation. Within the garment-making in-dustry are two branches which make possible an interest-ing and significant comparison between special factors making for and against successful labor organization. The cloak and suit industry has been well organized for years, while the dress and waist industry, within the jurisdiction of the same union, has been only a weak organization; in fact, at present it is a mere shadow of what it was at the end of the war period. How is this striking difference to be explained? Certainly not in the politics of the union and in the personnel of its leadership because that has remained a constant factor. The explanation must be found in the variable factors, which in this case are to be found both in the changes taking place in the industrial organization of these industries, in the degree of skill required, and in the type of workers with their set of attitudes toward organization. The facts of the requirement of greater skill, of more of a foreign element with attitudes favorable to unionism, of more men than women workers in the cloak and suit than in the dress and waist industry, throw light upon the far greater success of the same union in organizing the worker of the former than of the latter employment.

The history of the building trades of Chicago by Royal Montgomery[1] is the only detailed study yet published of organization and collective bargaining in building trades of an American city. It covers the period from 1900 and traces the rise and growth of the building trades in their many interesting phases. The crux of the study, however, centers around the explanation of the success of the trades in collective bargaining through an analysis of the economics of the building situation. In the first place, the nature of the business makes it comparatively easy to pass any increase of wages on to the consuming public with little or no loss and oftentimes with gain to the contractor. Then, too, on the basis of large contracts over limited periods the building business is so organized that the contractor and the construction companies find it advantageous to have strong unions with which to deal. Montgomery clearly defines this situation and indicates the rise, as a result, of an unusually high degree of organization,

[1] *Industrial Relations in the Chicago Building Trades.* Chicago: University of Chicago Press, 1927.

and also as a consequence of this situation the appearance of an unusual amount of waste and of abuses, as jurisdictional disputes, restrictive working rules, and uneconomical management procedures.

These four studies indicate the value for social science research of investigation into the institutional development and present status of trade unions in their actual setting in the local economic situation. From the study of each union in its particular industrial setting conclusions and hypotheses develop which may now be tested in wider comparative inquiries. These individual local studies are the first step in this larger program.

Certain phases of labor problems cannot be adequately treated by case studies of individual unions. Racial and immigrant factors are best ascertained by special projects. The study of the Negro in industry in Chicago, by Alma Herbst, is not only a contribution to the economic aspects of the series of studies in progress on the Negro in Chicago, but throws light on the problems in industrial and race relations of the rapid introduction of a new racial group into the labor market of a large metropolitan city.

The study of the Chicago labor market is now being planned as a co-operative project with the School of Commerce and Administration of the University. On the side of demand for labor this study will include the securing of data on points like the following: the demand for labor by the different types of industry; the demand for labor by occupational groups; the demand for labor by sex, age, and racial groups; the demand for labor by types and degrees of skill. On the side of labor supply the following points among others will be covered: the population of the Chicago area; the numbers of this population available for employment by age, sex, and racial groups; the natural increase of population by the excess of births over deaths; the additions to and subtractions from the various labor groups by immigration and by emigration; the different types and degrees of skill in the labor supply; the different training systems; methods of apprenticeship and improvership. The final part of the project has to do with systems of bringing demand and supply of labor together, as methods for obtaining and allocating labor by the employer; the policies and activities of private and public employment exchanges; special devices by employers; the nature and extent of unemployment; systems of wage payment; working conditions; rate of wages; numbers demanded by industry as over against transportation, trade, personal service, and public service. This project naturally leads into the study of the labor or personnel manager and the welfare plans of industry which is now being organized under the direction of Raleigh A. Stone.

Other studies in the labor series have treated the history of the Chicago and Illinois federations of labor and the actual workings of the workingmen's compensation law. The study, *The History of the Chicago Federation of Labor*, by Bigham, is peculiarly significant because it traces the development of the strongest city federation of labor in this country. Especially interesting in the evolution of its policies and the rôle of its leadership is the description of the part played by the federation in municipal and national politics. Two studies, one by Earl R. Beckner, *The History of Illinois Labor Legislation*, and the other by Eugene Staley, *The History of the Illinois State Federation of Labor*, supplement each other admirably, and taken together make clear both from the side of the legislature and of the labor organization movement how labor laws are enacted.

In a study, *Chicago Strikes and the Policing of Industry*, H. B. Myers studied in detail more than twenty of the outstanding strikes in the history of Chicago in the last generation. He reviewed the law relative to labor organizations (both statute- and court-made), the tactics employed in industrial disputes, and the actual application of the law in concrete situations. His analysis of the law, its all too frequent misapplication, and the actual workings of the labor injunction are important contributions.

This group of studies taken together contributes toward an adequate description of the labor movement, its organization, its status, and its problems in an industrial center of the first rank in the United States. As such, it has real historical value, but it also makes a contribution to the technique of social science research. Through careful and exacting research upon individual unions and special phases of the labor movement, it is now possible to proceed further and in selected concrete situations test out the conclusions and the hypotheses that have been drawn from these studies. Last, but not least, these studies have trained a group of students in the methods of field research as compared with the traditional library research. And the development in personality—in the capacity to make contacts with many different types of persons, in maintaining an objective and at the same time a sympathetic point of view, in learning how to evaluate information and the judgment and impartiality of the person interviewed—is not the least of the results of these studies because the best way to insure the ongoing of research in any field is the development of a research personnel.

Two remaining studies in the field of institutional economics will be briefly noted. The project, *The Chain Store: A Study of the Retail Business Organization of a*

Modern City, by E. H. Shideler,[1] employed the development of the chain store as an index for measuring the changes taking place both in the organization of the local retail business center and in local community organization. In tracing the stages in retail business organization from the village and the general store to the town and the separate special stores, to the city and the department store, and finally to the metropolitan city and the chain store, the author was able to state the interrelations in cause and effect between changes in business organization and in social life. Through case studies of local retail centers, like the Wilson Avenue district, he was able to show in some detail the play of factors in the rise and growth of such a center, the conditions under which the chain store makes its appearance, and the nature of the equilibrium which finally results. The outstanding finding of his study was the conclusion that the chain store is both a resultant of the predominance in the city of the business motive over the motives of sentiment and custom, and in its turn a most effective influence for the decline of neighborhood feeling and the increase of attitudes favoring standardization and impersonal and formal relations.

In *A Study of a Secular Institution, the Chicago Real Estate Board*,[2] Everett C. Hughes examines the origin and growth of the real estate board as a case of an economic or secular institution. As such, he places it in contrast with the type of organization, policies, and instrumentalities of cultural institutions like the church. The history of the Chicago Real Estate Board afforded an excellent opportunity for describing and analyzing the process by which a group of men carrying on activities of public interest by

[1] Manuscript in University of Chicago Libraries.
[2] *Ibid.*

interaction with each other and with the public develop control and code and functionaries, and become in fact an institution with standing in the community and a conception of its public function. The public rôles which the real estate board comes to assume are treated under the terms, "the protector of the landlord," "the watch-dog of the tax-payer," "the protector of the agent," "the mobilizer of land," "the control of the use of land," and "the development of the city."

This series of studies of the economic institutions of a metropolitan city, incomplete as they are at present, do furnish a new understanding of the complexity and intricacy of the immense mechanism of physical structure, technical devices, and involved human relationships that lies at the basis of urban society.

III. RECREATIONAL INSTITUTIONS

Recreational institutions, for the most part, are recent. In fact, they arose to meet the problems and situations of city life and are now being slowly extended into rural areas. In times past, play was considered an instinctive activity that needed no special encouragement or oversight except what the family, the church, and the school might be disposed to give to it. The settlement, the playground, and the motion picture, to mention only one outstanding example, respectively, of private, municipal, and commercialized recreation, are all creations of the last generation. Some, perhaps, would be disposed to deny to all these recreation agencies the character and status of an institution, and many would certainly not apply this term to enterprises of commercialized recreation. At any rate, there can be no doubt that the promoters of private and public recreation make their appeal to the public for support on the ground that they are agencies of character formation and as such performing a community function, while the critics of commercialized recreation assert that they also are efficient in the molding of personality which takes expression in unapproved forms of behavior. Accordingly, the relationship of all these enterprises to personal and social welfare and to community interest is well recognized.

With the co-operation of the Committee on Public Recreation of the City Club of Chicago, the Local Community Research Committee undertook a study of the distribution of all the recreational institutions of the city open to the public and attempted to make a census of their annual attendance. The large map showing the distribution of private, public, and commercial facilities by the picture symbols of the Russell Sage Foundation is now on display at the City Club. This map showed the predominance of commercial agencies of recreation in the zone of transition where other studies showed a concentration of poverty, juvenile delinquency, and boys' gangs, and a predominance of private and public agencies in better residential areas with families above the poverty line and with an absence of child crime and gangs. This map also brought out the concentration of commercial recreation at certain centers, as for instance, the presence in close proximity in one "bright light" area of three dancing palaces, a "wonder" motion-picture theater, two cabarets, and several cafés and restaurants. It was apparent from the map that in the period since the war motion-picture theaters and other enterprises of commercial recreation had been located with more intelligent calculation of community needs and population growth than had those of private and public recreation.

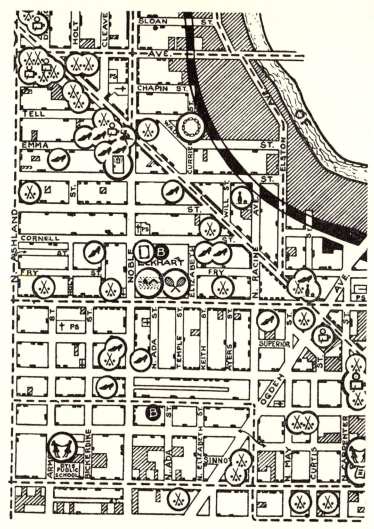

SECTION OF A RECREATION MAP OF CHICAGO PREPARED BY
THE LOCAL COMMUNITY RESEARCH COMMITTEE FOR THE
COMMITTEE ON PUBLIC PARKS AND RECREATION OF THE
CITY CLUB OF CHICAGO

The place in the life of the community of these recreational facilities may, perhaps, be gauged in part by the accompanying table of estimated attendance at Chicago's recreational institutions for the year 1925. Figures given here, although for most enterprises based on attendance

ESTIMATED ATTENDANCE AT CHICAGO'S RECREATIONAL INSTITUTIONS FOR THE YEAR 1925

I. Private recreation (facilities open to the public but privately supported)

1. Settlements and social centers	5,000,000
2. Athletic clubs, Sokols, and Turnvereins	3,500,000
3. Young Men's Christian Association (includes only recreational activities)	2,402,210
4. Boys clubs (outside of settlements)	1,500,000
5. Girl clubs (outside of settlements)	500,000
6. The Art Institute	973,586
7. Band concerts	1,500,000

II. Public recreation (facilities under governmental control)

1. Parks and small parks (includes only organized activities and omits visitors to parks)	32,000,000
2. Playgrounds (Board of Education)	7,683,696
3. Public Library and its branches	3,912,016
4. Community centers (Board of Education)	205,187

III. Commercial recreation (facilities operated as a business enterprise)

1. Motion pictures (total seating capacity 326,370)	120,000,000
2. Theaters and vaudeville	12,000,000
3. Public dance halls (capacity 117,646)	14,000,000
4. Pool halls and bowling alleys	25,000,000

counts, are tentative and not final. They are incomplete, inasmuch as certain enterprises are not included. The general proportions, however, between private, public, and commercial recreation will probably not be greatly changed with more complete and accurate data.

While these figures indicate the huge lead in attendance of commercial recreation over public and private, it must be remembered that the great bulk of recreation is still within the family and in congenial groups. Nevertheless, the enormous totals of attendance at commercial recreation are impressive when we recall that the motion picture, with its almost universal appeal, is little more than thirty years old.

No systematic attempt has been made to cover the field of recreational institutions despite their importance in city life. The most detailed study in this field was one made by Clark Tibbitts on *Social Forces and Trends in Settlement Areas* under the auspices of the Local Community Research Committee in co-operation with the Chicago Federation of Settlements and of the Wieboldt Foundation. This was not a study of the settlement as an institution so much as it was of the habitat of the settlement, elsewhere described as a Zone in Transition, or the industrial residential neighborhoods which serve for the first settlement of immigrant groups. In each of these separate neighborhoods the local history of the community was traced with its succession of immigrant groups and the trends and rapidity of population movement were so far as feasible forecast. The plotting of attendance showed quite unmistakably that while women, who had moved miles out of the neighborhood, would return to attend regularly the meetings of the mothers' clubs, there was only a thin scattering of boys and girls coming beyond a half-mile radius from the settlement. A special study of the recreational life of young people in settlement areas, undertaken in co-operation with Northwestern University Settlement, used the settlement dance as a laboratory to explore the mechanisms by which the process of Americanization was taking place and the problems of personal, familial, recreational, and industrial adjustment which these young people were experiencing.[1] A project in co-operation with Chicago Commons defined and analyzed the problems of boys' club work in an area where nearly every boy at an early age becomes a member of a gang. One contribution of this study was that it indicated the real but limited place in an immigrant area of boys' gangs of a Boy Scout troop, that is, for those boys who, for whatever reason, are not members of gangs.[2]

In the field of public recreation only one project has been developed beyond the preliminary stage, *A Study of a Small Park in the South Park System*, in co-operation with the National City Park and Planning Commission. This study surveyed by the sample method a community of approximately one hundred thousand people served by a small park and four playgrounds, and brought out interesting facts on the recreational activities that adults and children will travel farthest to attend.[3]

In the field of commercial recreation, maps have been prepared to show over a period of years the changes in the number and distribution of motion-picture theaters and public dance halls.[4] These disclose that both institutions steadily decrease in number but increase in size. The motion picture at first occupied remodeled store fronts; it now constructs its own ornate and magnificent structures. The motion-picture theater has come to have a decided economic significance in accelerating the growth and increasing land values in local business centers.[5] Maps made

[1] W. R. P. Ireland, *Factors in the Americanization of Immigrant Youth* (unpublished manuscript in possession of the Committee).

[2] Chester Scott, *A Study of Juvenile Delinquency in a Settlement Neighborhood* (manuscript in University of Chicago Library).

[3] F. F. Stephan (manuscript in possession of the Committee).

[4] Many of these maps were prepared by Daniel Russell and others in connection with his study, *Public Dance Halls in Chicago*.

[5] Lois K. Holley, *The Study of Motion Picture Theaters*.

by Daniel C. Russell show that the so-called dancing palaces were concentrated in Chicago in three areas, respectively, on the North Side, the West Side, and the South Side of the city. Plotting attendance at four of these enterprises showed that the attendance, instead of being local, was now over an area of several miles in radius and in fact practically city-wide.[1] Taken in conjunction with the disappearance of the neighborhood "movies" and dance halls and the rise of the automobile, these facts indicate the desire of youth to escape from the local community and to find adventure and romance in the larger outside world of the city. This situation results in promiscuity in the social relations of youth, that is, intimate relations and behavior with other persons who are known perhaps only in the setting of this recreational center and otherwise are quite anonymous. In a study of girl delinquency Evelyn Buchan makes the distinction between delinquency triangles of the neighborhood type, of mobility, and of promiscuity. The triangles of mobility and of promiscuity seem to afford an index of the change in neighborhood and personal relations taking place in city life.[2]

An interesting study has just been completed by Paul G. Cressey of the "taxi-dance hall."[3] The taxi-dance hall is so called because each dance, lasting often less than sixty seconds, is paid for separately at the rate of a dime a dance. It has been known as "the closed dance hall" by social workers who have investigated them because the only patrons are men, as the women in attendance are instructresses who are paid one-half of the receipts from the

[1] Maps in the possession of the Committee.

[2] See R. E. Park, *The City*, pp. 152–53.

[3] Paul G. Cressey, *The Study of the Taxi-Dance* (in manuscript).

patrons who dance with them. The taxi-dance, with an origin that can be traced variously to the Barbary Coast dance of San Francisco, to the dancing schools, and to the cabaret, was especially devised to meet the social and recreational needs of those men handicapped by racial marks, as are the Chinese, Japanese, and Filipino, by physical defect, by social timidity, or by any other trait which makes it difficult or impossible for them to secure partners at public dance halls. Consequently the taxi-dance hall opens up a new occupation for women entertainers who are the centers of a new and interesting world of recreational life, a world that has commercialized feminine grace and charm in so crude and sensual a fashion that it has aroused the censorship of certain public officials and the concern of social agencies.

In the study of our recreational agencies we are brought face to face with the play of social forces that seem to exert a determining influence upon the social attitudes of childhood and youth. This seems to be the basis of the present concern about the effects of the motion picture, the automobile, and the dance hall.[1] This also appears to be the dominating motive of those who are devoting their lives to the promotion of settlement activities, Y.M.C.A. and Y.W.C.A. work, and boys' and girls' club work. As yet no disinterested study has been made and published of the effects either of commercial or private and public recreation upon the personality development of children and youth. Much remains to be discovered both of practical and of theoretical importance by means of the launching of fundamental studies in this field of the influence of leisure-time activities upon conduct and personality.

[1] John H. Mueller, *The Automobile: A Study of Its Social Consequences* (University of Chicago Library).

IV. INSTITUTIONS OF FORMAL SOCIAL CONTROL

Our political institutions and our institutions of social work, while historically of different origin, are both attempts to control human behavior in the public interest. The state in the past has placed its chief reliance upon force and severity while social work has attempted to substitute investigation and expert treatment. The many studies of public and private institutions completed or undertaken will not be taken up here because an entire chapter on "Urban Growth and Programs of Social Control" has been set aside for their consideration.

Under this heading two studies will be discussed, not because they would be classified here primarily, but because they throw some light on the political process and the problems faced by institutions of public and private welfare. The study of the gang by Frederic M. Thrasher is an example of a project which leads to a better understanding not only of a practical problem but also of the entire social and political structure of a modern city. For the finding that boys' gangs are concentrated in the zone of transition in the river wards of the city was supplemented by the discovery that in the natural course of the development of the gang, the gang itself or its members graduate into the criminal gang or into the political machine. The boys' gang, though not itself an institution, was the forerunner oftentimes of a secret society, "The ———Athletic and Benevolent Association," under the patronage of a politician.[1]

The study of *Organized Crime* by John Landesco[2] con-

[1] See Thrasher, *The Gang*, p. 70, for a chart indicating the place of the gang in the evolution of the different types of group that compose the social order.

[2] *The Illinois Crime Survey*, Part III, *Organized Crime in Chicago*, pp. 815–1100.

firmed the conclusions arrived at in the study of the gang. It also showed concretely and with a wealth of detail over the period of twenty-five years the interlocking relationships of politics and organized crime. It explained why during this entire period all the crusades launched against the different forms of organized crime, such as gambling, sexual vice, bootlegging, and gang activities, have only served to consolidate the criminal elements and to syndicate their activities into a huge organization that seems now to have obtained nation-wide ramifications. It has disclosed that the present power of organized crime is derived not only from huge contributions for political protection and for defense funds against conviction by legal action, but also from local neighborhood sentiment and from ties of friendship between criminals and politicians. It has shown why organized crime has been able to extend its reach into certain normal economic activities of society, as labor unions and merchant associations, and to exert control by violence and by graft.

This analysis of the growth and the present power of organized crime presents a problem to agencies of law enforcement and of social work that in all probability cannot be solved by current methods of procedure. New and experimental techniques are required for programs both of community organization and of social treatment. The existing crime situation shows the failure of our institutions to meet the problems of a heterogeneous urban society, especially under the test of prohibition.

The police department is vitally and intimately involved in the protection of the community from crime and vice. The efficiency and proper management of the police force is a matter of fundamental importance to the community. In co-operation with Northwestern University, the Chicago Crime Commission, and the Institute of Criminal Law and Criminology, and at the request of the commissioner of police, William F. Russell, the Local Community Research Committee is now engaged in a systematic study of the Chicago Police Department. The opportunity to introduce specific administrative improvements leading to greater police efficiency is an unusual one.

v. TWO SPECIAL INSTITUTIONAL STUDIES

Quite apart from the fourfold classification suggested in the foregoing, and developed in the present chapter, are the institutions of prehistoric man in the Chicago region. The Department of Anthropology, with the support of the Local Community Research Committee, has undertaken a comprehensive program of research, combined with student training in archaeological methods, intended to recover the institutional life of the Indian tribes which occupied the region before the coming of the white man.

This program is in full swing; during 1929 a part of the work was done in co-operation with the Smithsonian Institution. Each summer is devoted to intensive field work, in 1927 in Jo Daviess County, in 1928 at Joliet, in 1929 at Quincy, where Indian mounds are being excavated in accordance with the most highly perfected technique.

In the autumn, winter, and spring months the results of the summer's excavations are carefully studied. The relationship of Illinois to neighboring areas is becoming clear, and it appears likely that Illinois will be a valuable field for the study of the contacts and diffusions of culture.

Related to these investigations are Mr. Sapir's studies in linguistics. With the co-operation of a native, Mr. Sapir has made extensive studies of the Grebo language and institutions, studies that have involved interesting applications of the kymograph and the artificial palate. In another direction, Mr. Sapir is studying the language of the Navaho Indians, and of the Athabascans.

At this point reference may also be made to the study of an institution which transcends community and national boundaries, but which has a profound influence on local affairs, international war. Three years ago Mr. Quincy Wright developed a large-scale outline for the study of the causes of war, which after successive revisions in the light of general discussion was accepted by the Local Community Research Committee as a co-operative project calling for five years' work. The units proposed and the tentative order of studies are exhibited in the accompanying table. The final year of the period would be devoted to completion of studies already begun and to summarizing results.

A Joint Committee was established comprising Mr. Wright, chairman (political science), Mr. Schmitt (history), Mr. Viner (economics), Mr. Cole (anthropology), and Mr. Lasswell (political science). The studies have proceeded according to the schedule laid down, and significant results are foreseen. During 1929–30, in addition to research carried on in Chicago, other work is proceeding in Washington, in Japan, and in the Tyrol. Mr. Schmitt spent the summer in Europe in connection with his studies of the outbreak of the World War, and Mr. Wright spent the autumn in the Far East in connection with the Institute of Pacific Relations.

VI. CONCLUSION

The institutions of a community afford one of the best approaches to the study of the community. For the institution always represents a vital aspect of community life, because it is charged with or assumes responsibility for

some communal function. Consequently, the problems of
the institution can always be stated and studied in terms
of the economic and social changes taking place in the
community.

Year	No. of Project	Studies
1927–28...	1	Antecedents of wars since 1815
	2	Combat situations in animals, savages, and children
	3	War frequency, pretexts, recruiting, and propaganda
	4	Armament expenditures
	5	Transfers of territory since 1815
1928–29...	6	War attitude of individuals
	7	Influences controlling foreign policy
	8	Economic dependence of states since 1815
	9	Consequences of international debtor-creditor relation
	10	Areas of hostility since 1815
	11	Newspaper treatment of foreign affairs
	12	Influence of school textbooks
	13	Determination of war promoters and profiteers
	14	Comparative land utilization
	15	Historic changes in causes of war
1929–30...	16	Variations in position of war-waging class
	17	Effects of overpopulation
	18	Disturbances of balance of power
	19	Effect of changes in war technique
	20	Effect of changes in methods of pacific settlement
	21	Effect of different commercial policies
	22	Cause and effect of armament races
	23	Minority and nationality dissatisfaction since 1815
1930–31...	24	Influence of types of political leadership
	25	National sports, spectacles, and amusements
	26	Position of war in systems of international law
	27	Position of violence in systems of private law
	28	Influence of types of civic education
	29	Literature of war and peace

The survey just completed of the wide range of institutions that were classified under the headings, cultural,
economic, recreational, and political (including social
work) has perhaps been sufficient to indicate both the
necessity and the promise of further work in research upon

the institutional life of the community. Our present institutions are meeting the full force of the social changes of the present. They were organized with reference to situations that have now passed. Many of them recognize the need for readjustment and modification. It is apparent that the readjustment can be made with a minimum of stress and strain and of social loss through the medium of research. And research in the field of institutions promises to throw new light from an unexpected source upon hitherto baffling questions of social organization, social control, and personality development.

CHAPTER X
PERSONALITY STUDIES

I. THE INFLUENCE OF MEAD AND THOMAS

The study of human personality has an impetus, a tradition, and a more or less distinctive orientation at the University of Chicago, due especially to the influence of George H. Mead and William I. Thomas. Mr. Mead, who has been a member of the department of philosophy since 1894, has been formulating an inclusive theory of the development of the self which has drawn the attention of successive University generations to the deep consideration of fundamental issues. His approach is philosophical, in the sense that his chief preoccupation is with the elimination of the subjective-objective dichotomy from the description of mental processes in relation to surroundings. But his approach is scientific in the sense that his training included laboratory work in physiological psychology, and that his speculations have been disciplined and chastened by the procedures and findings of the natural sciences. Mr. Mead's analysis of stimulus and response has legitimized the objective position of psychological acts in the behavior sequence. His account of the rise of the self through the process of "playing the rôle of the other" furnishes a vantage ground from which the statements by Cooley, Freud, Watson, Bechterev, and other representatives of current movements in sociology and psychology may be surveyed. The unpretentious yet penetrating influence of Mead is traceable in the work of many scholars and scientists who have been associated with the University of Chicago, even though many of them have never been under his immediate direction, for his ways of thinking have become more and more the common property of several departments in the institution.[1]

Joining to his abstract interests an indefatigable zeal for the acquisition of facts, William I. Thomas, who was connected with the Department of Sociology from 1894 to 1918, left an especially abiding stamp on research. In the third volume of *The Polish Peasant in Europe and America*[2] he and Florian Znaniecki printed in full the autobiography of a Polish immigrant to the United States. Since then the autobiography has been systematically used as a means of disclosing the developmental history of the individual, and of illuminating that which Ellsworth Faris has aptly termed "the subjective aspect of culture."

Thomas's contribution was more than a convincing demonstration of the importance of autobiographies for social research. He and Znaniecki went on to formulate conceptions of the nature of personality which have been widely employed. Especially in the methodological note to the third volume are found distinctions which are particularly relevant to the study of personality. Temperamental attitudes are the original and fundamental group of attitudes of the individual which exist independently of any social influence. The character attitudes are organized and fixed by social influences operating on the temper-

[1] Among his articles may be cited "Social Psychology the Counterpart of Physiological Psychology," *Psychological Bulletin*, VI (1909), 401–8; "What Social Objects Must Psychology Presuppose?" *Journal of Philosophy, Psychology and Scientific Methods*, VII (1910), 174–80; "The Social Self," *ibid.*, X (1913), 374–80; "The Genesis of the Self and Social Control," *International Journal of Ethics*, XXXV (1925), 251–77.

[2] First published in Boston (Richard Badger, 1918). 5 vols. Republished in New York (Alfred Knopf Inc., 1927). 2 vols.

amental base. The life-organization of the individual is the individual's conception of himself and his rôle in society, and involves the use of intellectual methods to control social reality rather than reliance upon automatic and instinctive impulses. The child comes into the world without a character or a life-organization, and achieves these by subsequent development in relation to changing social situations. The child becomes self-conscious, and in this process he takes himself not only for an object, but he makes life, as he throws it ahead of him in imagination, a project. Eventually he formulates principles of action and organizes his life in ways which seem likely to further his life aim. Since personality is an active process which grows up in response to changing social situations, types of personality may be defined with reference to their ability to adjust to a changing moral world. There is the philistine (conforms to conventional patterns), the bohemian (open to novel patterns, but unable to achieve a stable character or a career), and the creative personality (maintains a consistent life-organization in a changing world, and is capable of making an original contribution to culture). Personalities may also be characterized by the degree to which they are disposed by temperament or experience to respond to the desire for new experience, the need for security, the desire for recognition, and the desire for response. The more firmly the social organization is fixed in tradition, the more the individual's life will be tightly integrated within the social order, and the less he will be able, in consequence, to accommodate himself to a new and looser social order. This is the clue which is used to explain the very considerable disorganization of the Polish immigrant in America.

It has been essential to characterize, even so briefly,

the work of Mead and Thomas in order to sketch the background of current research on personality problems at the University of Chicago, and to explain the general orientation of those specific investigations which the research funds of the Local Community Research Committee have facilitated. Their work is part and parcel of the social science heritage in this situation, and theories and problems tend to be formulated more or less explicitly with reference to their conceptions.

The actual monographic output and contemplated projects in this field will be passed in review according to a very simple scheme. First will come those investigations which describe qualitatively the types of personality which function in various social situations. Then reference will be made to the researches which have undertaken to measure personality differences according to various scaling procedures. Finally attention will be paid to exhaustive examinations of individual subjects.

II. TYPES OF PERSONALITY

Every situation in which interacting personalities participate can be considered from the point of view of the relationships of dominance and submission which develop in the course of this interaction. Robert E. Park and Ernest W. Burgess have defined the person as "an individual who has status," and explicit in this concept is the notion that personality cannot be profitably isolated from social contexts.

Frederick M. Thrasher, who found 1,313 gangs in the city of Chicago, described a number of specialized rôles which appeared in the gangs, and which varied with the complexity of the activities and enterprises of the individual gang. The rôles included the "Brains," who planned things for the gang to do; the "Funny Boy," who often disguised bold criticism in a jesting manner; the "Show-off," who blustered, bragged, and bluffed; the "Goat," who was an easy mark for the others; and the "Goofy Guys," who joined some peculiarity to their "dumbness." The vocabulary of the gang shows a great deal about the aspects of the individual which acquired significance in this relationship. The nicknames were infinite in their variety, but representative ones were these: the fat boy was often "Tubby," the slender boy was "Slim," the small boy was "Shrimp," the handsome boy was "Sheik," the peculiar one was "Goofy," the unmanly one was "Siss," the hard one was "Dirty," the homely one was "Ugly," the foreigner was "Dago," the dark-complexioned lad was "Nigger," the overbearing boy was "Lord." Thrasher examined the marks of leadership, saying that the natural leaders were game, and usually thought clearly in the excitement of a crisis, usually backed their daring with physical prowess, and were quick and firm in decision, and imaginative. Some leaders relied on daring, others on bullying; there were heroic and obliging types. In the primitive democracy of the gang the tyrant could not last forever, and the leader who made mistakes would pass quickly into the category of the "has-beens." So there was much mobility in the definition of the individual's rôle in the group, due to the incessant conflict of one personality with another.[1]

If the participants in a certain culture meet new problems of adjustment, they modify the division of labor, whether wittingly or not, and new personality rôles arise and old ones alter. This process is clearly described for the Jewish community by Louis Wirth. He characterizes the

[1] See chaps. xvii and xviii in *The Gang* (Chicago, 1927).

personality types which are found in the segregated Jewish community, the rabbi, sexton, councilman, slaughterer, circumciser, marriage broker, Talmudic student, righteous individual, hangers-on in the synagogue, jester, apostate, and beggar. When the Ghetto is breaking down, an area of second settlement in such a city as Chicago develops the *Lodgenik*, or joiner, the emancipated woman, the philanthropic lady who does charity work in the old Ghetto, and the nearly emancipated man who clings to a small beard.[1]

A managerial group which is to be found in American municipal government was the object of Leonard D. White's investigation. He spent five months in the field studying the city managers in selected cities, and in his volume on the subject devotes a chapter each to the managers of Cleveland, Cincinnati, Kansas City, Pasadena, and Dayton. He then ventures to make some comparative remarks about the city managers as a class. Physically, he says, they are formed under the pressure of unremitting hard labor. They differ very widely in the degree of nervous tension which they sustain on the job. They resemble each other in their courageousness. The managers are "practical men" who are primarily interested in specific definite, immediate matters. "They are men who *do* things, and who like to think of themselves as men who do things rather than talk about things to do." As a group they are narrow in their range, usually more concerned about the physical problems of the city than its moral and intellectual problems. They are disinterested in the theory of government and of municipal administration either as art or science. They show intense loyalty to the interests of the city as a whole, rather than to favored factions. Emotionally they run the gamut from one extreme to another. Al-

[1] See chaps. vi and xii in *The Ghetto* (Chicago, 1928).

though a few are oratorical, most of them can speak from the platform with difficulty. One group comes to the annual convention for recreation and another for the exchange of experience.[1]

Even these preliminary characterizations of a group of executives suggests a variety of interesting inquiries. What are the traits of those who become interested in city management? How do their traits alter under the strains of office? Which are the traits which bring special success in a variety of managerial situations and how are those traits developed? Similar questions can be posed for diplomats, judges, officers, legislators, and other governmental and political classes, as indeed for every functional type in society.

The precinct captains of the city of Chicago have been the object of comparative investigation by Sonya Forthal, working under the direction of Harold F. Gosnell. The precinct captain is the party official on the lowest rung of the party ladder, and the literature about him is meager and undependable. A census of the captains was conducted in such wise that the selected precincts gave a fair sample of the political conditions in half of the fifty wards of Chicago. Each precinct captain was interviewed in order to elicit some definite facts which would permit exact comparison. The party, faction, age, color, occupation, birthplace, father's birthplace, years in Chicago, years in precinct, schooling, religion, sex, reason for entering precinct, years in politics, public offices held, methods of political organization, and services performed and favors sought for the precinct were tabulated. Each precinct was analyzed according to the economic, racial, nationalistic, and certain other prominent characteristics of the population.

[1] See especially chap. viii of *The City Manager* (Chicago, 1927).

Exact comparisons can thus be made between the precinct captains and the environments in which they work. Besides the quantitative facts, many qualitative impressions were recorded about the personalities of the men which subsequent studies may reduce to more exact form.

After having studied the rôle of the realtor in modern life, Everett C. Hughes was led to formulate the relationship between personality types and the division of labor in general terms.[1] Occupation selection operates in the urbanized world by mobilizing individuals from their family milieu and making them available at the points where competition will provide them with a task. Sometimes the mobilization is much more than a simple change in position away from the original neighborhood to the vicinity of the job. It may involve conversion, long professional training, and the development of esoteric skills and interests. The individual finds a "life-organization" in the occupational group which, in the case of the more mobile and esoteric occupational types, leaves the familial and neighborhood connections far behind.

Mr. Hughes comments that in the caste system the individual is born to a station and a sacred set of prerogatives, and that his personality is thus a stereotype. In a mobile world only a few are born in their station. Since the occupations are themselves new or changing, the individual financier or industrialist often is the "first generation," having many poor relations. Occupational selection upsets moral codes and remodels social organization, and a man's trade comes to have more significance to him than his family. Some individuals pass readily from one vocational rôle to another, maintaining a high level of produc-

[1] Chap. vii of *Personality and the Social Group*, edited by Burgess (Chicago, 1929).

.tivity, and constituting a distinct type.[1] The reformulation and illustration of Durkheim's conceptions is proceeding in the light of such empirical studies as Harvey W. Zorbaugh's *Gold Coast and the Slum* (Chicago, 1929) and Nels Anderson's *Hobo* (Chicago, 1923).

III. MEASUREMENT OF PERSONALITY DIFFERENCES

All the studies of institutions, like the family, necessarily undertake to discover how the cast of characters of the traditional pattern play their parts under new conditions. What is the actual meaning of "mother," "father," "oldest son," and the rest of the family under contemporary urban influences? Ernest W. Burgess reports that the study of life-history documents confirms the conclusion that the family, though conventionally treated as a social institution, has lost so many of its former collective activities that it has become a "mere unity of interacting personalities."[2] There is no static and permanent ordering of relationships of affection and duty, but a moving constellation of family bonds which loosen and tighten, and of family attitudes which shift and mutate as the situation is redefined. This is brought out especially in connection with the study of delinquents by Ernest W. Burgess and Clifford R. Shaw, and of adult criminals by Ernest W. Burgess and John Landesco.

Personality differentials may be sought among those who are similar in that they all commit an act like suicide. Ruth Shonle Cavan's volume on *Suicide* (Chicago, 1928) treats suicide as one of the solutions sought by disorgan-

---

[1] An analysis of personality types in relation to the fields of distinguished activity has been made by Fritz Giese in *Die öffentliche Persönlichkeit* (Leipzig, 1928).

[2] See chap. x of *Personality and the Social Group*, edited by Burgess (Chicago, 1929).

ized personalities. She divides her cases into those who suffer from vague and unidentified cravings, those with unfulfilled wishes for a particular type of thing, those with unfulfilled specific wishes, those with mental conflicts, and those with a broken life-organization. The first three categories refer to cases in which the conflict is supposed to be between the person and some element in the environment; in the fourth category the scene of the battle is within the personality. The volume contains statistics of the frequency of suicide among various populations, but the personality hypotheses are the most valuable points of departure for future work. The psychoanalyst would like to see whether more specific connections could be developed between the ways in which the person meets his early infantile and adolescent crises and his subsequent resort to self-destruction. Mrs. Cavan's procedure and theories owe much to the personal supervision of Ellsworth Faris.[1]

The researches to which allusion has thus far been made have dealt in qualitative, descriptive terms with the personality types which they have explored. Another group of studies, and one which it is proposed greatly to expand in the future, undertakes to apply some exact measuring procedure to the personalities observed, for the sake of discovering precise means of differentiation. An imposing battery of tests of mental and affective traits has been devised by modern psychologists, and several of these were applied by W. H. Cowley to political leaders, at the instigation and under the direction of Charles E. Merriam and L. L. Thurstone. The problem was to find out whether existing and specially invented psychological tests, administered in a laboratory, would show any stable dif-

---

[1] Mr. Faris is also interested in "The Sect and the Sectarian." See chap. xi in *Personality and the Social Group*, edited by Burgess (Chicago, 1929).

ferences between leaders and followers in the same situation, and leaders in one situation and leaders in another. Twenty-eight psychological tests were given to these subjects according to standard procedures and under standard conditions. Such traits were tested as aggressiveness, self-confidence, intelligence, emotional stability, finality of judgment, tact, suggestibility, and speed of decision. The preliminary results showed that the test scores differentiated clearly between leaders and followers in the same situation. Leaders in different situations showed different traits, suggesting that there are no common traits of leadership, which is to be treated as a function of original equipment as modified and functioning in situations with special requirements.[1] An effort was made to isolate the leader from the mere "headman," the leader being "an individual who is moving in a particular direction and who succeeds in inducing others to follow after him," while the headman is "an individual who, because of ability or prestige, has attained to a position of headship."

Psychometrical data are not the only kind which is capable of being exactly summarized. The morphological and physiological aspects of the personality can be stated with great precision in many instances. L. L. Thurstone, who has been particularly interested in the possibilities which are inherent in this approach, has stimulated and co-operated with work of this kind. Gilbert J. Rich, of the Institute for Juvenile Research of Chicago, has recently reported the results of his tests of a group of individuals who were rated by observers for excitability and aggressiveness. He measured the hydrogen-ion concentration of

---

[1] These conclusions are reported in "Three Distinctions in the Study of Leaders," *Journal of Abnormal and Social Psychology*, Vol. XXIII, No. 2 (July-September, 1928). The data are not yet published and available for criticism.

the saliva, the acidity of the urine, the alkali reserve of the blood, the creatinine content of the blood, and the creatinine excretion of the urine. He found that the least excitable individuals tended to have the most acid saliva and the most acid urine. Results of this general nature were predicted on the basis of what is known about the sympathetic and parasympathetic nervous systems, and the acid-base balance of the blood.

L. L. Thurstone has been investigating the connection between pupillary reflexes and the affective organization of the person. This work grew out of the observation by Ludlum, Elton Mayo, and others that the pupils of hysterics seemed to be wider than the pupils of obsessional neurotics. The problem has been to devise reliable procedures of measurement, and to choose subjects whose traits are judged by independent criteria.

The relationship between somatic conditions and mental life is the subject of a growing body of research, and the Personality Studies Committee of the Local Community Research is anxious to secure the personnel and to supply the laboratory facilities necessary to develop a promising attack. This program requires an adequate physiological laboratory, a biochemical laboratory, an anthropological laboratory, and special test equipment.[1]

An incident of Thurstone's work has been the development of a device for detecting neurotic traits in the individual. He devised a questionnaire which was given to entering college students, and on the basis of which predictions were made about the persons who would prove to be neurotic. The predictions were tested by the reports of

[1] Existing research methods and hopes are reviewed by William I. Thomas and Dorothy S. Thomas in chap. ix–xiii of *The Child in America* (New York, 1928).

those who subsequently watched the students in various life-situations, and by observation on selected individuals by the experimenter. The work as so far developed seems to show that the predictive value of certain answers is high, and also that some current hypotheses about formative influences on neurotic development are open to question. A provisional finding throws considerable doubt on the common assertion that position in the family is importantly associated with the development of neurotic traits.[1]

IV. PERSONALITY OF INDIVIDUAL SUBJECTS

The investigations which have so far been reviewed describe or measure a few features of many cases. Another series of researches concentrates attention upon individual cases, using detailed description and measurement in so far as possible. Starting with personal contacts with a wide variety of political types, Charles E. Merriam has initiated and supervised a series of monographs upon political leaders. In 1922 he published *The American Party System* in which he presented a provisional list of traits which characterized the political leader. The generalized political leader was said to have unusual sensitiveness to the strength and direction of social and industrial tendencies with reference to their party and political bearing; acute and quick perception of possible courses of community conduct with prompt action accordingly; facility in group combination and compromise—political diplomacy in ideas, policies, and spoils; facility in personal contacts with widely varying types of men; facility in dramatic expression of the sentiment and interest of large groups of voters, usually

[1] William Fielding Ogburn is conducting a series of studies which are designed to put various psychopathological hypotheses to a quantitative test.

with voice or pen—fusing a logical formula, an economic interest, and a social habit or predisposition in a personality; courage not unlike that of the military commander whose best laid plans require a dash of luck for their successful completion. Mr. Merriam called for a series of detailed investigations which would subject traits to more minute scrutiny, search for hereditary determiners, evaluate the rôle of various environments, and scrutinize the techniques of power, and developed a series of such studies in Seminar.[1] The most recent study, which was rendered possible through the aid furnished by the Local Community Research, is that of Carter Henry Harrison I, which was executed by Claudius Johnson (Chicago, 1928).[2]

Mr. Johnson's purpose was not to write another biography of the man who served five terms as mayor of the city of Chicago, but to analyze the equipment and tactics of Harrison as a political leader. After sketching the ancestral background, the early life, the private life, and the political career of the subject, Mr. Johnson discussed his physical characteristics, mental traits, and temperamental traits. Such topics are treated as Harrison's size and features, appearance and dress, strength and endurance, health, diet, sleep, exercise, energy, manner, and voice; his type of mind, capacity for observation, problem-solving ability, inventive ability, resourcefulness, judgment, foresight, mental poise, memory, capacity for details, capacity for mental development; his gentlemanliness, geniality, optimism, sense of humor, sense of fair

[1] See his *Introduction to Four American Party Leaders.*

[2] See Harold F. Gosnell, *Boss Platt and His New York Machine;* Roy Victor Peel, *James Gillespie Blaine* (MS); Margaret Carol Dunn, *Jane Addams* (MS); Pearl Louise Robertson, *Grover Cleveland* (MS); Marietta Stevenson, *William Jennings Bryan* (MS). Other studies are in process of completion.

play, goodness of heart, integrity and sincerity, social insight, personal insight, courage, dramatic qualities, love of pageantry, desire for applause and fame, sensitiveness to criticism, egotism, deficiency in tact, impatience and "temper," co-operativeness, and capacity for organization. The pertinent material was set out under these headings, thus forcing into prominence the points on the basis of which comparisons may be drawn with other political leaders. The literary tradition in biography tempts most writers to disguise the gaps in their knowledge with deft phrases, but Mr. Johnson's inventory method ruthlessly discloses the weak spots in his material. He is scientific in spirit, and the result is neither poetry, nor drama, nor romance. Emotional titillations are sacrificed in favor of hard thinking about the comparative significance of this personality history.

Half the volume is given over to the analysis of the political strategy and tactics of Mayor Harrison. The topics which are dealt with here include Harrison's efforts to secure nominations, his election technique, his group appeals, his relationship to certain institutional enemies, his legislative leadership, and his administrative leadership. Mr. Johnson seizes hold of many distinctions where the non-specialist in politics finds foggy and spurious simplicity.

Other lines of attack on the problem instituted by Merriam include the study of non-leader types, the examination of the special skills or techniques of leaders, leadership situations developing in types of social settings, the application of the known batteries of tests to leader and non-leader groups (with Thurston and Cowley) and the attempt to discover relations between patterns of political leadership and personality patterns unveiled by the methods of psychometrics, psychiatry, physiology, or various forms of constitutional studies. The basis for this attack was laid by Merriam in the Committee on Psychology and Politics in the National Conference on the Science of Politics in 1923, with the co-operation of Elton Mayo and Thurstone.[1]

These studies throw into sharp relief the disparity between what is reported and what would be valuable to know for the sake of understanding a single personality. One of the proposals which has been carefully considered by the Personality Studies Committee calls for the building up of a body of records about individuals who have been studied very intensively by almost every known method. The most voluminous contribution to such a record would be the verbatim report of a psychoanalytic interview, which may stretch over several months for an hour every day. If the methods and hypotheses of Sigmund Freud can be confirmed, the revolution will be consummated which he has begun in our ways of thinking about the whole range of psychotic, neurotic, and normal personality manifestations. At the present time the psychoanalytic records are in a very fragmentary and unsatisfactory state. Available documents are not verbatim records of what was actually produced by the patient, but the interviewer's recollection of what he considered to be important after the close of the interview. This is subject to distortion in many ways. What is wanted is a verbatim account of what comes out in the course of the interview, so that very fundamental hypotheses and questions can be carefully considered. Instead of vague innuendoes about the "suggestion therapy" of the analysts, it will be possible for a small group of

[1] A progress report summing up the results of several years of trial and error in this field is in preparation.

specialists to consider specifically such definite statements as these: "On page 40 you gave the subject the suggestion which eventually produced the dream on page 140 and finally established the belief asserted on page 240." "You have used the term anal-sadistic drive on page 600, but you have not taken into account the behavior recorded on page 1000."

Since the analytic interview is a huge document, and represents an enormous expenditure of energy on the individual case, opportunity should not be lost to correlate the results secured by this procedure with documents about the same case which are procured by other methods. The life-story of the individual might be solicited in the form of a written statement prior to the psychiatric interviewing. A biography should be prepared from material supplied by the family and acquaintances of the subject. Psychometrical and physical tests should be used. The essential problem is to find out the kinds of retrospective and prospective predictions which can be made on the basis of various kinds of personality records. What is the historicity of an analytical document of a certain type, when compared with an analytical document of another type, and an autobiography? What is the degree of accuracy in predicting behavior under control situations which can be achieved by using the material to be found in the interview record?[1]

[1] See Harold D. Lasswell, "The Problem of Adequate Personality Records: A Proposal," *American Journal of Psychiatry*, May, 1929.

CHAPTER XI

URBAN GROWTH AND PROBLEMS OF SOCIAL CONTROL

Much of the research conducted under the auspices of the Local Community Research Committee is not immediately connected with any proposal for improvement or change, but is directed solely toward the better understanding of the conditions of life in an urban community. Thus the determination of the boundaries and analysis of the social organization of the local communities of which Chicago is composed has no immediate reformist end. The measurement of opinion, the prediction of population, the analysis of the qualities of leadership, the discovery of the functions of a precinct committeeman, or the prestige value of public employment are in a way the analogue of "pure science" in the field of the natural sciences.

Other studies seek specific methods of improving social organization or procedures, or supply reasoned answers to a definite problem presented to the Committee. These are more in the nature of applied research, although of course they are as objective and thoroughgoing as are studies in the other class; and if they take the form of temporary social organization, they have perhaps in them an element of the experimental which more fully justifies characterizing the city as a laboratory.

I

A brief reference to some types of applied research will be followed by a more detailed statement of selected cases.

In 1914 a survey of Chicago Crime Statistics was undertaken by Miss Abbott, in connection with the Crime Investigation of the Chicago City Council directed by Mr.
Merriam. In 1923 the Cook County Jail Committee asked
for help in their important survey undertaken in co-operation with the Chicago Community Trust. Reference will
be made below to a request addressed in 1925 by the
Marshall Field Estate to Miss Edith Abbott to determine
the most advantageous location of a significant housing
development, and to another in 1927 by the Rosenwald
Fund, the directors of which asked her to co-operate in a
similarly important project. By reason of her long study
of the Chicago housing problem Professor Abbott was emi-
nently qualified to furnish aid in these undertakings. In
1928 the Rosenwald Fund again suggested co-operation in
providing for the placement of dependent Negro children
in foster-homes. While these pages were being written a
telephone request came from a group of persons desiring
to establish a memorial in the form of some community
service, asking for exact information as to the character
and social needs of the neighborhood. The answer depends
upon the systematic knowledge of the social life of the
community concerned, for the most part already at hand
in the Local Community Research organization. On January 21, 1929, Commissioner of Police William F. Russell
invited the University of Chicago, Northwestern University, the Institute of Criminal Law and Criminology, and
the Chicago Crime Commission to make an impartial and
comprehensive study of the Chicago Police Department.
The Local Community Research Committee mobilized a
professor of criminal law, a professor of sociology specializ-
ing in crime and its treatment, a professor of public administration, and the assistant business manager of the

University to serve on a Joint Committee to direct the study. These are a few among many illustrations of the type of research which is related to some specific problem which forms the primary subject matter of the present chapter.

Other pieces of research stand midway between the "pure" and "applied" categories, and in fact there is an imperceptible gradation between the two. Here some cases of research rather definitely bearing upon a program of reform or improvement are presented, together with some indication of results achieved in the practical world where results have become evident. Any student or worker in the social sciences, however, knows how slowly the wheels grind in social evolution, and it need surprise no one if the end-results in actual reform appear fragmentary.

Two studies have been mentioned elsewhere which deserve incidental reference here, *Factors Making for Success on Parole*, by Ernest W. Burgess, and the study entitled *Registration of Social Statistics*, by A. W. McMillen and H. R. Jeter, which is proceeding in co-operation with the Association of Community Chests and Councils. Both of these studies are directed toward very specific ends. The first sought and discovered a formula to predict the success or failure of a prisoner on parole; the second seeks a reasoned and uniform basis for keeping the records of welfare agencies.

Several studies in the area of government illustrate the nature of applied research. Under the supervision of Charles E. Merriam, Mr. Herman C. Beyle attacked the problem of public reporting, which is notoriously ineffective. Mr. Beyle developed tentative standards of reporting by examination of the municipal reports of Berlin, London, Paris, and Boston, and of such reports as those of Cooke in Philadelphia and Woods in New York. He then examined in turn the reports of each of the important public authorities in the Chicago region and laid bare their deficiencies and merits. The study concluded with a list of tentative conclusions as to what constitutes good reporting practice.[1]

In 1925 the Union League Club approached the Local Community Research Committee with a plan to make a directory of the civic agencies of Chicago. It was known that a great amount of civic effort was being expended, but in what directions, to what extent, and with what results was not clear. A co-operative enterprise was inaugurated in which the direction of the census was given to Mr. J. G. Kerwin, assisted by Mr. Edward M. Martin, secretary of the Public Affairs Committee of the Union League Club. Eventually a selected list of 526 civic organizations was prepared with a membership of 1,102,126 persons, employing 174 salaried officers, issuing 55 regular periodical publications, and commanding a combined budget for civic purposes alone of more than a million dollars per annum.

The study also revealed a lack of organization and co-ordination, to remedy which the Union League Club led the way in the formation of the Chicago Civic Conference. This body represents about fifty organizations, with close contact on the part of many more. It is intended to serve as a clearing-house of information and to promote civic interests through the medium of conferences and the distribution of literature, especially utilizing material from its members. A General Committee represents the members; an Executive Committee selects and supervises the

---

[1] Herman C. Beyle, *Governmental Reporting* (Chicago: University of Chicago Press, 1927).

officers. Thus in a preliminary way some order is being secured in the field of civic effort, while the independence of each group is maintained in full. There is no element of indorsement by the Chicago Civic Conference, as in the social work field.

The problem of general administration in a city as large as Chicago is of great practical importance. There is general agreement that the present municipal organization is wasteful, extravagant, and irresponsible. More than ten years ago the Chicago Bureau of Public Efficiency proposed the city-manager plan for Chicago. In order to secure recent and first-hand information as to the operation of this form of municipal government, to raise the question of its adaptability to Chicago, and to restate its fundamental presuppositions, Leonard D. White undertook a survey of the problem and published, in 1927, *The City Manager*. In addition to furnishing a record of actual experience in a number of leading cities, this volume analyzed the standard patterns of behavior of the city managers in their official relationships, and emphasized the fundamental problems facing this significant group of executives. Since the publication of the volume, interest has been renewed in the application of the plan to the city of Chicago, and the International City Managers' Association has affiliated with the University of Chicago.[1]

At the request of Mayor Dever, Mr. White made a survey of the conditions of municipal employment in 1924, revealing the conditions which had lowered the morale of the city service, and offering constructive proposals for change.[2] Under the direction of Mr. White and Mr.

[1] Leonard D. White, *The City Manager* (Chicago: University of Chicago Press, 1927).

[2] Leonard D. White, *Conditions of Municipal Employment in Chicago: A Study in Morale* (City of Chicago, 1925).

Wooddy, a study of administrative areas was undertaken, opening up a field for further intensive work.

Under the direction of Mr. Gosnell, Mr. David M. Maynard completed a study of the referendum in Chicago, revealing gross negligence and at times unmistakable fraud in counting referendum ballots. Evidence gathered by students of the University has been of value to the county judge in prosecuting for violation of the ballot laws.

Another governmental and political problem was studied by Mr. W. B. Philip in *Chicago and Down State*, under the supervision of Mr. Jernegan, while still another study was made of the Chicago delegation in Congress.

In the field of public finance, Mr. Leland has in progress an extensive study of the cost of government of the state of Illinois. Several units of this study are approaching completion. The growth of governmental expenditures since the admission of Illinois to the Union has been ascertained. Monthly expenditures have been analyzed since 1890. The cost of the Illinois General Assembly has been ascertained. The cost of maintaining public employment agencies has been determined. The costs for maintaining parks have been analyzed, and military expenditures discovered.

Under Mr. Leland's direction, Mr. Chamberlin is conducting a study of *The Taxation of Insurance Companies*. Mr. Leland has been closely identified with the Illinois Tax Conference, and assisted in the writing of the 1928 annual report of the State Tax Commission.

Mr. Merriam has been acting chairman of the Cook County Committee on Consolidation of Local Taxing and Governing Bodies.[1]

Social control of the use of property on a larger scale

---

[1] See above for studies in regional planning and police.

develops through the modern municipal invention of zoning. In a series of studies prepared under the immediate direction of the law school, Mr. Newman F. Baker described the character of a zoning ordinance and its application by judicial and administrative methods. These studies were published with the aid of the Local Community Research Committee in a single volume in 1927,[1] and do much to illustrate the constitutional and legal difficulties encountered in any attempt to deal with housing on a large scale.

Of all the studies, however, which look forward to administrative or legislative reform, the largest and most varied are the studies of welfare institutions conducted chiefly under the supervision of members of the School of Social Service Administration. The members of this School have worked out a systematic and comprehensive program intended eventually to deal with the whole range of welfare agencies and institutions in Chicago and its region.

The studies made with the help of the Local Community Research Committee divide themselves into four main groups:

1. A survey of the Chicago housing problem and the population elements in the community.

2. The public social services of Chicago, Cook County, and the state of Illinois; the organization of the agencies developed for the care of the destitute; and the provision made for the special groups usually spoken of as "wards of the state."

3. Studies dealing with the various aspects of the problem of dependency and delinquency among the children

---

[1] Newman F. Baker, *The Legal Aspects of Zoning* (Chicago: University of Chicago Press, 1927).

and young persons as this problem presents itself in the oldest of all the juvenile courts.

4. Studies in Negro life.

5. A number of miscellaneous studies undertaken at the request of agencies or groups in the community desiring help in the formulation of a policy for which they were responsible and for which a substantial piece of research was necessary. In many cases these agencies have made contributions that could be matched by the Local Community Research Committee. Of these the most notable undertaking was that dealing with the budgets used for dependent families by the great relief societies of the community—the United Charities and the Jewish Social Service Bureau. This study resulted in the substantial inquiry into *The Income and Standard of Living of Unskilled Laborers in Chicago*, by the late Leila Houghteling.

The studies of housing and population to be published in final shape during the coming year were begun twenty years ago at the request of the late Charles B. Ball, who was for many years the chief of the Sanitary Bureau of the Department of Health. Reports of investigations in selected areas have been published from time to time in the *Journal of Sociology* and in other journals. In order to collect the necessary facts regarding overcrowding and the enforcement of the various provisions of the tenement-house code, a house-to-house canvass in certain of the deteriorated areas of the city was first undertaken in the winter of 1908–9. The groups of blocks canvassed in the year 1908–9 were taken from the area that had been covered in an earlier investigation, the study of *Tenement House Conditions in Chicago*, which had been published by the City Homes Association in 1901. In the preparation of this report a house-to-house canvass had been made in three of the most densely populated neighborhoods of the lower "West Side," the old tenement-house district lying between the two branches of the river, lying also between wide stretches of railroad tracks, and inclosed by a dense semicircular belt-line of manufacturing and commercial plants and lumber yards. Three districts were selected for this intensive study by a committee of the City Homes Association. The first of these was a group of forty blocks lying betweeen Halsted Street and the river, in the Italian and Jewish quarter east and south of Hull House; the second, a group of eight blocks in the Bohemian district toward the south branch of the river; and the third, a group of ten blocks in the old Sixteenth Ward, now the Thirty-third Ward, in the Polish region toward the north branch of the river.

The districts which were investigated in 1900 were revisited in order to ascertain how far conditions might have changed since that time. A careful house-to-house canvass was therefore made again in each of the blocks in the congested Polish district on the Northwest Side and in a sample area in each of the other two districts. In the following year new districts were selected for study in the Polish section near the gates of the steel mills in South Chicago, in the Polish-Lithuanian district back of the yards, in the district of the lower North Side known as "Little Sicily." As the inquiry was prolonged, new districts were selected in areas of the city not previously canvassed until a large number of sections and many different national groups were included in the sample. Twenty-five different districts were canvassed. One of these had been entirely taken over for business purposes at the time of the recanvass; and the recent material, therefore, covers twenty-four districts in seventeen different wards.

These surveys were continued winter after winter by groups of graduate students until a considerable body of material was collected bearing upon the subject of tenement-house conditions in Chicago and the enforcement or lack of enforcement of tenement-house legislation.

The selection of the particular areas chosen for investigation was determined by a number of factors. Areas in different parts of the city were selected in order to include homes of all types in the various tenement districts.

It was hoped that a sufficient number of districts could be so canvassed to secure a representative sample of the houses in the deteriorated areas of the city. Single blocks were rarely investigated, for it was no part of the plan to pick out the worst blocks, district by district. Instead of single blocks, groups of blocks were most frequently chosen, the number of blocks in a neighborhood varying from four to forty. The 151 blocks finally canvassed may properly be called a fair sample of the conditions in the industrial sections of the city where the poor are obliged to live.

The districts canvassed were widely scattered, in order to make certain of the inclusion in the sample of the various types of housing and to avoid concentration on any single area of deterioration. Moreover, it was hoped that the interest of various groups of people in the different sections of the city might be secured and that their interest in better housing might be aroused. Political reasons were also a factor in the choice of areas. The support of different aldermen for a more adequate appropriation for tenement-house inspection could, it was hoped, be secured by reports showing the condition of tenements in their own wards.

The canvass of the 151 blocks covered 6,165 buildings, including churches, schools, fire stations, and similar buildings, and 15,163 different apartments or households. The 6,165 buildings in the districts canvassed included 4,299 houses used only for residence purpose, 1,420 buildings

NUMBER OF HEADS OF HOUSEHOLDS OF SPECIFIED NATIONALITY, BY DISTRICTS
(RECANVASS AND 1923–26 ORIGINAL CANVASS DATA)

Nationality	Number of Heads of Households	Percentage Distribution
Total all nationalities.	15,163	. . . .
American.	2,711	17.88
White.	882	5.82
Colored.	1,829	12.06
Foreign.	12,188	80.38
Bohemian.	385	2.54
British.	40	.26
Chinese.	17	.11
Croatian.	150	.99
French.	28	.19
German.	484	3.19
Greek.	382	2.52
Irish.	196	1.29
Italian.	3,001	19.79
Jewish.	86	.57
Jugoslav.	10	.07
Lithuanian.	1,340	8.84
Magyar.	244	1.61
Mexican.	375	2.47
Polish.	4,591	30.28
Russian.	100	.66
Scandinavian.	135	.89
Serbian.	67	.44
Slovak.	411	2.71
Slovenian.	14	.09
Spanish.	26	.17
Ukranian.	106	.70
Other European.	37	.24
Other.	9	.06
Not reported.	218	1.44

for residence and business purposes, 357 buildings used only for business, and 107 other buildings. The distribution of the population by nationalities in these 151 blocks canvassed is indicated in the accompanying table.

During the period from January 1, 1924, to January 1, 1927, all the districts investigated before 1920 were recanvassed. To the Local Community Research Committee this material was a valuable record of the housing problem of the poorer districts of Chicago in the first two decades of the twentieth century; and at the request of the directors of the survey, Miss Edith Abbott and Miss Sophonisba P. Breckinridge, assistance was given to enable them to have these districts revisited once more in order to record the post-war changes.

On a few points, notably rent, the districts that were canvassed for the first time during the period 1919–27 represented conditions that were very different from those of the pre-war canvass, but in the main the tenement-house provisions of the city ordinance remained unenforced and apparently unenforceable. In social legislation, it has been well said that "the life of the law lies in its enforcement." Housing standards as laid down in tenement-house codes may seem to be reasonably high. But when one turns from the printed ordinances to look at the houses in which the poor are actually living in Chicago, it is clear that the standards of housing tolerated and the standards of housing as set forth in the letter of the law are very different.

Along with the study of the tenements went the study of the people of the tenements and the population changes over nine decades as recorded by the United States Census. The areas selected were colonies of immigrants. An interesting, large-scale colored map was prepared showing the distribution of nationalities in Chicago at the close of the war; and a study was made of the various Polish communities, the Italian settlements, the Czech and Slovak colonies, the Ukranian settlements, the Jugoslav communities, Slovenians, Croatians, and Serbians, the White Russians, the Greeks, the Bulgarians, and the recent Mexicans. The history of the housing problem, or rather the various housing problems, of Chicago is traced back to the early days of the prairie metropolis. Nationality maps for the Hull-House area show the coming and going.

From time to time the studies have been put to practical use. Data have been presented not only to the Public Health Department but to committees of the City Council dealing with the tenement-house problem and with the location of parks and playgrounds. The taking over of one of the most congested blocks in the original Polish area for a small park known as Pulaski Park was due in part to the setting out of the congested conditions prevailing in that district. More recently one of the directors of the survey has served two important enterprises providing experiments in better housing, the Marshall Field Estate and the Julius Rosenwald Fund. A special report on various sites for improved housing development was prepared at the request of the Marshall Field Estate, and special data were also secured for the Rosenwald Fund in connection with the provision of model houses for Negro tenants.

II

Another series of inquiries carried by Miss Abbott and Miss Breckinridge that have yielded practical results are those dealing with the public welfare work in the state of Illinois and particularly in the Chicago region. This field has been considered very important, first, because of the questions of human welfare involved in the support of the dependent, delinquent, and defective members of the community, including, in the United States, the treatment of 350,000 insane in state hospitals, the care and education of 54,000 feeble-minded, the provision for nearly 600,000 prisoners, the methods of dealing with more than 200,000 children in the care of public institutions or agencies, the 50,000 deaf or blind, and an undetermined number of destitute and sick handled by outdoor relief officials and by other local authorities with little or no supervision from state boards or departments.

The subject is also important because of the great costs involved, recent estimates indicating that something more than $900,000,000 were expended by the state and local agencies of the United States in the field of social welfare, of which $150,000,000 was by central and $750,000,000 by local authorities. These costs are great so far as the taxpayer is concerned, but unfortunately in spite of the large expenditures they are either so inadequate or so unintelligently expended that the care of the "wards of the state" is neither humane nor scientific.

The outstanding problems in this field may be briefly summarized as follows:

1. *Questions of cost.*—The most interesting of these is the subsidy system. Little is known of its extent or the disadvantages suffered by the communities in which it exists. The actual costs of the public social services are unknown at the present time, and problems of cost accounting are involved in an attempt to determine them accurately. Problems of centralized purchasing and marketing are also involved. Questions of corruption and extravagance in administration are also important but difficult to analyze.

2. *Statistics of the public social services.*—Various problems are involved such as recording and reporting on the character and volume of work done. The practical outcome of a study of these problems, as well as those included in cost, should be the standardization of methods not only

for state boards and institutions but for local institutions as well. An adequate study in this field should ultimately be the basis for a national program. The United States Census, the United States Children's Bureau, and a Committee of the American Statistical Association are all interested in some parts of the work in this field.

3. *Personnel.*—Next to cost this is the most important problem in the field. The whole system of spoils politics is involved, and, more recently, the difficulties in the application of civil service methods to the public social services. The inefficiency of the personnel has for more than a century involved not only needless waste of the taxpayers' money but great human suffering.

4. *Interstate and what may be called "regional relationships,"* (a) where co-operation seems essential, for example, the Whitin plan of disposing of prison goods; (b) where there are essential or apparent conflicts of interest, for example, the ancient and still perplexing problem of "settlement" in the care of the destitute.

5. *Professional practices or techniques involved* in the scientific treatment of mental diseases, the education of the feeble-minded, prison administration involving the labor, educational, physical, and mental welfare of men and women in prisons and reformatories, methods of educating the deaf and blind, and also in the problems of centralized purchasing, cost accounting, direction of personnel, and institutional domestic management, e.g., dietetics, nutrition, etc., as well.

6. *The differences between law and practice in social legislation.*—It is always easier to have laws passed than to get them enforced. This is especially true in regard to legislation relating to the disadvantaged members of the community.

7. *The conflicts between local and state interests,* which are responsible, for example, for the continuation of incompetently managed county poorhouses and county jails, mothers' allowances on a county basis, etc., with no control by the state authority.

8. *Methods of study.*—Two methods were possible in selecting among these interesting topics and pursuing these inquiries: (a) the study of certain subjects, such as the problem of personnel, or the subsidy system, or the care of the blind, might be studied in all sections of the country; or (b) the study of all the problems found in a given state or region could be analyzed and set out.

The School began the study of *Public Welfare Administration in Illinois,* using the latter method, because, while it would be extremely interesting to study some one problem common to all our states, it was obviously too costly to be considered.

For several years the School of Social Service has been studying the problems involved in the administration of the various institutions and agencies dealing with the "three D's" in Illinois or in Cook County. The method has been to study the laws under which they were created, the development of the administration in relation to the social problems involved, and the conditions in the institution or agency at the present time with an attempt to measure them according to modern needs and modern standards. For only a few of these has help been given by the Local Community Research Committee, but a report of the administration of the oldest of the hospitals for the insane; of the institution for the feeble-minded; of the Illinois "Soldiers' Orphans Home"—an institution erected at the close of the Civil War by misguided benevolence to provide for the children, most of them *not* orphans of veterans, which has continued a wasteful and socially harmful existence on down to the present day, when it remains the sole provision of the state of Illinois for its dependent children —and a number of others have been completed or are near completion. *The Prison System in Illinois*, *The Pontiac Reformatory*, *The Prison Labor System*, and a report on *The Cost of the Public Welfare System of Illinois, 1909–1927* have been completed. At the present moment an attempt is being made to complete this series of studies by adding *A Study of the Illinois Poor Law and Its Administration*, *A Study of the Institutions of Cook County*, and *A Study of the System of Public Subsidies ot Private Institutions in Illinois*. A chapter from the subsidy study appeared in the June, 1929, number of the *Social Service Review*.

With reference to the county organization, the plan includes *Oak Forest*, the great almshouse and infirmary, housing about 4,000 persons at a time, the *Administration of the Blind Pension Fund*, and a study of *Relief-Giving under the Poor Law in Cook County outside of Chicago*. The plan for the Oak Forest study has contemplated several approaches. Records for the entire population of Oak Forest on December 1, 1928, have, for example, been copied, and this information, hitherto nowhere available although essential to any analysis of the population, will make known the age distribution in the institution, the sources of admission, and the physical condition of those admitted. It will reveal what groups Oak Forest contains and to what individuals the institution ministers.

A sufficient number of case histories has likewise been obtained to be illustrative of all the leading types within the institution as well as of certain features of the existing admissions system and certain deductions as to the times when alternative methods of care might have been substituted.

Study of the administration and of the buildings and their equipment has been continuous as has also been the consideration of Oak Forest in relation to the community and to other existing facilities for the care of the groups and types which find their way into Oak Forest.

Another interesting subject is that of relief-giving under the Pauper Law in Cook County outside Chicago. Attention should perhaps be called to the fact that the establishment of the County Welfare Bureau, which gives relief in Chicago under the Pauper Law, was greatly facilitated by an investigation made under the direction of the School in connection with the so-called "Advisory Committee." This study brings together the facts on which a sound county-wide plan can be based.

Interviews have been made with the thirty supervisors who give relieve under the Pauper Act, and the data obtained with reference to the amounts of money expended and the number of families aided. In addition to this, a study has been made of the conditions under which a considerable number of the families asked and received aid. The cordial co-operation has been secured of the county public health nurses and the Chicago Tuberculosis Institute nurses, both of whom now are under the general direction of the County Bureau of Public Welfare. Not only has an interesting body of data been obtained but a relationship has been established, it might be said, between the County Bureau of Public Welfare and the thirty independent relief-giving officials, so that a fair beginning toward a County Relief Service may be said to have been made.

III. THE PROBLEM OF DEPENDENCY AND DELINQUENCY AMONG YOUNG PEOPLE

With reference to the studies in this field attention should be called to the fact that they are in a sense a continuation of the studies that have already been published by the School of Social Service Administration and its predecessor, the Chicago School of Civics and Philanthropy. For example, there have been already published the results of investigation dealing with: the delinquent wards[1] and the truant wards of the Juvenile Court,[2] the administration of the Aid to Mothers Law in Illinois,[3] a study of the Juvenile Court in its other aspects,[4] a study of the Cook County Detention Home,[5] and a study of the treatment of delinquent children in Cook County and Illinois, which is ready for publication and will appear in the *Report of the Illinois Association for Criminal Justice.*

Recently at the request of the officers of the Juvenile Court sixty of the 186 odd justices of the peace and police magistrates who are supposed to hold court in Cook County outside of Chicago have been interviewed. A considerable number of the sessions of their courts have been attended, and information obtained especially with reference to their dealings with young offenders, with problems of domestic discord, and certain other aspects of their

---

[1] *The Delinquent Child and the Home*, by Breckinridge and Abbott, published by the Russell Sage Foundation.

[2] *Truancy and Non-Attendance in Chicago*, by Abbott and Breckinridge, published by the University of Chicago Press.

[3] *United States Children's Bureau Publication No. 82.*

[4] *United States Children's Bureau Publication No. 70, A Summary of Juvenile Court Legislation in the United States*, by S. P. Breckinridge and Helen R. Jeter; and *No. 104, The Chicago Juvenile Court*, by Helen R. Jeter.

[5] By Savilla Millis, published by the Board of Commissioners of Cook County.

jurisdiction which have special social significance. This study will be followed by further examination of the relation between the decisions of these justices as examining magistrates, the findings of the grand jury, and the decisions of the Criminal Court. With reference to these enterprises, it might be said that studies in the regional area have not been ignored. The effort of the School is, however, always to leave, if possible, as the result of their research a report which contributes to the knowledge of the situation and also a piece of good administrative machinery; and this, for the moment, does not seem practical in connection with areas outside of Cook County.

The studies now under way then have to do chiefly with the group of dependent children, and they are in part statistical and historical, and in part are being made after the method of experimentation. For example, a study of the use by the Juvenile Court of the so-called "Boarding Fund," which enables the Court to provide carefully selected foster-home care for any dependent or neglected child, is being carried on by one of the University Fellows, Miss Marian Schaffner, and by one of the Leila Houghteling Fellows, Donald Hartzel; but the Boarding Fund was especially important as applied to the care of the Negro children for whom no provision has been made in the past either along the lines of institutional care or of foster-home care, and this is the subject of a piece of co-operative experimentation made possible by a gift from the Rosenwald Fund, matched by the Local Community Research Committee, and making use of the funds granted to the Court for boarding purposes.

Along with the study of foster-homes has gone the inquiry into the care of other dependent children. As has been said, the only provision made by the state of Illinois for its dependent children is the old Home for Soldiers' Orphans established after the close of the Civil War, at Normal, Illinois. Miss Alice Channing, now of the United States Children's Bureau, made a study of this antiquated institution with help from the Committee; and that study may, it is hoped, be followed by some field studies at a later date.

On a smaller scale, there has been a series of studies made of the assignment of dependent children in Cook County to the institutions in Chicago and Cook County. This has been made possible in part through the organization of what is known as the Joint Service Bureau, and an analysis of the needs of these children is especially facilitated by a gift from the Community Trust to the Bureau, and by the Bureau to the Local Community Research Committee. The organization among the Jewish and Catholic philanthropic agencies was much closer than among Protestant and non-sectarian agencies, and the possibilities of effecting closer relationship among the latter group had never been studied. The combined results of these two pieces of work will serve to throw new light on the important problem of community organization in behalf of dependent children. Another aspect of the problem of dependency was dealt with in a study to which the Local Community Research contributed, of *The Illinois Adoption Law and Its Administration*, by Miss Elinor Nims, which has been published in the series of monographs by the School of Social Service Administration. And still another study bordering on the problem of dependency is a monograph published in the same series, made possible by contributions of the Rotary Club of Chicago, entitled *The Young Cripple and His Job*, by Marion Hathway. This report was the basis for both continued experimental work by the Rotary Club and of certain extensions of work by the Vocational Guidance Bureau of the Board of Education.

IV. STUDIES IN NEGRO LIFE

On all sides is recognized the importance of understanding the process of adjusting the Negro population to the conditions of a northern urban metropolis. Problems of many kinds arise from this adjustment and many groups are interested from various points of view, going back at least to the volume *The Negro in Chicago*, published after the race riots of 1919.

The Local Community Research Committee now is assisting five studies in Negro life, and in 1929–30 will add a sixth. These are: standards of living of the Negro population; placement of dependent Negro children; the Negro family; the Negro in business in Chicago; the Negro woman in Chicago industry; the Negro in politics.

The study of Negro standards of living is similar to Miss Houghteling's study of the standards of living of unskilled labor in Chicago. It is conducted under the supervision of Miss Abbott and Miss Wright, and will be completed in September, 1929.

The study of the placement of dependent Negro children was suggested by the Rosenwald Foundation and is a matched fund project, the Foundation offering $5,000 for a period of three years commencing in 1928–29. It is conducted in close contact with the county relief authorities and with private agencies, and is affording unusual opportunities to participate in and formulate policies for the direction of this function.

The study of the Negro family is also a co-operative project, being suggested to us by the Chicago Urban

League. It is now in its second year and is yielding satisfactory results. It is in charge of a Joint Committee representing the Urban League and the Local Community Research Committee.

The writing up of the materials on this study of the Negro family is now in progress. The study consists of an introduction to the fundamental problems of the Negro family in four parts. The first part, based upon published autobiographies, biographies, and documents, deals with the origin of the family in slavery and among the free Negro class that existed in this country almost from the time that Negroes were first introduced. The last chapter in this section gives a brief description of the development of the family since emancipation. Part II gives an analysis of available statistics on the Negro family in the United States. Part III is concerned with the Negro family in Chicago. Chapters in this section deal with the character of the Negro community; analyses and interpretation of census statistics on the Negro family for fifty-one census tracts; family disorganization represented in desertions, non-support, illegitimacy, and juvenile delinquency; the ecology of family disorganization and the relation of family disorganization to social classes. Part IV gives analyses of the processes of disorganization and the integration of the Negro family. An extensive classified bibliography has been worked out to accompany the study. Besides the Bibliography, the Introduction, Parts I, II, and several chapters of Part III have been written up. It is hoped the whole study will be completed some time during the summer quarter of 1929.

The study of the Negro in business in Chicago was interrupted a year ago when the research assistant went to Atlanta to participate in a study of the Negro in industry in the South. Upon his return in the spring of 1929 the study was resumed upon a matched fund basis with the Rosenwald Foundation, and will be concluded in September. It is supervised by Mr. Millis. Schedules for about four hundred Negro business-houses had been collected by June 30, 1929.

The study of the Negro woman in Chicago industry was interrupted during the year by illness, but has again been resumed and will be completed in the near future. It is conducted by Miss Alma Herbst and supervised by Mr. Millis.

Mr. Gosnell will initiate a study of the Negro in politics in the year 1929–30.

A joint committee to advise on the Negro studies has been created consisting of Mr. White, chairman, Miss Abbott, Mr. Millis, Mr. Gosnell, and Mr. Ogburn.

V. MISCELLANEOUS STUDIES

Among the miscellaneous studies to which attention might be called are those undertaken for the survey which preceded the building of the new County Jail. These were Miss Edith Abbott's resurvey of the statistics of crime in Chicago and Mr. Beeley's study of *The Bail System in Cook County*, which was a unit of the *Survey of the County Jail* made possible, in part, by the Community Trust; in part, by contributions from the School; and, in part, by the Local Community Research Committee. In this study Mr. Beeley attempted to work out methods by which the dependability of persons detained in jail because unable to furnish bail might be sufficiently ascertained to allow a selection of those prisoners who could safely be granted their freedom on their own recognizance. It is an interesting forerunner of Professor Burgess's later study, *The Pre-*

dictability of Success on Parole, and Dr. Sheldon Glueck's Massachusetts studies in the same field, which have been long under way and are discussed in the *Harvard Law Review* for January, 1929.

The Committee has contributed to the preparation of the case records of social agencies in Chicago for publication, which enabled the School to proceed with its program of making source material in this field available for careful study; four volumes of documents, two by Miss Abbott, *Immigration: Select Documents and Case Records* and *Historical Aspects of the Immigration Problem: Select Documents;* and two by Miss Breckinridge, *Family Welfare Work in a Metropolitan Community: A Series of Social Case Records* and *Public Welfare Administration: Select Documents,* have been published, a series of *Mental Hygiene Records from a Behavior Clinic for Children* are in preparation, and a series of *Medical Social Case Records* have been published.

The most important contribution, however, as has been said, is Miss Houghteling's scholarly and illuminating study, which has great interest from the point of view both of content and of method.

Studies of the work of women and children in the truck gardens of the region were published by the United States Children's Bureau,[1] *Work of Children on Illinois Farms,* and by the *Social Service Review;*[2] a *Study of the Juvenile Detention Home* was made for the Citizens Committee of the County Board and published by Mr. Cermak, the president of the Board; a "study of the work of one of the most successful committees providing scholarships for working children" was made at the request of the Committee, which

[1] *Publication No. 168.*   [2] I, 194.

wished an effective survey of their work to determine its value after fifteen years of continued service;[1] and the Helen Crittenden Memorial Fund asked for a study of the *Chicago Social Service Exchange,* the results of which have also been made available by publication in the series of "Social Service Monographs."

Another small but interesting piece of work undertaken under the supervision of the School is an inquiry into the history of the development of the Illinois law governing the status of women. Illinois is one of the states in which the idea of equality for married women was embodied at an early date in legislation. Those responsible for this legislation held the view that equality of rights meant equality of responsibility. There are many points, such as independent domicile, separate citizenship, statutory heirship, etc., on which neither the women nor the lawyers are unanimous. Before undertaking an ambitious nation-wide inquiry the National League of Women Voters thought a small exploratory inquiry might be illuminating, especially in view of the very wide interest in the subject of family problems today. A small gift from the League matched by the Committee is being used to trace (1) the attitude of the courts, (2) the sources of agitation for change, (3) the general response of the legislature, (4) the present administration of some of the more important portions of the law. It is hoped that the activities of the state and local League may be given perhaps a more constructive social character in this particular field.

[1] Esther Ladewick, *Scholarships for Children of Working Age, Social Service Monograph, No. 6.*

CHAPTER XII

SOCIAL SCIENCE RESEARCH AND THE COMMUNITY

Social science research offers many tangible benefits to the community, as the foregoing chapters have made apparent. Countless others will no doubt flow from the projects outlined in this book as understanding further proliferates into control. But there remains for deserved emphasis a hitherto largely neglected advantage of social science research—the intrinsic significance of social understanding itself. Only when a man comes to himself does he become a man. So also when a community calls upon itself and finds itself at home, it acquires in the persons of its members the dignity of self-consciousness; it becomes then material for art as well as for science. Contrary to the popular impression of science as cold-blooded, scientific research is the surest way to sustained imaginative warmth and appreciation. Particularly would this be true of a science social in intent as well as in content.

Social science at its best is indeed both scientific and social: it exemplifies an analytic technique for the isolation of elements and a clairvoyance for the whole dissevered through analysis. It is science in that it deals with change, dissecting it into processes. It is social in that it seeks to maintain the sense of community and indeed to further it, through the scientific technique. In concluding the description and evaluation of the Local Community Research Committee's work at the University of Chicago, let us by elaborating this distinction emphasize the significance for the community of the resulting self-consciousness and appreciation.

I

In the modern city more perhaps than anywhere else on earth, as Mr. Park has suggested,[1] is present in condensed, rapid, observable form the social mobility that makes fruitful research possible. Natural science arose when the heavens and the earth, from being static and sacred, were conceived to be dynamic and secular. Science is made likewise possible in the social field by such changes as psychologically impel attention and invite control. Curiosity has been described as the mother of natural science. Gossip might be said to be the mother of social science; for gossip is the easy way to celebrate changes already transpired and to make two events grow where but one grew before. Justice Oliver Wendell Holmes has distinguished philosophy from gossip in terms of background; social science may, in like mood, be distinguished from gossip in terms of exactitude and disinterestedness. The exactitude renders it science, the disinterestedness renders it social. A more systematic word upon types and levels of change may help to clarify the relation between the University as research center and the community as laboratory.

There is, first, the type of change that is just change. It represents the lowest level. Geology and astronomy reveal a background for biology which makes the past tenure of all life only a moment in the eons of our earth. Change that knew nothing of itself nor, for all the evidence that we have, was known anything of, went on nevertheless. Change that is just change is in no sense, however, restricted to inanimate nature. Bodily development from infancy is largely unconditioned by consciousness. The basic

[1] Robert E. Park, "The City as a Social Laboratory," *supra*, pp. 1 ff.

muscular and glandular processes of the most canny scientist go on without his yea or nay. What is true of both nature and man as individual seems to be equally true of men in groups. Social processes are real, and they go on whether we as individuals will it or even know it. Not that we may not know it and that our knowing may not make a difference. Where it can and where it cannot make a difference is for science to inquire: and the wise scientist will respect his material whether it reveals him potent or impotent. But it is well for us to see that knowledge alone does not condition the fact of change. A full recognition of this simple fact would cure the community of that naïve, and oftentimes pathetic, notion that all we have to do to keep things as they are is to let them alone. No social status quo can ever be maintained by doing nothing. If one genuinely wishes to stay where he is in a stream, he must swim—upstream. Most social change of the past has gone on quite as unknowingly as has geological change in nature, and that which has been known has been known generally when it was too late to do anything about it.

Then there is the change that is known as it transpires. It represents the second level. Natural and social processes do come to consciousness. Gossip, as has been suggested, is the ancient method of keeping in contact with social processes while they are going on. The daily newspaper serves a similar purpose on a large scale. The self-conscious person and the socially sensitized can be cognizant of a tremendous amount of change approximately while it is happening. That this enlargement of cognizance marks progress in the vocation of being human is certain. The limits of cognizance are not prescribed and certainly have not yet been reached. Such consciousness of change demands, however, no special knowledge of the past; it may occur largely divorced from preoccupation with the future. To know that change is happening while it is happening is certainly an advance over not knowing it at all; but so to apprehend change is certainly not science. At worst it is gossip, at best artistic narrative.

Not only is it not science; it is not even human merely to watch the passing show. Human beings have interests in change, preferences for outcomes. Our reach directs our grasp, else what's our reaching for? Knowledge itself is at least partially motor rather than merely contemplative: to know is to cast the weight of one's vital reserves in favor of something, against something.

It is, then, this change which may be foreknown that constitutes the third type. It is this, of course, with which we are most intimately concerned. For it is in the possibility of so understanding social data and forces as to previse change that there lies the hope of human improvement. When men know what is going to happen before it happens, then in many cases it need not happen at all, unless desired. This is the fate "which," as Shakespeare says, "happily foreknowing may avoid." Prevision, however, implies postvision, and both imply much more vision than the ordinary man has or can get by ordinary means. Common sense and lay intuition, even though feminine, have reached their limit of social cognizance. Research is the community's emancipation from immediacy and unexpectedness. This emancipation, however, comes hard: it tests both the wit and will of men; it requires the invention of new methods of understanding, new tools of analysis; it implies new views of human nature, new theories of education, new conceptions of government; it demands a type of character that must be created in the process; and it promises personal and social rewards unique in quality, challenging in prospect. Such knowledge of the community's life and changes is science. How to turn this knowledge, as it accumulates, to count for the sake of community is a major problem for a social science that has matured into responsibility.

This is doubly difficult because of the very technique of science. Science is analytic. It does not grasp things as a whole. Thus to know things is, at the low level, common sense; at the high level, mysticism. Neither of these is science. Scientific clarity in the social field, as elsewhere, comes from the tearing apart of elements that go to make a community. Whatever control arises from this method of understanding is also logically and likely piecemeal; and from such control some parts of the community profit more than others, and not infrequently at the expense of others. A historical glance will set this difficulty into relief.

Pari passu with the growth in modern times of natural science there came into effective action a revolutionary political philosophy—a doctrine of the contractual origin of government for the protection of individualistic rights. This theory of government passed over into a legal notion that social change to be legitimate must arise from a meeting of minds in contract. Contract requires a consideration, a *quid pro quo*, in which only the interests of the contracting parties are of direct concern. To be sure, the state in imposing the conditions of contract is presumed to safeguard the interests of the community; but the state in turn is itself, according to the theory, the result of a contract in which not community, but private interests, were the direct desiderata. Early political science and even later economic theory have suffered not merely from an atomistic methodology borrowed from natural science but also from atomistic assumptions regarding the nature of the state and, in the sequel, other institutions as well. Not that the common welfare, not that community, were not regarded as good; but no machinery had evolved for aiming at these goods directly, no machinery indeed except individualistic interests.

At the best, it was hoped that these communal interests in being ignored would be furthered. It was indeed more than hope; it was also trust. Was there not an "invisible hand" that brought social good out of honest self-seeking? There was, of course—as long as basic religious and moral assumptions remained undisturbed by the spirit of science whose ravages they were to repair. But this was not for long. The spirit of science led to discoveries, to technologies, to methods of controlling and exploiting nature. The advantages that came from these went to the strongest, or to the first on the ground, or to the craftiest. And the social sciences that had borrowed their methods from, and shared their assumptions with, natural science had no distributive wisdom with which to meet the exploitative efficiency of applied science. As soon as natural resources became property, they became private property; and law existed to sanction, and government to protect, private property. As Blackstone had it: "So great, moreover, is the regard of the law for private property, that it will not authorize the least violation of it; no, not even for the general good of the whole community." It is clear that against such odds, any theological agency was likely to be as ineffective in preserving community interests as it was invisible in its operation. "Each man for himself and the devil take the hindmost"—this was the bravado of early industrial optimism; but the impotence of this optimism left the maxim eventually to become a sardonic epitaph for those who aimed at but did not enter the promised land.

If one wishes further evidence of the disintegrative effect of this analytic approach to life, let him consider the view of art that grew popular in the nineteenth century and has persisted into the twentieth. What natural science practiced and social science assumed, the artist bodied forth as a philosophy of life. Walter Pater concluded in *The Renaissance* that the "love of art for art's sake" is the truest wisdom, "for art comes to you professing frankly to give nothing but the highest quality to your moments as they pass, and simply for those moments' sake." The justification Pater gave for generalizing this atomism into a philosophy of life was that science, as it was commonly understood, had decomposed the whole world into discrete atoms out of which consciousness must get its materials, "unstable, flickering, inconsistent."[1] With artists and literary men, like Pater, to make accessible to everyone what scientific men regarded as fundamental and politicians a raison d'être of states, the atomistic view came to prevail in life as it had prevailed in nature and politics.

Now the nineteenth century was a period of unprecedented population growth in the West and the age of the expansion of cities. The modern cities were naturally, therefore, the communities that suffered most from a natural science (social science corroborating) that permitted power to fall into the hands of the strong, or of the crafty, or of the lucky; and an art and a philosophy that detached each moment's flickering consciousness of each of these detached human elements and made it its own mean-

[1] Cf. Walter Lippmann, *A Preface to Morals*, chap. vi, for a more complete orientation of this philosophy of art. I am indebted to Lippmann for the suggestion.

ing and reward. If rights are natural and inalienable, if unto God the things that are God's, if art for art's sake, then business is business and capitalism is purged. The Gold Coasts and slums of cities survive to become the material and to constitute the problem of social science come of age. It may well be argued indeed that law and the state exist not more to safeguard the visible interests common to contracting parties than the invisible welfare common to all those affected by the remote consequences of contracts as well as by non-contractual forms of conduct.[1] To say the least, genuine social science should not in straining for scientific exactitude wholly forget the need for solicitude. Its interest in community welfare will become, as between conflicting elements, disinterestedness. To see social science research over any fair perspective is to discover that the community has as vital an interest in this aspect of social science as in the characteristics of exact knowledge and efficient control; for the question will ever recur: Who control whom for what?

II

One way of seeing what, in this larger sense, the community may expect from social science research is to make clear what such research does for those who pursue it as a vocation. To adopt this procedure in assessing the contribution of social science is unusual, but may be allowed to be judged upon its merits. We may without compunction devote ourselves to this general inquiry here, because the concrete advantages of social research have already been so well indicated, directly and indirectly, in preceding chapters. As Miss Jeter has said regarding the empirical

[1] John Dewey, *The Public and Its Problems* (New York, 1927), has indeed based a whole theory of the rise and function of government and law upon this conception.

method of population prediction, so with regard to social science itself as method, "Confidence in the method becomes largely a matter of confidence in the person applying the method."[1] As we extend the perspective from the five years envisaged in this volume to all the years brightened by the prospect of the new laboratory at the University of Chicago, the truer does Miss Jeter's remark become. Far more true than for natural science is it that what social science can do for a community depends upon what the community thinks of social scientists. And what it thinks, we may well believe, will depend upon what they are. We may fool all the people part of the time, and part of the people all the time, but not all the people all the time. What qualifications have social scientists for such community control as, fortune favoring, long and genuine research will bring?[2]

What qualifications they have for this heavy responsibility may be assumed to come from their work. We begin with a general prevision of what their work does for them, then pass to a more specific consideration of the explanatory conditions under which they work, and at last summarize what they can contribute by dedicating themselves with their vocation to the community. Accurate knowledge of social data certainly has value as a propaedeutic to inner contentment. It has often been claimed, and truly enough, that the study of astronomy carries great personal satisfaction. It shows one his place in the vast universe: it deflates his pride, but also gives him a sense of being a part of an encompassing system which he may contemplate in

[1] *Supra,* chap. v.

[2] It may relieve the other contributors to this volume of any embarrassment and the author of this chapter of immodesty, if he here state that he is *in* but hardly *of* the group. They are scientists who do the work, he a philosopher who talks about it.

its majestic motion. To know has its first great advantage
in making the knower at peace with things. "To know," as
Aldous Huxley has said, "is pleasant; it is exciting to be
conscious." Knowledge purges fear, that greatest corrupt-
er of peace, and it furnishes a means whereby the soul may
objectify itself. This certainly is no more true of natural
than of social knowledge. We are indeed a part of the
world of nature, but in society we live and have our very
being. To objectify one's self upon social data is, therefore,
more difficult for the very nearness, but also more mean-
ingful when achieved. To lose ourselves in the very processes that constitute ourselves certainly has eventual advantages. No more truly and literally are our bodies com-
pounded of chemical and physical elements than our minds
are molded of social and cultural patterns about us. Social
science, particularly at the University of Chicago,[1] has already taught us that. The oldest human wisdom—already
old enough when Western Europe was young, to be in-
scribed as a Delphic maxim—is self-knowledge. What is
not old, however, is the realization that self-knowledge
cannot be got by social nescience, by withdrawal from the
world. That way, as we now know, lies contraction and
eventual atrophy. Self-knowledge comes only from understanding the social factors that constitute the self. If to
know all is to forgive all, as the French proverb has it, then
from intuition of the social pattern revealed in research one
may expect not merely a mind wise in its own ways, en-
larged in scope, and purged of its sharpest biases, but also
a personality enriched in sympathy. So much their subject matter contributes to social scientists.

Even more is contributed by the setting of their work.

---

[1] See Harold D. Lasswell's account, *supra*, of the social psychology that
forms the background of the Chicago research group, chap. x.

The social science research fostered by universities—to which we confine our attention for the moment—is almost invariably carried on by, certainly always in the atmosphere of, teachers. Now with all their well-known debits, teachers are not noted for any mercenary or highly competitive spirit. More than perhaps any other research profession in the modern world, they are expected to, and largely do, keep their eyes off such wealth as is competitive. Working for a modest salary, with a limit easily reached, and not likely to be indefinitely expanded, they come to work with their eyes fastened more upon the community than is likely to be true of any other class. This is but to repay in kind the community's interest in them. They have been educated wholly or partly at community expense, are subject to an unusual surveillance by the community, and get their modest incomes from community or philanthropic funds. They are remarkably well prepared to be disinterested in dealing with social materials. In the modern world of industry and finance, but not of it, they are prepared to be observers without more than a minimum bias due to material expectancy. If disinterestedness constitutes, as suggested, a major criterion for social science, then the research that goes on in such a setting as is here envisaged, is likely to be social as well as scientific.

Not that all research upon social problems is found in universities; not by any means. Industrial concerns that but yesterday awakened to the necessity of carrying a charge for pure science are today adding to their scientific staff psychologists, economists, and other students of human and social processes. The tendency in this direction is in all probability hardly more than well begun. Such research activity may and will uncover valuable data. It is science when carefully done; but it is not social science, in

the honorific sense here given to the term; for it aims not at
general welfare, except by attribution; but rather at private gain. It need not be, and seldom is, downright anti-
social. It may indeed, and usually is, social in outcome;
but in primary intent it is non-social. It is an appendage of
business competition and must be made to produce financial gain. The social pattern involved breaks off in someone's pocket, and must resume again with someone's
scheme for further profit.

In the University, however, the atmosphere is such that
disinterestedness is as natural a response to community
problems as it is to the secrets of nature, where in the same
sort of environment no one thinks of profiting personally
from discoveries that net millions to those who exploit
them. And yet the disinterestedness of the university re-
searcher is not lack of interest; it is wholeness of interest
rather than fragmentary bias toward profit as goal. A
purely aesthetic attitude might indeed show as much interest in a strike as in its settlement, as much in a war as
in peace, as much in pathological personalities as in normal
ones. But the teacher does not have purely an aesthetic
interest: enough of public spirit has gone into his training
to make such complete moral neutrality unlikely. His motive will be found in that which is largely independent of
economic categories. While he may not have genius for following into execution such ideas as arise for community
betterment, he nevertheless will be vitally concerned in
whatever aims to set up or maintain the generalized forms
of peace and welfare. Sufficiently detached and aesthetic
in attitude to organize his own life around a vision of social
unity, and thus secure for himself inner peace, he will be
sufficiently implicated in common concerns as to work

against whatever disrupts the community and thus disturbs his own personality synthesis.

So much for the conditioning fact that our social scientist is a teacher. What is equally important, where true, is such an organization of research as makes knowledge easily communicable and enthusiasm contagious. So much is to be known, and needs to be known, about the community's life that no one man can become competent upon more than a fraction of any given field. But if specialists can be thrown fruitfully together so that they make a community while studying one, they supplement each other's knowledge, they reinspirit each other's morale, and they make of each a center for understanding the whole. Such organization of even social research has been rare. It is the realization of this ideal of organization in the new laboratory at the University of Chicago[1] that raises hope of increasingly fruitful work among this group. Francis Bacon's *New Atlantis* has descended upon the Quadrangle at Chicago: "The end of our foundation," as Bacon said of his, "is the knowledge of causes and secret motions of things; and the enlarging of the bounds of human empire, to the effecting of all things possible." A whole community pictured in the mind of each scientist in co-operation with many like-minded colleagues and an interest in maintaining the inner picture as a prized object through preserving its objective counterpart furnish an ideal for research in the community that measures up to the highest human aspiration.

III

Indeed if, as one passes from the research organization itself into the community, one seek a single statement for the contribution that the former might make to the latter,

---

[1] See White's description of the laboratory, *supra*, chap. ii, p. 1 ff.

it may be said that research can contribute to the community nothing else so good as this attitude of mind in all citizens. To say so might well be thought to be the pathetic fallacy of an academic mind, projecting its own standard of excellence into the community at large. There is no doubt not only a place for, but also a necessity for, action that surpasses in vital force the mild activity of the academician. To know is not all that is needed; but it is the basic need for community welfare. It is natural for the research man to believe that nothing could be better for the community than to generalize the conditions that beget his own preoccupation. But even if this belief be well founded, as we shall argue, before it could be made effective a connecting link must be found between those devoted to pure research and those with engineering minds who order the business of the day and bring to pass whatever of the dream is workable in the world of affairs. The community needs nothing else so much as men who, even though they themselves be not scientists, can understand science and adapt its results to community needs.

Fortunately, the university can itself contribute something toward this need also. Its contribution is found on the educational side of its function, as contrasted with the purely research side. As educators, research workers come constantly in contact with those who before they have gone far into research will quit the academy and go into active service in the world of affairs.

This contact with students is the social scientist's constant reminder of the habits, the prejudices, the occupations, the aspirations of the community, which all together go to make up his data as a scientist. A representative student group—and a wise university will seek to keep its students representative—is the community in miniature.

It is, however, more amenable to change than is the community itself. It is the future community caught in the act of becoming. The plasticity of youth reflects the dynamic aspects of community life as the inflexibility of age betrays its static aspects. Present to be taught and developed, students keep academic research workers ever hopeful of effective improvement through social understanding. Present, moreover, in occupational and cultural variety, at a time while cultural prejudices and conflicts of economic interests are both at a minimum, they thrust upon the scientific mind the just claims of all interests and furnish it also with a social norm in the self-regarding joy of a co-operative enterprise.

So much they do to the social scientist. He, in turn, discovers to them their individual capacities, sensitizes them more or less to his way of looking at things, to his goals, to his incentives, and sends them back into the larger community with pride in what they have to give. What they have to give makes for change, but for change in the direction of the goals the scientist envisages. The end, however, of a community in which all interests are recognized and adjusted, to which the scientist himself may in his isolation leap at once, the students as citizens must approach through means furnished by the community itself, which resists change in the name of fixed interests and established classes. In order to give his own creative capacity to the community, the student must get a living from the community; and in order to do this he must fit himself occupationally and emotionally into pre-existing molds. The goals glimpsed in the laboratory grow dim in the market place and progress toward the goals, here logical and rapid, becomes there slow and uncertain. But the effect does not wholly disappear. So far as it remains, higher education is justified by its children. Technological efficiency can perhaps be learned short of the university—in trade schools or in industrial apprenticeship. But along with each method goes a certain type of mind. If, as Professor Alfred North Whitehead has said, there is in the immediate future "to be less security than in the immediate past, less stability," then we must face the fact that, as he further observes, "the fixed person for the fixed duties who in older societies was such a godsend, in the future will be a public danger." The open mind for change, the sensitization for new situations so much called for by a complex civilization in which new class interest arises and must be accommodated—this develops most fruitfully away from the smoke of battle, in an atmosphere of disinterested research. It is almost certain that the community has much more to gain from education done in a research atmosphere than done outside such an atmosphere.

Once developed, this interest in the community as a whole remains to be awakened by evolving situations in society itself or restimulated by ever more accessible reports upon social researches. Citizens educated in an atmosphere of research become thus the outposts of science in its efforts to be of service to the community. They become leaders in their own right, and in their leadership they reflect a spirit of conciliation that comes from understanding that no interest has an unconditional claim save that of the community as a whole. They become organizers and entrepreneurs in their own right and reveal in their functions the basic wisdom which treats morale as the key to industrial efficiency and social good will. They become professional practitioners and reveal an ability to follow superior insight no less than to lead those who grope more than they. As they have been youthful representatives of the community to the university, so they become thus sometimes in ways seen, sometimes in ways obscure, its representatives to the community. What they represent peculiarly—better, that is, than can those technologically skilled in the occupations themselves—is the disinterestedness that makes skill and exactitude into social science. Given such a liaison, what more than their mind perpetuated in fellow-citizens can scientists contribute to the community?

IV

The first and obvious answer to that question can be had better by looking about one than by reading a book. The results of science are on every hand. The power, the convenience, the luxury that puts, according to some estimates, at every elbow the power equivalent of a half-hundred slaves—these are what science, natural and social, have contributed to the community. But what has social science itself contributed? It has contributed statistics and all that goes with that ingenious and exact method of measuring and recording human interests and change. Methodological improvement is the major thing thus far contributed. Change can do little for us, except make us victims, until we are able to observe it. But observing it, we can do little to control it, until we can measure it. And, consequently, the emphasis we have put, and must continue to put, upon refining old methods of observing and measuring, of inventing new methods, of applying both old and new in new territories to see what further modifications are necessary for a growingly universal social mensuration. We must believe, with Plato, that "the art of measurement would do away with the effect of appearances, and, showing the truth, would fain teach the soul at last to find rest in the truth, and would thus save our life." But unless the way of acquiring this desideratum and the specific results that grow out of its application make men whom the community will trust either to wield power or expertly to advise those who do wield power, social science will either leave the community where it is or harm it.

Whatever of culture, of art, of religion, of science men get independently of the job at which they make their living is dependent upon leisure; and leisure is itself the result of both natural and social science, though its distribution is largely the result of social science. The older social order allowed the leisure to be appropriated by the few. But leisure is now progressively passed around to all classes of the population in proportion either to the general discernment of their rights in relation to their utility, or to their power as asserted in organization with or without recognition of rights. It is of course this wresting from an unwilling community of increased leisure or other rights that social engineering on a scientific basis might supplant by just adjudication. Indeed increased industrial arbitration preceded by increased participation of workers in profits and control indicates already the ripening fruits of social intelligence. It is not too much to say that industrial clashes and even international warfare can be avoided, if at all, only by the temper that social research fosters. The most far-reaching if not also the most basic thing here is the progressive capitalization into rights of the interests of as yet unrecognized classes. The majority of men have yet to enter into anything like the privileges of civilization. Their interests involve crucially the welfare of the community because from sheer number they constitute the major part of the community.

It is growingly clear, however, that number in itself is not an ultimate category for humanity. Quantitative research eventuates as emphasis upon quality of life. Less than ever before need a community be a sheer victim of excessive population. The more or less covert application of the by-products of scientific research has already called attention to the beneficence of population control by actually controlling it in part. The creation of power by natural science makes it necessary for social science to adjust population intelligently to machine production and agricultural fertility.

An optimum population rather than a haphazard population, be the latter maximum or minimum, is one of the larger goals of social intelligence. The largest goal, to which the population question is a major means, is such appreciation of the needs of classes and such knowledge of social causation as will lead to a complete institutionalization of the principle of revolution—a progressive and peaceful adjustment of conflicting interest-claims functioning as rights. Social harmony as the final goal of social science can permit progress only by being conceived as a moving equilibrium. Further reasons for believing that the scientific mind is the longest step toward, and the greatest factor in, this eventuation will be given below. For the moment we have sought to get clear the larger type of hope that moves at the heart of the social science enterprise. While scientists themselves often give the impression of indifference as to uses made of their methods and techniques, it is not unfair to say that, since scientists are also men, these humane hopes are more compatible with a science that is social than with any thorough-going indifferentism. The major part of the energy that goes into the scientific movement derives directly or indirectly from such hopes as have been here sketched.

V

It is much for men to know what they want; it is more for them to know how to get what they want; but it is the last stage of wisdom for them to learn how to want what they eventually get. The first marks the level of common sense; the second marks the level of science; the third marks the level of philosophy. That the satisfaction of the wants of men constitutes the meaning of life and the basic criterion may here be assumed. In so far as one departs from this assumption as standard, one rationalizes the wants of some special class of men into specious pre-eminence. In learning this, philosophy differentiates it-self from theology. In accepting this, social science prevents itself discriminating against common-sense classes in the name of some unthought-out philosophy. For social science to see its problem, when it rises above mere means as it will in moments of reconnaissance, as that of adjusting interests—repressing none, sublimating the minimum, satisfying the maximum—is for it to achieve a solid ethical orientation.[1]

Knowing both that human wants lead initially to inventions of means of satisfaction and that they also temper themselves eventually to the means available, the social scientist who is philosophically inclined is likely to see in an aesthetic attitude toward social data a means, on the one side, of socializing wants and, on the other side, a compensation for what is lacking of complete satisfaction. The end-result of any improvement from social science or elsewhere will be an improved state of mind in human individuals. If the scientist has found happiness in a way of life that requires a modicum of possession and permits a maxi-

---

[1] Walter Lippmann has presented in *A Preface to Morals* (New York, 1929) a striking picture of one such ethical orientation for the man of science.

mum of creation, it is natural for him to think that his greatest contribution is after all dissemination of his way of looking at things. What is more, he is demonstrably right. Human happiness cannot be achieved in such distributed fashion as to be an all-community asset merely by emphasizing the acquisitive ideal, because the competitive spirit cannot be satisfied by having less than the other fellow nor by having an equal amount but only by having more. It is demonstrably impossible for every man to have more than the other fellow, even if it could be proved the way of happiness. The creative ideal on the other side makes happiness possible with equal goods and does not make it impossible with less possession than the other fellow, if there be compensations for economic disparity. If one cannot through differential possession reap power and prestige, one's happiness must be found in understanding rather than in power.

VI

It should now be clear why we have elected to dwell upon the way social science affects its devotees. We have done so because of two factors, without either of which we cannot communicate the spirit of the enterprise to which this volume is devoted. The first is that science *is* a way of life to the scientist; it is a way of life that realizes the maximum of happiness for him; it is a way of life for which recruits must constantly be made if its career is to prosper; and it is a way of life with such superior claims upon human attention that it need only be understood to be appealing. Not least of the preoccupations of those who direct the social laboratory at the University of Chicago is, as we have seen, this one of the continuous renewal at ever higher levels of ability of those who carry on the work. Connected with this is the belief that the best way to

equalize the competition between business with its visible
lure of money and power, and science as a vocation without
personal wealth and with little show of power is to call the
attention of an industrial civilization to the rôle played by
social intelligence even in the business man's life. Now
social intelligence is, of course, not all shut up in laboratories. The business man has it in the field of his success. The
lawyer has it in the field of his success. Every citizen has
it in so far as he adds to the name citizen the functions of
citizenship. Its possession is a matter of degree, and it is
self-rewarding in so far as possessed. To make men self-
conscious of the portion they do possess and cognizant of
its rôle in their personal lives is to encourage its increase
among men, and this in turn is to facilitate by educational
evolution what historically has been generally achieved by
revolution, if at all—an economical adjustment of group
claims through the discovery by them or for them of some
common interest. If social knowledge possesses in any
measure what we have claimed for it in high measure, it is
clear that it is a virtue of citizenship and should be distributed as far as is humanly possible. One way after all to
get a harmonious society is through the development of
peaceable men.

The other factor that impelled us to emphasize the
character result of social research is the fact that its personal benefits to the specialist do not stay locked up in his
specialism. We have indicated that a mastery of social
data not merely enlarges the mind and reduces its prejudices but promotes also a growth of sympathy. From
the latter quality social understanding tends strongly to
pass into reform through the power that knowledge constitutes. The latest social scientist is much like the first
great one in this respect: when peace has been won through

contemplation of a completed pattern, the heart is stirred by the recognition that the pattern is instinct with human life and hope. Then comes the impulse, now as in Plato's day, to forsake the peace of contemplation for the disquietude of the cave where fellow-men stumble unoriented to the light. The social scientist is so remade through the process of getting his knowledge that he cannot easily regard the knowledge as something for its own sake. He must share it with his community.

> But thou wouldst not *alone*
> Conquer and come to thy goal,
> Leaving the rest in the wild.

In so far as he has mastered his community as data and reduced its changes to descriptions, his opinion as to policies is superior to the opinions of less well-informed citizens. Results of tendencies, consequences of proposed actions, he will be able to foresee with at least some measure of probability. In telling men what are the means to their ends, he will be indispensable as an expert. He may have at times, also, to correct sophistication by reminding them that the ends of life for all alike are just common experiences that all prize, plus the rare experience that comes from achieving one's own good in such way as to facilitate the same quest on the part of others.

Developing thus through unbiased devotion to community a non-economic interest in economic processes, a non-competitive interest in competition, academic researchers may dependably be expected to become interested in the community for its own sake, in it as a variegated and absorbing pattern of multiform forces. Let a man in a calm moment sit down and paint in imagination the diverse elements that go to make a community—the physical habitat, the housing, means of transportation, the back country, different interests that form themselves into groups—social, economic, religious, political, educational motifs all woven into the picture. Then let him animate this passive canvas with the pains and fatigues, the throbbing passion, the pulsing ambitions, the concealed inferiorities, the vaunted superiorities, the acclamation, and the resentment that vivify the group life of man. Touch the picture to pathos with children playing in crowded streets. Such a man will feel in greatly expanded form the fascination that captivates the onlooker at a horse race or a partisan at a football game as the senses feast upon the colors and scents and expectancies fused into a complex whole. If he then endow this picture of a community with a local habitation and a name, with memories, with the pride of possession, and a challenge to willing sacrifice, he will understand the aesthetic motif in social research. One who gets this vision for the first time will have found a day up to which will slope in significance all other days of his life and down from which, if he cannot maintain it, will slope all subsequent days. The social scientist is he who has achieved and can maintain with some consistency this aesthetic interest in some actual community.

VII

To see thus in imagination the diverse patterns that go to make up a human community is to become socialized intelligently. This is not the only type of socialization. One may be socialized emotionally. This is the historic type. But as the Chinese in the legend could not have roast pig until the house was burned down, so historically men have experienced the finest human thrill of apprehending a community only when it was in danger of dissolution by war, by famine, by insurrection.[1] It was the imminent ravage of the Holy City, until one stone would not be left upon another, that led Jesus into his touching apostrophe to Jerusalem. It was the nadir of internecine disaster, the presence of honored dead, and the sobs of the bereaved that led Pericles into his immortal eulogy of Athens.

Since the vitality of communities is not sufficient to maintain continuous menaces to themselves, men have experienced the community but rarely. Normally they have lived for themselves and for very small groups. It may be said indeed that the problem of creating a large, secular community and maintaining it in beauty and health depends upon a method of achieving in times of peace and prosperity the appreciation of community that men have traditionally felt only in time of war and disaster. What is true of one's country is even more true of cities. For cities are not often threatened with destruction from within; and when they are threatened from without, the nation rather than the city becomes the object of solicitude. What loyalty does arise for a city, however, comes from sources similar to war. Chicago assumed a certain majesty in citizens' hearts through the Haymarket Riot and the Great Fire. It is very difficult to get such response from constructive episodes, though some pride was awakened in Chicago by the World's Fair and the same promises to be true also of the Century of Progress. If the imagination could be stirred by persisting peaceful factors as it is by intermittent and precarious ones, then the problem of good government and happy citizenship would be solved together. Men will not stand to see polluted a thing that they love.

[1] For fuller development of this point, see George H. Mead, "National-Mindedness and International-Mindedness," *International Journal of Ethics*, XXXIX (July, 1929), 385–407.

Mere disciplining of the imagination is not enough, however, to make a community a constant aesthetic object. The imagination builds its eidola of what it knows most intimately. The natural scientist most frequently describes his preoccupation, from the moon to the atom, in terms of a quest for beauty. If men are to enshrine the community in their affections through imaginative appropriation of it as a gorgeous pattern, they must be trained in apprehending, comprehending, and manipulating the social processes that go to make it up. To see only its parts is to be willing to squander its resources; to see it as a community is to wish to preserve and enjoy it. Only those who see the community impartially can see it whole. Others when they look at the community will see only their labor union, or their business, or their family. The scientific observer, if fortunately associated with others whose total knowledge includes all its parts, will himself come to sense it as one process. Wholeness of vision is what lends aesthetic enchantment. When violence alone gives a sense of the whole, then violence serves a great ethical purpose. But it is a poor artist who can paint no other scenes than those of carnage. With the imagination disciplined to see the community in all its interactions, the community can become an object of priceless appreciation in peace as well as in conflict.

With the acquisition of such prestige, the city can reap its share of patriotism. The city is not intrinsically inferior to the nation in soliciting the admiration of men. Historically, it has been superior. The first community above the family that challenged the attention and love of men was the city. This first secular love of men will be at the end of civilization as it is at the beginning of the word itself. Materially, the city is the superior social object. In it men have achieved the fullest control yet achieved over the environment of their daily lives. Refrigeration and central heating almost at last subdue even the weather. Burdens are lifted by machinery, work is made compatible with cleanliness, luxuries become necessities, and man at last masters his physical fate. Socially, the city offers undreamed-of variety. No want of man for which it does not offer some satisfaction.

> Something to see, by Bacchus, something to hear at least!
> There, the whole day long, one's life is a perfect feast.

Moreover, the city specializes in the business of creating new wants. Creative work, infinite amusement, increasing leisure; and then, lest its excellencies cloy, occupational insecurity for many, clattering noise for all, lurking selfishness, corrupt administration of common affairs. The city is the place where men have at least created the content of good living; the full form of it awaits readier intelligence and completer co-operation.

This fact constitutes not merely, as has already been indicated, a deep motivation for so directing change as to relieve the city of its evils, but also motivation for making the city through complete understanding of it an object of sensitive appreciation and of moral devotion. To the man who knows enough to survey its total processes, imagination becomes a storehouse of unending delight. For every citizen so trained, his city will become a Jerusalem and into the folds of imagination he will in fair weather, as well as foul, gather her as a hen gathers her chicks under her wings. With the vision of her complexity, her gaiety and pathos, her resources and potentialities for improvement, his own city may become to every citizen what Athens was to Pericles:

Our laws secure equal justice for all in their private disputes, and our public opinion welcomes and honours talent in every branch of achievement, not for any section of reason but on grounds of excellence alone. And as we give free play to all in our public life, so we carry the same spirit into our daily relations with one another. We have no black looks or angry words for our neighbour if he enjoys himself in his own way, and we abstain from the little acts of churlishness which, though they leave no mark, yet cause annoyance to whoso notes them. . . . . Yet ours is no work-a-day city only. No other provides so many recreations for the spirit—contests and sacrifices all the year round, and beauty in our public buildings to cheer the heart and delight the eye day by day. . . . . We are lovers of beauty without extravagance, and lovers of wisdom without unmanliness. Wealth to us is not mere material vainglory but an opportunity for achievement; and poverty we think it no disgrace to acknowledge but a real degradation to make no effort to overcome. Our citizens attend both to public and private duties, and do not allow absorption in their own various affairs to interfere with their knowledge of the city's. . . . . Let us draw strength . . . . from the busy spectacle of our great city's life as we have it before us day by day, falling in love with her as we see her, and remembering that all this greatness she owes to men with the fighter's daring, the wise man's understanding, and the good man's self-discipline in its performance.

For such a city men will die in time of need; but, greater the achievement, for her they will live in uneventful times. Their riches gained at her expense become ashes; her unification and completion, their success and pride. The only way to live thus in the presence of a soul-growing and self-rewarding community is so to have comprehended her parts that one can continuously present her as a whole to himself. Social science research has as its first result this presentation to the scientist and as the final result the creation in all citizens of an appreciation of the community in its wholeness and beauty.

APPENDIX I

LOCAL COMMUNITY RESEARCH PUBLICATIONS

BOOKS AND MONOGRAPHS

ABBOTT, EDITH. *Historical Aspects of the Immigration Problem: Select Documents.* "The University of Chicago Social Service Series." Chicago: University of Chicago Press, 1926. Pp. xx+881.

————. *Immigration: Select Documents and Case Records.* Chicago: University of Chicago Press, 1924. Pp. xxii+809.

BAKER, N. F. *The Legal Aspects of Zoning.* "Materials for the Study of Business." Chicago: University of Chicago Press, 1927. Pp. xii+182.

BECKNER, EARL R. *A History of Labor Legislation in Illinois.* Social Science Studies No. XIII. Chicago: University of Chicago Press, 1929.

BEELEY, ARTHUR. *The Bail System in Chicago.* Social Service Monograph No. 1. Chicago: University of Chicago Press, 1927. Pp. xi+189.

BEYLE, HERMAN C. *Governmental Reporting in Chicago.* Social Science Studies No. X. Chicago: University of Chicago Press, 1928. Pp. xxiii+303.

BRECKINRIDGE, SOPHONISBA P. *Family Welfare Work in a Metropolitan Community: Selected Case Records.* "The University of Chicago Social Service Series." Chicago: University of Chicago Press, 1924. Pp. xvii+938.

————. *Medical Social Case Records: Submitted in the 1927 Case Competition of the American Association of Hospital Social Workers.* Introduction by Sophonisba P. Breckinridge. Social Service Monograph No. 3. Chicago: University of Chicago Press, 1928. Pp. xi+176.

————. *Public Welfare Administration in the United States: Select Documents.* "The University of Chicago Social Service Series." Chicago: University of Chicago Press, 1927. Pp. xxiii+786.

WILLIAMS, DOROTHY, AND SKINNER, MARY E. *Work of Children on Illinois Farms.* United States Department of Labor, Children's Bureau, Bulletin No. 168. Pp. 48.

Chicago Civic Agencies: A Directory of Associations of Citizens of Chicago Interested in Civic Welfare, 1927. Published for the Public Affairs Committee of the Union League Club of Chicago and the Local Community Research Committee of the University of Chicago. Social Science Studies No. VI. Chicago: University of Chicago Press, 1927. Pp. viii+315.

DUDDY, E. A. *Agriculture in the Chicago Region.* Social Science Studies No. XV. Chicago: University of Chicago Press, 1929.

FRYXELL, F. M. *The Physiography of the Region of Chicago.* Social Science Studies No. V. Chicago: University of Chicago Press, 1927. Pp. viii+55.

GOODE, J. P. *The Geographic Background of Chicago.* Social Science Studies No. III. Chicago: University of Chicago Press, 1926. Pp. xi+70.

GOSNELL, H. F. *Getting Out the Vote: An Experiment in the Stimulation of Voting.* Social Science Studies No. IV. Chicago: University of Chicago Press, 1927. Pp. ix+128.

HATHWAY, MARION. *The Young Cripple and His Job.* Social Service Monograph No. 4. Chicago: University of Chicago Press, 1928. Pp. xiv+130.

HOUGHTELING, LEILA. *The Income and Standard of Living of Unskilled Laborers in Chicago.* Social Science Studies No. VIII. Chicago: University of Chicago Press, 1927. Pp. xvii+224.

HUGHES, E. A., AND STUENKEL, F. *The Social Service Exchange in Chicago.* Social Service Monographs No. 8. June, 1929. Pp. xiii+115.

JETER, H. R. *Trends of Population in the Region of Chicago.* Social Science Studies No. VII. Chicago: University of Chicago Press, 1927. Pp. xv+64.

JOHNSON, CLAUDIUS O. *Carter Henry Harrison I: Political Leader.* Social Science Studies No. XI. Chicago: University of Chicago Press, 1928. Pp. xiii+306.

LADEWICK, ESTHER. *Scholarships for Children of Working Age.* Social Service Monographs No. 7. May, 1929. Pp. xi+104.

MERRIAM, C. E., AND GOSNELL, H. F. *Non-Voting: Causes and Methods of Control.* Social Science Studies No. I. Chicago: University of Chicago Press, 1924. Pp. xiii+287.

MILLIS, S. *The Juvenile Detention Home in Relation to Juvenile Court Policy: A Study of Intake in the Cook County Chicago Juvenile Detention Home.* Published by the Citizens' Advisory Committee on the Cook County Juvenile Detention Home. Pp. 96.

MONTGOMERY, R. E. *Industrial Relations in the Chicago Building Trades.* "Materials for the Study of Business." Chicago: University of Chicago Press, 1927. Pp. xi+340.

MOWRER, E. R. *Family Disorganization: An Introduction to a Sociological Analysis.* "The University of Chicago Sociological Series." Chicago: University of Chicago Press, 1927. Pp. xvii+317.

NIMS, ELINOR. *The Illinois Adoption Law and Its Administration.* Social Service Monograph No. 2. Chicago: University of Chicago Press, 1928. Pp. xvi+127.

PALMER, VIVIEN M. *Field Studies in Sociology: A Student's Manual.* Social Science Studies No. XII. Chicago: University of Chicago Press, 1928. Pp. xix+281.

PARK, R. E., AND BURGESS, E. W. *The City.* "The University of Chicago Studies in Urban Sociology." Chicago: University of Chicago Press, 1925. Pp. xi+239.

PARK, ROBERT E. Chapter I, "Sociological Research," in the volume *Social Science Research*, edited by Wilson Gee (article based on Chicago local community research studies). (In press.)

Parole and the Indeterminate Sentence: The Workings of the Indeterminate-Sentence Law and the Parole System in Illinois. Report to Honorable Hinton G. Clabaugh, chairman, Parole Board of Illinois by the Committee on the Study of the Workings of the Indeterminate-Sentence Law and of Parole in the State of Illinois. August, 1928. Pp. i–vii; p. 277. Part I, "The History and Development of the Parole System in Illinois," by Andrew A. Bruce, pp. 3–63; Part II, "The Workings of the Parole Board and Its Relation to the Court," by Albert J. Harno, pp. 67–120; Part III, "Parole and Rehabilitation of the Criminal," by John Landesco, pp. 123 201; Part IV, "Factors Determining Success or Failure on Parole," by Ernest W. Burgess, pp. 205–68.

Region of Chicago Base Map. Chicago: University of Chicago Press, 1926.

RHOADES, E. L. *The Chain Store and the Packing Industry.* "Studies in the Packing Industry." University of Chicago Press, 1929. Pp. 31.

————. *The Management of Chain Meat Markets.* "Studies in the Packing Industry." University of Chicago Press, 1929, Pp. 28.

Chain Stores and the Independent Meat Retailer. "Studies in the Packing Industry." University of Chicago Press, 1929. Pp. 16.

SCHULTZ, H. *Statistical Laws of Demand and Supply with Special Application to Sugar.* "Materials for the Study of Business." Chicago: University of Chicago Press, July, 1928. Pp. xix+228.

STALEY, EUGENE A. *The Illinois State Federation of Labor.* Social Science Studies No. XVI. Chicago: University of Chicago Press. (In press.)

THRASHER, F. M. *The Gang: A Study of 1,313 Gangs in Chicago.* "The University of Chicago Studies in Urban Sociology." Chicago: University of Chicago Press, 1927. Pp. xxi+571.

WARNE, C. E. *The Consumers' Co-operative Movement in Illinois.* "Materials for the Study of Business." Chicago: University of Chicago Press, 1926. Pp. xiv+420.

WHITE, LEONARD D. *The City Manager.* Social Science Studies No. IX. Chicago: University of Chicago Press, 1927. Pp. xvii+355.

————. *Conditions of Municipal Employment in Chicago: A Study in Morale.* Submitted to the City Council of the City of Chicago, June 10, 1925. Published by the Press of John F. Higgins. Pp. 114.

————. *The Prestige Value of Public Employment in Chicago.* Social Science Studies No. XIV. Chicago: University of Chicago Press, 1929.

WIRTH, LOUIS. *The Ghetto.* "The University of Chicago Sociological Series." Chicago: University of Chicago Press, 1928. Pp. xvi+306.

WOLF, H. D. *The Railroad Labor Board.* "Materials for the Study of Business." Chicago: University of Chicago Press, 1927. Pp. x+473.

WOODDY, C. H. *The Chicago Primary of 1926: A Study in Election Methods.* Social Science Studies No. II. Chicago: University of Chicago Press, 1926. Pp. vii+299.

ZORBAUGH, HARVEY W. *The Gold Coast and the Slum.* "The University of Chicago Sociology Series." Chicago: University of Chicago Press, 1929. Pp. xv+287.

ARTICLES

BURGESS, ERNEST W. "The Determination of Gradients in the Growth of the City," *American Sociological Society,* Vol. XXI (1927).

————. "What Social Case Records Should Contain To Be Useful for Sociological Interpretation," *Social Forces,* Vol. VI, No. 4 (June, 1928).

————. "Residential Segregation in American Cities," *Annals of American Academy of Political and Social Science.* Philadelphia (November, 1928), pp. 1–11.

BURGESS, ERNEST W. "The Changing American Family," in *Religious Education*.

————. "Is Prediction Feasible for Social Work?" *Social Forces*, VII (June, 1929), 533–45.

————. "Family Tradition and Personality Development," in *Proceedings of the National Conference of Social Work* (1928), pp. 322–30.

————. "The Family and the Person," in *Personality and the Social Group*, edited by E. W. Burgess (Chicago, 1929).

————. "The Use of Census Data in Local Community Studies," in *Proceedings of the National Conference of Social Work* (1928), pp. 634–37.

COLSON, MYRA HILL. "Negro Home Workers in Chicago," *Social Service Review*, II, No. 3 (September, 1928), 385–413.

DOUGLAS, P. H. "Wages in 1928," *American Journal of Sociology*, May, 1929.

DUDDY, E. A. Published in *American Elevator and Grain Trade*, October, November, and December, 1928: "The Grain Elevator Capacity of the United States and Its Regional Distribution", "The Use of Elevator Space as Determined by Operating Efficiency Ratios";"History of Elevator Capacity and Location in the Chicago Market."

————. Published in *Distribution and Warehousing*, October, November, and December, 1928: "Regional Distribution of Public Merchandise Warehouse Space in the United States"; "History of Public Merchandise Space and Location in the Chicago Market"; "History of Household Goods and Furniture Storage in Chicago, with Factors affecting Plant Location."

FRAZIER, E. FRANKLIN. "The Negro Community, A Cultural Phenomenon," *Social Forces*, VII, 415–20.

————. "The Negro Family," *Annals of the American Academy of Political and Social Science*. CXL (November, 1928), 44–51.

GOSNELL, H. F. "Characteristics of the Non-Naturalized," *American Journal of Sociology*, XXXIV (March, 1929), 847–55.

LASSWELL, HAROLD D. "The Problem of Adequate Personality Records: A Proposal," *American Journal of Psychiatry*, VIII (May, 1929), 1057–66.

LELAND, S. E. "The General Property Tax," *National Real Estate Journal*, October 1, 1928, pp. 21 ff.

————. "The Scientific Assessment of Land," *ibid.*, October 29, 1928, pp. 46 ff.

————. "Valuing Buildings for Taxation," *ibid.*, November 12, 1928, pp. 25 ff.

LELAND, S. E. "Real Estate Taxation in Foreign Countries," *ibid.*, January 7, 1929, pp. 64 ff.

———. "Separating the Sources of State and Local Revenue," *ibid.*, February 4, 1929, pp. 44 ff.

———. "The Classified Property Tax," *ibid.*, March 4, pp. 48 ff.; April 1, 1929, pp. 36 ff.

———. "Theories Underlying the Use of Special Assessments," *ibid.*, April 15, 1929, pp. 94 ff.

McMILLEN, A. W. "A Registration Area for Social Statistics," *Journal of the American Statistical Association*, XXIV, No. 165, 68–69.

McMILLEN, A. W., AND JETER, H. R. "Statistical Terminology in the Field of Family Welfare," *Social Service Review*, II, No. 3 (September, 1928), 357–84.

———. "The Results of a First Year's Program for the Central Registration of Social Statistics," *Journal of American Statistical Association*, XXIV, No. 165–A, 174–79.

MONK, A. T., AND JETER, H. R. "The Logistic Curve and the Prediction of the Population of the Chicago Region," *Journal of American Statistical Association*, December, 1928.

SAPIR, E., ASSISTED BY BLOOAH, C. G. "Some Grebo Proverbs," *Africa*, II, No. 2 (April, 1929), 183–85.

———. "Rational Economics," *American Economic Review*, December, 1928.

THURSTONE, L. L. "A Mental Unit of Measurement," *Psychological Review*, Vol. XXXIV, No. 6 (November, 1927).

———. "Three Psychophysical Laws," *Psychological Review*, Vol. XXXIV, No. 6 (November, 1927).

———. "Psychophysical Analysis," *American Journal of Psychology*, XXXVIII (July, 1927), 368–89.

———. "Psychological Examinations for College Freshmen," *Educational Record*, April, 1927.

———. "Theory of Attitude Measurement," *Psychological Review*, XXXVI, No. 3 (May, 1929), 222–41.

———. "An Experimental Study of Nationality Preferences," *Journal of General Psychology*, I, Nos. 3 and 4 (July-October, 1928), 405–25.

———. "Fechner's Law and the Method of Equal-Appearing Intervals." *Journal of Experimental Psychology*, XII, No. 3 (June, 1929), 214–24.

———. "Attitudes Can Be Measured," *American Journal of Sociology*, XXXIII, No. 4 (January, 1928).

THURSTONE, L. L. "Measurement of Opinion," *Journal of Abnormal and Social Psychology*, Vol. XXII, No. 4 (January-March, 1928).

———. "The Unit of Measurement in Educational Scales," *Journal of Educational Psychology*, November, 1927.

———. "Norms for the 1927 Psychological Examination," *Educational Record*, April, 1928.

———. "The Phi Gamma Hypothesis," *Journal of Experimental Psychology*, Vol. XI, No. 4 (August, 1928).

———. "The Absolute Zero in Intelligence Measurement," *Psychological Review*, Vol. 35, No. 3 (May, 1928).

WHITE, LEONARD D. "Morale and Prestige Values in Public Employment," *International Journal of Ethics*, XXXIX (April, 1929), 257–68.

LOCAL COMMUNITY RESEARCH STUDIES COMPLETED BUT NOT PUBLISHED

ABBOTT, EDITH. Housing and Population in Chicago.

ANDERSON AND BROWN. The Case of Abraham Bernstein.

ARNOLD, L. Development of the Book to 1880.

BARROWS, E. Extent of Trade Union Organization among Women in Chicago.

BIGHAM, T. C. Chicago Federation of Labor.

BLAINE, LOUISA. A Problem in the Chicago Milk Market.

BROWN, E. Chicago Typothetae.

CARMICHAEL, LILLIAN. Street Trades in Relation to Juvenile Delinquency in Chicago.

CHANNING, ALICE. The Illinois Soldiers' Orphans' Home.

CLARKE, HELEN I. Uniform Areas for City-Wide Agencies.

COLE, FAY-COOPER. The Archaeology of Jo Daviess County.

COLSON, MYRA. Homework Among Negro Women in Chicago,

CONWAY, PAUL. The Apartment House Dweller: A Study of Social Changes in Hyde Park.

CRESSEY, PAUL G. The Closed Dance Hall in Chicago.

DANKERT, CLYDE. The Furniture Industry in the United States as Shown by the Census Reports 1849–1925.

DAVIS, ELIZABETH. State Institutional Care of Feeble Minded in Illinois.

DINSMORE, J. C. Investigation of Purchasing Methods in Use by Chicago Charities.

Douglas, P. H. Measuring the Movement of Real Wages for 1926–28.

Duddy, E. A. The Warehousing Industry in Chicago.

Duflot, J. L. A Social Psychological Study of the Failing Student in High School and College.

Dummeier, E. Marketing of Pacific Coast Fruits in Chicago.

Dunn, Margaret. Jane Addams as a Political Leader.

Ellis, L. E. Chicago Delegation to Congress.

Evans, Louis E. Pontiac Reformatory.

Ferebee, E. E. Agricultural Implements Industry.

Ficek, Karel F. Milk as a Type Case of Social Control.

Freund, R. Begging in Chicago.

Glick, Clarence Elmer. Winnetka: A Study of a Residential Suburban Community.

Graham, Irene. Negroes in Chicago, 1920; An Analysis of United States Census Data.

Hayner, N. S. The Hotel: The Sociology of Hotel Life.

Himan, Elizabeth. The Study of the Chicago and Cook County School for Boys.

Hoijer, Harry. The Causes of Primitive Warfare.

Hosford, B. Study of Protestant Orphanages in the Chicago Region.

Ireland, W. R. P. The Study of the Process of Americanization among Polish Young People in a Settlement Neighborhood.

Irwin, Merle. The Study of Outdoor Relief under the Pauper Act in Cook County outside of Chicago.

Kahn, J. United States Rubber Supply.

Kresinova, Miroslova. The Knit Goods Industry.

Leland, S. E. A Report on Certain Aspects of the Tax Situation in Illinois.

Liebtag, G. A Statistical Analysis of the Petroleum Refining Industry.

Lieffer, M. H. The Boys' Court of Chicago.

Magee, M. Manufacture of Women's Wear in Chicago.

Maynard, David M. The Referendum in Chicago.

Maynard, William Simpson. The Use of Prisoners' Labor and the Disposition of Prison-Made Goods in Illinois State Institutions.

McGill, H. E. Land Values, an Ecological Factor in the Community of South Chicago.

McKinney, Madge. Certain Characteristics of Citizens.

McReynolds, Cora Seville. The Training and Placement of the Adult Handicapped Worker in Chicago.

MOORE, COYLE E. Cost and Administration of Public Welfare in Illinois 1904–25.

MYERS, EARL D. Juvenile Delinquency.

MYERS, HOWARD B. The Policing of Labor Disputes in Chicago: A Case Study.

MYERS, ROBERT JAMES. A Statistical Account of the Development of the Men's Clothing Industry.

NELSON, JEAN THOMAS. A History of the Policy of the United States toward Naturalized Citizens Abroad.

O'DONNELL, CYRIL. The Lumber Industry.

OGBURN, W. F. Fertility According to Occupations and Social Classes.

———. Ranking of Different Influences in the Last Presidential Election.

———. Variability in Birth-Rates in Different Civilizations.

PALMER, DWIGHT L. Some Social and Business Aspects of Storage.

PALMER, J. Cook County Survey of Market Research Data.

PRAEDAHL. Theory of Plant Location (translation).

RAUBER, EARLE. The Place of Power in Civilization.

RECKLESS, W. C. The Natural History of Vice Areas in Chicago.

RICH, E. A. Heart Disease Mortality in Chicago.

RIGG, STERLING F. Janitors' Union.

———. Milk Wagon Drivers' Union.

ROBINSON, T. H. Chicago Typographical Union No. 16.

SANDERS, W. B. The History and Administration of the State Prisons of Illinois.

SCOTT, CHESTER. The Study of Juvenile Delinquency and Recreation in a Settlement Neighborhood.

SCHULTZ, HENRY. The Statistical Law of Demand and Henry L. Moore's Contribution to It.

SHAPIRO, DENA EVELYN. Indian Tribes and Trails of the Chicago Region: A Preliminary Study of the Influence of the Indian on the Early White Settler.

SHAW, CLIFFORD. Juvenile Delinquency.

SNIDER, HYLA. Development of Methods of Food Preservation.

SORRELL, LEWIS CARLYLE. Transportation and Traffic in Industry.

STEADMAN, ROBERT FOSTER. Protection of Public Health by Governments in the Region of Chicago.

STEPHAN, F. F. Public Recreation in Chicago.

———. Some Social Aspects of the Telephone.

STONE, URSULA BATCHELDER. The Baking Industry with Special Reference to the Bread-baking Industry in Chicago.

STRATTON, HERMAN J. Factors in the Development of the American Pottery Industry, 1860–1929.

TIBBITTS, R. C. Immigrant Groups in Chicago.

———. Social Forces and Trends in Settlement Neighborhoods.

TOWNSEND, A. J. The Germans in Chicago.

WEAVER, A. J. The Organization and Dissemination of Market News in the Grain Trade.

APPENDIX II

ADAMS, MARY FAITH (Mrs. Charner M. Perry), Assistant Registrar, University of Texas, Austin, Texas.

AITKENS, JAMES, Research Assistant, University of Chicago.

ANDERSON, CLARENCE, O.

ANDERSON, NELS, Assistant Professor of Sociology, Seth Low Junior College.

ARNOLD, LUELLA (Mrs. Victor Kaufman). Instructor in Commercial Subjects, Northeastern High School, Detroit, Michigan.

BARROWS, EMILY (Mrs. Harold N. Weber), formerly Instructor of Economics, Wellesley College, Wellesley, Massachusetts.

BATCHELDER, URSULA (Mrs. R. W. Stone). Research Assistant, School of Commerce and Administration, University of Chicago.

BECK, NORMAN, Instructor in Political Science, University of Missouri.

BECKNER, EARL R., Associate Professor, Department of Economics, Butler University, Indianapolis, Indiana.

BENJAMIN, GRACE, Probation Officer, Cook County Juvenile Court, Chicago.

BEYLE, HERMAN, Assistant Professor of Political Science, Syracuse University.

BIGHAM, T. C. Assistant Professor of Economics, University of Arkansas.

BITTERMAN, HENRY J., Instructor, Department of Economics and Business Organization, Ohio State University, Columbus, Ohio.

BOLTON, WENDELL H., Research Assistant, Department of Economics, University of Chicago.

BROWN, CARROLL, Instructor, Harrison Technical High School and Commerce and Administration Department, American School, Chicago, Illinois.

BROWN, EMILY CLARK, Assistant Professor of Economics, Wellesley College, Wellesley, Massachusetts.

BROWN, WILLIAM O., Assistant Professor of Sociology, University of Cincinnati, Cincinnati, Ohio.

BRYAN, MALCOLM H., Assistant Professor of Economics, University of Georgia.

BURKE, WILLIAM, Assistant Professor, Graduate School of Social Service Administration, to be Associate Professor at Washington University, St. Louis, Missouri.

CARMICHAEL, LILLIAN, Case Worker, Juvenile Protective Association, Chicago.

CARTER, W. P., Acting Assistant Professor of Sociology, University of Missouri, Second Semester, 1927, 1928.

CHAMBERLAIN, VELL B., Research Assistant, Department of Economics, University of Chicago.

CHANNING, ALICE, Assistant Director, Child Labor Division, Children's Bureau, Washington, D.C.

CHRISTENSEN, ALICE, N.

CHRISTENSON, CARROLL R., Assistant Professor of Economics, Lewis Institute, Chicago, Illinois.

CHURCHILL, ROGER.

CLARKE, HELEN I., Assistant Professor of Sociology, University of Wisconsin.

COCHRANE, MARY ELIZABETH, Research Assistant, Local Community Research.

COE, VIRGINIUS F., Research Assistant, Johns Hopkins University.

COLSON, MYRA HILL (Mrs. H. A. Callis), Instructor, Tuskegee Institute, Alabama.

CONWAY, PAUL, Graduate Student in Law, Harvard University.

COOK, LLOYD, Assistant Professor of Sociology, Kansas State Teachers College, Emporia, Kansas.

CRAVEN, IDA, Editorial Assistant, *Encyclopedia of the Social Sciences*, Fayerweather Hall, Columbia University, New York City, New York.

CRESSEY, PAUL F., Instructor in Sociology, University of Chicago.

CRESSEY, PAUL G., Assistant Professor of Sociology, Evansville College.

DANKERT, CLYDE E., Graduate Student, Department of Economics, University of Chicago.

DAVIDSON, C. B., Wheat Pool, Winnipeg, Manitoba, Canada.

DAVIDSON, PHILIP G., Professor of History, Agnes Scott College, Decatur, Georgia.

DAVIS, ELIZABETH, Psychiatric Social Worker, South Side Child Guidance Clinic, Chicago, Illinois.

DUFLOT, JOSEPH L., Professor of Sociology, Texas State Normal College, Canyon, Texas.

DUMMEIER, E. F., Professor and Head of Department of Economics, Washington State University.

DUNN, MARGARET. (Deceased.)

ELLIS, ETHAN L., Assistant Professor of History, Rutgers College, New Brunswick, N.J.

ELRICK, SUSAN (Mrs. R. F. Posanski).

ENGLE, ROBERT H., Assistant Professor of Marketing, Purdue University, Lafayette, Indiana.

ERRANT, JAMES W., Assistant Professor of Political Science, University of Oklahoma.

EUBANK, CHARLES, Director of Personnel Research, Kimberly-Clark Company, Neenah, Wisconsin.

EVANS, LOUIS EARL, Director, Joint Service Bureau, Department of Child Placing, Chicago.

FEREBEE, E. E., Assistant Professor of Commerce and Administration, Washington and Lee University, Lexington, Virginia.

FOLEY, C. C., Business, Seattle, Washington.

FORTHAL, SONYA, Research Assistant, University of Chicago.

FOSTER, JR., SCHUYLER, Instructor in Political Science, Ohio State University.

FRAME, BENJAMIN H., Assistant Professor of Economics, University of Missouri.

FRANK, J. L.

FRAZIER, E. FRANKLIN, Research Secretary, Chicago Urban League.

FREUND, H. ROGER, Secretary, Committee on Under-Privileged Boys, Y.M.C.A., Detroit, Michigan.

GIVIN, GRACE. (Alabama.)

GOETZ, ROGER, Auditor, Plibrico Jointless Fire Brick Company, Chicago, Illinois.

GRAHAM, IRENE, Research Assistant, Graduate School of Social Service Administration, University of Chicago.

GREEN, LORRAINE, Member Research Committee, Chicago Urban League.

GROBBEN, MARGARET, Graduate Student, Department of Economics, University of Chicago.

HABER, S. L.

HAHNE, E. H., Associate Professor of Economics, School of Commerce, and Assistant Dean, College of Liberal Arts, Northwestern University, Evanston, Illinois.

HALFANT, DAVID M. (Deceased.)

HANSON, VICTOR, Professor of Political Science, Shanghai College.

HATHWAY, MARION, Instructor in Sociology, University of Washington, Seattle, Washington.

HATHORN, J. B., Instructor in Education, Sam Houston State Teachers College, Huntsville, Texas.

HERBST, ALMA, Instructor in Economics, Ohio State University.

HERRICK, MARY J., Chicago Public Schools.

HEWETSON, H. W., Professor of Economics and Business Administration, Kansas Wesleyan University, Salina, Kansas.

HIRSCH, ELIZABETH, Case Worker, Jewish Social Service Bureau, Chicago.

HOIJER, HARRY, Research Assistant, University of Chicago.

HOSFORD, BERTHA (Mrs. Arthur P. Butler), Director Joint Service Bureau, of the Protestant and Non-Sectarian Child-Caring Agencies of Chicago.

HUGHES, EVERETT, Assistant Professor of Sociology, McGill University.

IRELAND, W. R. P., Research Assistant, Local Community Research.

JENKINS, HARRY P., Research Assistant, Department of Economics, University of Chicago.

JOHNSON, C. O., Professor of Political Science, Washington State University.

JOURNEY, ROCKWELL CRESAP, Professor of Economics and Sociology, Alma College, Alma, Michigan.

KINNEY, LEILA, Investigator, United States Children's Bureau.

KNOWLTON, HORACE, Special Investigator, Purchasing Agent, University of Chicago.

LADEWICK, ESTHER, Case Worker, Jewish Social Service Bureau, Chicago.

LANDESCO, JOHN, former Field Research Worker in Illinois Parole Study and Research Director of Study of Organized Crime (Illinois Association of Criminal Justice); Research Director Organized Crime Survey, Local Community Research Committee and Institute of Criminal Law and Criminology.

LAWRIE, ELINOR, Assistant, Medical Social Service Department, University Clinics, University of Chicago.

LAVES, W. H. C., Assistant Professor, Political Science, Hamilton College.

LEIFFER, MURRAY H., Assistant Professor of Sociology, Garrett Biblical Institute, a Member of Research Staff, Chicago Church Survey.

LIEBTAG, CARL FERDINAND, Investment Analyst, Down-Town Office, University of Chicago.

LIND, ANDREW W., Assistant Professor of Sociology, University of Hawaii, and Member of Research Group in Race Relations.

LUESSING, MARGUERITE.

MACAULEY, ROBERT.

MacGILL, HELEN E. G. (Mrs. Everett Hughes).

MAGEE, MABEL, Assistant Professor of Economics, Wells College, Aurora, New York.

MAYNARD, DAVID M., Professor of Political Science, Lake Forest College.

MAYNARD, WILLIAM S., Probation Office, Cook County Juvenile Court, Chicago.

McKINNEY, MADGE, Assistant Professor, Political Science, Hunter College.

McREYNOLDS, CORA S. (Mrs. William S. Miller), formerly Vocational Adviser, Bureau of Vocational Guidance, Board of Education, Chicago.

McREYNOLDS, ROSS A., Statistician, National Metal Trades Association, 1021 Peoples Gas Building, Chicago, Illinois.

MERTZ, ALICE (Mrs. Henry Miller), Visitor, New York Charities Aid Association, New York City.

MILLIS, SAVILLA (Mrs. V. D. Simons), Research Assistant, Local Community Research Committee, University of Chicago

MONTGOMERY, ROYAL E., Associate Professor of Economics, Cornell University, Ithaca, New York.

MOORE, COYLE E., Associate Professor of Sociology, Florida State College for Women.

MONROE, DAY, Assistant Professor, Home Economics, University of Chicago.

MYER, MAURICE B., Junior College, Arkansas City, Kansas.

MYERS, EARL D., Assistant Professor of Social Economics, Graduate School of Social Service Administration, University of Chicago.

MYERS, HOWARD B., Chief of the Bureau on Statistics and Research, Illinois Department of Labor.

MYERS, ROBERT JAMES, Assistant Professor of Economics, Grinnell College, Grinnell, Iowa.

NELSON, JEAN THOMAS.

NIMS, ELINOR, Assistant Professor of Sociology, University of Kentucky, Lexington, Kentucky.

NORCROSS, CARL.

O'DONNELL, CYRIL, Instructor in Economics, De Paul University, Chicago, Illinois.

PALMER, DWIGHT, Research Department, Bullocks Store, Los Angeles, California.

PARRATT, SPENCER D., Research Assistant, Local Community Research.

PEARSON, RUTH, Teacher, High School, Chicago, Illinois.

PERKINS, CAROLINE, Member of Board of Control for the Feeble-Minded, Faribault, Minnesota.

PHILIP, WILLIAM B., Professor of History, Bradley Polytechnique Institute, Peoria, Ill.

RAUBER, EARLE L., Research Assistant, Department of Economics, University of Chicago.

REDFIELD, ROBERT, Assistant Professor of Anthropology, University of Chicago, Social Science Research Council Fellow.

REICH, NATHAN.

REILLY, WILLIAM JOHN, Associate Professor of Business Administration, University of Texas, Austin, Texas.

RIGG, STERLING F., Research Assistant, Department of Economics, University of Chicago.

RISCH, ERNA, Research Assistant, Local Community Research.

ROBERTSON, PEARL, High School, Bozeman, Montana.

ROBINSON, THOMAS HOBEN, Assistant Professor of Sociology, Colgate University, Hamilton, New York.

ROBISON, GEORGIA, Fellow in History, Columbia University.

ROPER, MARION WESLEY, Kansas State Teachers College, Professor of Sociology, Emporia, Kansas.

ROYSE, J. B., Instructor in Economics, Crane Junior High School, Chicago.

RUSSELL, DANIEL, Professor of Sociology, Agricultural and Mechanical College of Texas.

SANDERS, WILEY B., Professor of Sociology, University of North Carolina.

SCHMIDT, JOHN W.

SCHUMAN, FRED, Instructor in Political Science, University of Chicago; and Fellow Social Science Research Council.

SCHWEINITZ, DOROTHEA DE, Research Associate, University of Pennsylvania.

SCOTT, CHESTER, Staff Worker on Research Institute of Juvenile Research.

SETTERLUND, ELMER, Professor of Sociology, Kansas Wesleyan University.

SHAW, CLIFFORD, Sociologist, Chicago Behavior Research Fund.

SHOCK, NATHAN W., Research Assistant, University of Chicago.

SMITH, MARIAN B., Social Worker, South Side Child Guidance Clinic, Chicago.

SNIDER, HYLA, Instructor, Frances Shimer School, Riverside, Illinois.

STALEY, A. EUGENE, Social Science Research, Fellowship, 1929–30.

STEADMAN, ROBERT F., Assistant Professor of Political Science, Syracuse University.

STEPHAN, FREDERICK F., Assistant Professor of Sociology, University of Pittsburgh.

STRATTON, HERMAN J., Professor and Head, Department of the Social Sciences, Illinois College, Jacksonville, Illinois.

STUENKEL, FRANCELIA, Instructor of Case Work, Lutheran Deaconesses Home and Hospital, Chicago.

TAKEUCHI, STERLING H., Research Assistant, University of Chicago.

TALLE, H. O., Teacher of Public Speaking and Political Economy, Luther College, Decorah, Iowa.

THOMAS, R. G., Assistant Professor of Economics, Purdue University, Lafayette, Indiana.

TIBBITTS, ROY CLARK, Local Community Research Assistant to Professor Ogburn.

TOWNSEND, ANDREW J., Professor of History, Chicago Normal College, Chicago, Ill.

UTLEY, CLIFTON M., Research Assistant, University of Chicago.

VERRY, ETHEL, Superintendent, Chicago Orphan Asylum, Chicago; Instructor in Social Economy, Graduate School of Social Service Administration, University of Chicago.

VOLKERT, MONA, Research Assistant, United States Children's Bureau.

WEAVER, A. J., Professor of Economics, Berea College.

WEIBEL, BESSIE, Field Investigator, United States Children's Bureau.

APPENDIX

WILCOX, SIDNEY W., Statistician, Bureau of Business Research, University of Pittsburgh, Pittsburgh, Pennsylvania.

WILLIAMS, DOROTHY (Mrs. W. W. Burke), Special Agent and Investigator Boys' Court, United States Children's Bureau.

WILSON, RUTH (Mrs. W. H. C. Laves), Clinton, New York.

WIRTH, LOUIS, Assistant Professor of Sociology, Tulane University, Director of Child Behavior Clinic.

WOLF, HARRY, Associate Professor of Economics, University of North Carolina, Chapel Hill, North Carolina.

WOOD, IRIS, Social Worker, Jewish Board of Guardians, New York City.

WOODDY, CARROLL, Assistant Professor of Political Science, University of Chicago.

ZIEGLER, HARRY GARRETT, Halsey Stuart and Company, Chicago.

ZORBAUGH, FREDERICK M., Local Community Research.

ZORBAUGH, HARVEY, Assistant Professor Educational Sociology, New York University (in charge of Social Behavior Clinic).

ZUBER, WILLIE (Mrs. Alvan D. Battey), Case Worker, The United Charities.

INDEX

Abbott, Edith, 130, 142, 145, 195, 205, 206, 215, 217, 218; member of Joint Committee on Registration of Social Statistics, 23

Addams, Jane, 4

Adler, Herman M., 13

Adoption law of Illinois and its administration, 214

Agriculture, growth and development in Chicago area of, 82, 84

Almshouse, Oak Forest, 210

American Association of Hospital Social Workers, 93

American Association for Organizing Family Social Work, 92

American Museum of National History, 45

Anderson, Nels, 8, 128–29, 130, 185

Anthropometrics, laboratory in Social Science building for, 25, 31

Anti-Saloon League, 141

Archaeology: laboratory in Social Science building for, 25, 30; research assistants of University in, sought by other institutions, 45

Association of Community Chests and Councils, 23–24, 40, 64, 196

Arts, effects of growth of the city on, 69

Athens, 244, 246

Attitudes: method of measurement on specified questions, 107–12; national and racial attitudes of a group of students, 110–112; scales, 108–11; subjects for which scales are in preparation, 110; unit of measurement in educational scales, 109

Atwater, Pierce, representative of Community Chest, Wichita, Kansas, 24

Aurora, 85

Automobile, influence of, upon social attitudes of childhood and youth, 169, 170; rôle of, in development of amusement centers, 127

Bacon, Francis, 232

Bail system: Chicago, 112; Cook County, 217

Baker, Newman F., 200

Ball, Charles B., 201

Baltimore, 53

Banks and banking: as centers of trade in local communities, 116, 125; studies in process, 155

Basic social data; see Data

Beckner, Earl R., 160

Beeley, Arthur, 112, 217

Behavior Research Fund, 13–14

Behaviorism: affected by change of environment, 11; child study and behavior clinics established, 13–14; the individual and social problems, 12–15; influence of leisure-time activities, studies needed, 170; mental-hygiene records from a children's clinic, publication, 218; see also Recreation

Berlin, 78, 81, 196

Better Government Association, 141

Beyle, Herman C., 64, 196–97

Bigham, T. C., 160

Birth-rate: base for measurement, 70; social classes compared with occupational classes, 95

Bishop Museum, 45

Book- and job-printing industry, industrial relations compared with the newspaper industry, 156–57

Booth, Charles, 5–6

Boston, 53, 78, 81, 196; Judge Baker Foundation, 13; South End House, 4

Woman: equal rights, development of
Illinois law on status of women,
study of, 219; labor in truck gardens, 218

Woods, Robert, 4

Wooddy, Carroll H., 18, 43, 199

Wright, Quincy, 30, 66, 174–75, 215;
chairman of Causes of War Subcommittee, 23

Wu, C. C., 131

Young, Erle F., 48

Young Men's Christian Association
College, 62

Znaniecki, Florian, 178–79

Zones; *see* Regions

Zoning ordinance and its applications,
study of, 200

Zorbaugh, Harvey W., 8, 129, 133–35,
185

SOCIAL SCIENCE STUDIES

*Directed by the Local Community Research Committee
of the University of Chicago*

THE UNIVERSITY OF CHICAGO PRESS